P9-DBO-068

THE COMPLETE IDIOT'S GUIDE® TO

Stock Investing

by Sarah Young Fisher, CFP, and Susan Shelly

ALPHA

A member of Penguin Group (USA) Inc.

ALPHA BOOKS

Published by the Penguin Group

Penguin Group (USA) Inc., 375 Hudson Street, New York, New York 10014, USA

Penguin Group (Canada), 90 Eglinton Avenue East, Suite 700, Toronto, Ontario M4P 2Y3, Canada (a division of Pearson Penguin Canada Inc.)

Penguin Books Ltd., 80 Strand, London WC2R 0RL, England

Penguin Ireland, 25 St. Stephen's Green, Dublin 2, Ireland (a division of Penguin Books Ltd.)

Penguin Group (Australia), 250 Camberwell Road, Camberwell, Victoria 3124, Australia (a division of Pearson Australia Group Pty. Ltd.)

Penguin Books India Pvt. Ltd., 11 Community Centre, Panchsheel Park, New Delhi—110 017, India

Penguin Group (NZ), 67 Apollo Drive, Rosedale, North Shore, Auckland 1311, New Zealand (a division of Pearson New Zealand Ltd.)

Penguin Books (South Africa) (Pty.) Ltd., 24 Sturdee Avenue, Rosebank, Johannesburg 2196, South Africa

Penguin Books Ltd., Registered Offices: 80 Strand, London WC2R 0RL, England

Copyright © 2011 by Sarah Young Fisher, CFP, and Susan Shelly

THE COMPLETE IDIOT'S GUIDE TO and Design are registered trademarks of Penguin Group (USA) Inc.

International Standard Book Number: 978-1-61564-088-1
Library of Congress Catalog Card Number: 2011901233

13 12 11   8 7 6 5 4 3 2 1

Interpretation of the printing code: The rightmost number of the first series of numbers is the year of the book's printing; the rightmost number of the second series of numbers is the number of the book's printing. For example, a printing code of 11-1 shows that the first printing occurred in 2011.

Printed in the United States of America

Note: This publication contains the opinions and ideas of its authors. It is intended to provide helpful and informative material on the subject matter covered. It is sold with the understanding that the authors and publisher are not engaged in rendering professional services in the book. If the reader requires personal assistance or advice, a competent professional should be consulted.

The authors and publisher specifically disclaim any responsibility for any liability, loss, or risk, personal or otherwise, which is incurred as a consequence, directly or indirectly, of the use and application of any of the contents of this book.

Most Alpha books are available at special quantity discounts for bulk purchases for sales promotions, premiums, fund-raising, or educational use. Special books, or book excerpts, can also be created to fit specific needs.

For details, write: Special Markets, Alpha Books, 375 Hudson Street, New York, NY 10014.

Publisher: *Marie Butler-Knight*
Editorial Director: *Mike Sanders*
Executive Managing Editor: *Billy Fields*
Senior Acquisitions Editor: *Paul Dinas*
Development Editor: *Lynn Northrup*
Senior Production Editor: *Kayla Dugger*

Copy Editor: *Louise Lund*
Cover Designer: *William Thomas*
Book Designers: *William Thomas, Rebecca Batchelor*
Indexer: *Celia McCoy*
Layout: *Brian Massey*
Proofreader: *John Etchison*

Contents

Appendixes

Introduction

It seems like almost everyone is interested in the stock market. Even those who aren't invested in the market understand that its performance affects the economy, and that the economy affects the market. Learning the best way to invest in the stock market, however, can seem confusing and even overwhelming.

The language of the stock market is daunting. Terms such as "fundamental analysis," "market data," "international indexes," "buying on margin," and others can leave a beginning investor wondering if they'll ever be able to put it all together. And the thought of needing to research companies before deciding to buy their stock can make it seem like investing might just be too darned much work.

But wait a minute. Really, how hard can it be? After all, people have been investing in and making money in the stock market since the country was founded. Granted, investors used to be primarily upper-crust financial types—a sort of old boys club that dominated Wall Street and knew the ins and outs of the investing game. But these days, with more and more folks like you and me jumping into the stock market, the mysterious curtain has fallen away, and we are free to jump in and take our turns at investing.

The Internet, in particular, has made stock market investing more accessible and understandable. Not only can we set up online brokerage accounts that allow us to buy and sell stock whenever we think it's a good idea, we can access unbelievable amounts of reliable, useful information—much of it at no cost.

If you've picked up this book because you want to learn more about the stock market and begin with a strategy of long-term investing, you are to be congratulated. All in all, the market has proven to be the most profitable investment over time. It's risky business if you're looking for big gains in the short term, but if you're willing to jump in and stay in for the long haul, chances are very good that you'll realize a good return on your investment. You're apt to need a little advice along the way, but taking time to read this book and learn about how the stock market works and the best ways to invest your money will give you a great start.

How to Use This Book

The Complete Idiot's Guide to Stock Investing is written in five parts, each part covering a different aspect of investing.

Part 1, Are You Ready for the Stock Market?, tells you exactly what the stock market is, how it got started, and why, despite its ups and downs, it's still the best place to park your money. It also helps you take a good hard look at your own financial situation and assess whether it makes sense for you to begin stock market investing at this stage of your financial life.

Part 2, What Kind of Investor Are You?, provides lots of information about different kinds of stock, and which kind might make sense for you. You also learn about mutual funds and exchange traded funds (ETFs), and how investing in them differs from stock investing. Because investing is not without risk, you learn how to evaluate your risk tolerance and recognize different types of investment risk. You also read about the differences between trading and investing, and learn why it's so important to choose stocks that create a diversified portfolio.

Part 3, Getting Started: One Step at a Time, discusses the ins and outs of finding stock with which to build your portfolio. You learn where to access information about companies offering stock and the industries in which they're contained, and what's important to know about those companies. Once you learn about financial statements, balance sheets, ratios, and other information that affects the financial health and outlook of a company, you'll be able to predict where a company is heading and determine whether buying its stock is a good idea.

Part 4, The Mechanics of Investing, walks you through the basics of finding a broker to help you with your investments, and also shows you how to invest on your own, with minimal or no help from a broker. You learn how to order stock, and the different types of orders you can use. You also discover some tricks of the trade in the form of trading strategies to maximize your investments and minimize your chances for loss. And, because the market is one big roller coaster ride, you learn about effective investing in both good times and bad.

Part 5, How Are You Doing?, helps you get some perspective on your investing performance and assess how your portfolio is coming along. Investments are like children in that they bear watching, and you get a handle on what you should be looking for (and looking out for) and how to tweak your portfolio as necessary. Because taxes are an inevitable part of investing, you also get an overview of tax matters you're likely to encounter along the way, and learn how to maximize your earnings by avoiding paying more to the IRS than necessary. We also share some information about investment clubs, so you can decide if that option might make sense for you.

Extras

All chapters contain sidebars, intended to offer additional advice and information. Here's what to look for:

> **DEFINITION**
>
> In these boxes you'll find simple definitions for selected keywords and concepts about stock investing.

> **TAKING STOCK**
>
> These boxes provide helpful tips and advice to help you get the most out of your stock investing experience.

> **CRASH!**
>
> These cautionary notes warn you of common errors that could derail your investment strategies.

> **SHARE THIS**
>
> These boxes provide interesting facts and snippets of information related to the stock market and investing.

Acknowledgments

The authors would like to thank the many people who provided time, information, and resources for this book. Especially, we are grateful to the editors at Alpha Books, and to Gene Brissie of James Peter Associates. A special thanks to Paul Dinas for his usual guidance and direction, and to Lynn Northrup for her exceptional editing skills, patience, and humor.

Susan offers a very special acknowledgment to Bert Holtje for his wisdom, support, and encouragement, and is proud to call him a friend.

Sarah expresses sincere thanks to Don Gross, CFA; Vince Rudisill, Hershey Trust Company; Michael Hinerdeer, Kuntz Lesher Capital, LLC; and Ed Monborne, CPA—they are wonderfully gifted people who exhibit patience and possess the ability to present their knowledge with simplicity.

Trademarks

All terms mentioned in this book that are known to be or are suspected of being trademarks or service marks have been appropriately capitalized. Alpha Books and Penguin Group (USA) Inc. cannot attest to the accuracy of this information. Use of a term in this book should not be regarded as affecting the validity of any trademark or service mark.

Are You Ready for the Stock Market?

This part introduces you to the history of the stock market, its structure, and the basics of how it operates. You learn how stock is traded, understand the major stock exchanges, and become acquainted with indexes, which are gauges of stock market activity based on the performance of a particular group of stocks. You also get an overview of how the Great Depression came to be, and read about the bull and bear markets that have followed it. And you learn that, historically, the stock market is the best long-term investment.

Having said that, stocks aren't for everyone, and you learn why. If your personal financial house isn't in order, you probably should put stock investing on hold. By the time you finish Part 1, you should feel more confident about understanding what the stock market is all about, how it operates, and how you can benefit from it.

What Is the Stock Market?

In This Chapter

- How the stock market works
- Buying and selling stock
- Understanding why companies offer stock
- Different types of stock
- The ups and downs of owning stock
- Getting a handle on stock exchanges and indexes

If you've picked up this book, it's most likely because you're looking for some clear and easily understandable information and advice about investing in the stock market. The world of stock market investing can seem daunting and complicated. You'll encounter a lot of terms you might not know, and you'll need to be open to learning about some new concepts and techniques. When you get right down to it, however, it's not all that difficult. Just think of the stock market as a giant auction, with people buying and people selling stock.

This chapter will provide a clear idea of exactly what the stock market is and how it works. You don't need to be a genius to understand the stock market, and you don't need to be rich to own stock. You just have to be willing to learn and get involved in investing your money. With that said, let's get started on learning about this entity called the stock market.

How Does the Stock Market Work?

The *stock market* is a generic term that encompasses the trading of *securities*. The trading occurs within organized markets called exchanges, which you'll read more about later in this chapter.

> **DEFINITION**
>
> The **stock market** is the organized securities exchange for stock and bond transactions. **Securities** are investments that represent evidence of debt, ownership of a business, or the legal right to acquire or sell an ownership interest in a business.

Have you ever been to an auction, or at least know how one works? When you bid on something, whether it's an antique clock, a cow, or a car, you inform the auctioneer of your desire to buy the object for sale. You don't actually buy the object from the auctioneer, because he doesn't own it. It's his job to match up people who want to buy the objects with those who want to sell them, and to get the highest price he can for the sellers.

That's pretty much how the stock market works. It's like a big auction where, every day, people buy and sell stocks. It's much more complicated than an auction selling cars or household items, of course, because the stock market operates on various levels with multiple buyers and sellers. Similarly, though, the price of the stock depends on supply and demand. If a lot of people want to buy the same stocks, the price of those stocks will increase. If nobody's bidding, the price will drop. The selling price of stocks is determined by how much a buyer is willing to pay, just as the price of auction goods is.

Buyers

People buy stocks that they believe will increase in value over time. You probably know that the price of stocks goes up and down, sometimes very slowly, and sometimes quite dramatically.

Just like those folks bidding on the clock at the auction, smart investors are always looking for good deals on stocks. They pick a stock that they believe will be a good investment over time and, if the price looks right, they'll put in an order with their broker to buy it. If they think the price is going to fall, they'll wait to buy.

When you want to buy a stock, you inform your broker, who plays the same role as the auctioneer. He passes along the information that you want to buy, and either electronically or through a human broker you get matched up with a seller. As the buyer, you get to decide if you're willing to meet the asking price for the stocks. If you are, a deal is made and you receive notification of the trade.

Sellers

People who own stock decide to sell it for different reasons. These could include needing cash; deciding that the stock is too risky; concluding that it is not in line with your ethical, social, or moral values; reaching a point where you want to shift your money into investments that are completely safe and nonvolatile; or (and this is the scenario investors hope for) to lock in or harvest your gains or appreciation.

When an investor wants to sell stock, he informs his broker, who, again, performs the role of the auctioneer and works to find his client a buyer. Once a price is agreed upon, the seller passes along his stock to the buyer.

How Stock Works

A share of stock represents a little piece of ownership in a company. When you buy 1 share, or 1,000 shares, you're buying a piece, the size of which is contingent on the number of shares you buy and the total number of outstanding shares of a company. This entitles you to share in the success of a company, but also makes you a partner if the company should fail.

Companies issue stock to raise money so that they can continue to grow and become more profitable. Most companies that offer stock to the public have been around long enough to become established, and need to raise additional capital in order to continue growing.

Some companies sell their stock to the public, while others—usually smaller companies—sell their stock privately. Private placements—the sale of a relatively small amount of stock to selected investors as a means of raising capital, not offered to the public—allow the business owners to retain control over who owns its stock, while still raising capital. And they can often avoid having to register with the Securities and Exchange Commission (SEC), a requirement for publicly held companies. In this book, however, we'll primarily be discussing and learning about stock that is publicly offered and traded.

Publicly Traded Companies

All corporations have stock, but not all corporate shares are sold to the public. Once a company has sold stock through an *initial public offering (IPO)*, however, it no longer controls who can buy its stock. A company in that position is called a *publicly traded company*. IBM is a publicly traded company; Cargill is a privately held company.

> **DEFINITION**
>
> An **initial public offering (IPO)** is the first sale of stock by a private company to the public, and is a course of action necessary for a company to be permitted to sell its stock publicly on an open exchange. A **publicly traded company** is one that offers its stock for sale on an open exchange to whomever chooses to buy it.

All of the companies listed on any of the stock exchanges are publicly traded companies. They got to be publicly traded through IPOs, when a company's stock is sold publicly for the first time. You'll learn more about IPOs in Chapter 17.

Companies issue stock in order to raise capital, presumably to reinvest into the business so it can continue to grow. Publicly traded companies can also use stock as a form of compensation for employees, its board of directors, and officers.

Once a company goes public and offers its stock for sale, it is required to comply with regulations issued by the SEC, which generally keeps a pretty close eye on public companies. Company officers are required to provide reports each year about major shareholders, which company officers own stock, and other information. Going public, however, is an effective way of generating capital, which is why most companies do so.

Different Types of Stock

You'll hear and read about a lot of different types of stock, such as growth stock, blue chip stock, penny stock, value stock, income stock, cyclical stock, counter-cyclical stock, emerging growth stock, established growth stock, interest sensitive stock, and defensive stock. Some of those names, such as blue chip stock, penny stock, and income stock, refer to how a stock is perceived by the market or whether it pays a hefty dividend, while other names, such as cyclical stock or defensive stock, refer to how a stock reacts to particular economic conditions. You'll learn more about those different kinds of stock throughout this book. The two kinds of stock that people most often talk about are *common stock* and *preferred stock*. You'll learn more about these stock varieties in Chapter 17, but for now, let's take a quick look at how they differ:

- **Common stock** is the most widely traded of any type of corporate security. Hundreds of millions of shares of common stock are traded every day on the major stock exchanges. Investors like common stock because it comes in many flavors and it's easy to buy and sell. You can buy stock in the morning and, if you wish, sell it before the market closes the same day. Owning common stock also entitles shareholders to vote at shareholders' meetings and to receive *dividends* issued by the company. Owning common stock, however, is not a guarantee that you'll receive dividends.

- If you own **preferred stock,** you're entitled to some perks that you wouldn't get with common stock. However, you usually aren't entitled to vote at the annual shareholders' meeting. Just as with common stock, there are different flavors of preferred stock, some of which you'll learn about in Chapter 17. Exactly how preferred stock works varies from company to company, as it can be structured in different ways. Sometimes called "preferred shares," this type of stock is considered to be a sort of hybrid between a bond and a stock.

DEFINITION

Common stock is a type of security that entitles you to a share in the ownership of a company. Holders of common stock are entitled to **dividends,** which are payments made to stockholders. **Preferred stock** is a special type of security that provides some preferential treatment to owners, but usually doesn't include voting rights.

Benefits and Risks of Owning Stock

If the company makes a profit or grows its earnings over time, you as a shareholder generally share and benefit from that profit. This profit is usually reflected by an increase in the market value of the stock. If the company loses money, however, the value of your shares will decrease as other investors unload their shares of the stock. One of the first rules of stock market investing is that there are no guarantees.

On the other hand, owning preferred stock gives you predictability of your income stream but does not allow the holder to benefit from the upside experienced by common stock holders.

Ideally, as with any sort of investment, when you invest in stock you want to buy low and sell high. That means, of course, that when you decide to sell your investment you'll get much more for it than you paid. The same is true when you purchase a home or a painting or gold or baseball cards. The hope is that you'll be able to sell your investment for more—hopefully a lot more—than you paid for it.

The price of a stock can rise significantly over time if a company has good earnings and good prospects for future growth. That price, however, can also fall significantly, sometimes for reasons over which the company has no control, like the collapse of a particular market, such as housing, or a natural disaster.

You'll read a lot more about the benefits and risks associated with owning stock later in this book, so for now just keep in mind that both are factors to consider.

Understanding Stock Exchanges

When you buy and sell stock, you generally do it on a *stock exchange*. There are numerous stock exchanges, both domestic and international, and some are much better known than others.

> **DEFINITION**
>
> A **stock exchange** is an institution that hosts a market where stocks and other securities can be bought and sold. The facilities provided for trading can be physical or electronic.

Most companies are listed on just one stock exchange, although there is no rule limiting them to that. Some companies, like Walgreens and Charles Schwab, trade on both the New York Stock Exchange and the NASDAQ. And some international companies, such as British Petroleum (BP), trade on both domestic and foreign exchanges.

Basically, stock exchanges are businesses that are looking to earn profits and grow. Stock exchanges make money in various ways, including charging companies initial and annual fees to be listed. Some stock exchanges, including the New York Stock Exchange and NASDAQ, are publicly held companies with stock that is traded just like that of Home Depot and Coca-Cola.

The New York Stock Exchange

Founded in 1792, the New York Stock Exchange (NYSE) is the largest exchange in the world, with its listed companies valued at somewhere around $12.25 trillion in mid-2010. The four trading rooms of the NYSE are located on Wall Street in Lower Manhattan, but the exchange's main building is located at 18 Broad Street. There are more than 3,600 companies listed on the NYSE, which is open for trading Monday through Friday from 9:30 A.M. to 4:00 P.M.

SHARE THIS

The New York Stock Exchange's grand building at 18 Broad Street in Manhattan opened on April 22, 1903, a year after its target completion date. The building, which was projected to cost $1 million to construct, ended up costing $4 million, an astounding amount for that time. Among the features of the building were air conditioning, a paging system called annunciator boards, skylights, and entire walls of windows.

Traders on the floor of the NYSE buy and sell stock for investors in an auction-style setting. Except for a few very high-priced stocks, all stocks can also be traded electronically—and in fact, most of them are.

In 2007, the NYSE merged with Euronext N.V., a Paris-based stock exchange with subsidiaries in five other European countries. The official name of the exchange is NYSE Euronext, although it continues to be known as the New York Stock Exchange.

NASDAQ

NASDAQ, letters which once stood for The National Association of Securities Dealers Automated Quotation System, is not technically a stock exchange, although it serves as one. NASDAQ is actually a computerized market, but it's considered an exchange because many companies are traded on it.

Headquartered in New York City, NASDAQ (which claims that its original name is obsolete because its 1971 founder, the National Association of Securities Dealers, no longer exists) was the world's first electronic stock market. It's the largest electronic market in the United States, and the fourth largest in the world.

NASDAQ merged with the London Stock Exchange in 1992 and with the American Stock Exchange in 1997. In 2007, NASDAQ acquired the Philadelphia Stock Exchange, America's oldest exchange. Many of the more than 3,200 companies listed on NASDAQ are technology firms, including Dell, Microsoft, and Apple.

The American Stock Exchange

The American Stock Exchange (AMEX) was once a primary competitor of the New York Stock Exchange, but today is considered a less competitive exchange on which mostly smaller companies are listed. Started in the years following the Civil War, the AMEX was known as the "New York Curb Exchange" because traders met and conducted their auctions in the streets of New York City. It became known as the American Stock Exchange in 1953.

The AMEX was purchased by NASDAQ's parent company in 1998, but continued to operate as an active stock exchange. In 2008, it was acquired by NYSE Euronext, and the information contained on the AMEX website was integrated onto the NYSE site. Although the AMEX is owned by the NYSE, it continues to conduct business as its own entity.

Foreign Exchanges

Stock exchanges operate around the world. There are the Cayman Islands, London, Iceland, Moscow, Kuwait, Thailand, Hong Kong, Indonesian, Australian, Ghana, and Swaziland stock exchanges, along with dozens more in countries across the globe.

Investors sometimes are attracted to foreign markets because they hear or read about huge returns and want to get a piece of the action. While it's possible to buy stock on foreign exchanges, you'd need to work with a brokerage firm that is experienced in foreign markets. Remember that a fair number of foreign companies are listed on American stock exchanges, and that investing in one or more of those may be easier than in those listed only on foreign exchanges. You can also get in on foreign stocks through mutual funds or exchange traded funds (you'll learn more about these in Chapters 8 and 9), which entails less risk than the direct purchase of stock on a foreign exchange.

CRASH!

You should conduct a significant amount of research before buying any stock, but you should be particularly diligent before buying stock on a foreign market. Be aware that regulations concerning the sale of stock vary from country to country. And circumstances within a country that you may not even be aware of can affect the value of stock. If you're tempted to trade in foreign markets, be sure you do a lot of homework and get good advice from a broker.

Over the Counter Market

The stock of companies that are not listed on a stock market trades on the over the counter (OTC) market. The OTC market isn't centralized, and some stock sold on the OTC market isn't regulated by the SEC, so it's generally a more risky investment than stock traded on an exchange. Companies with stock traded over the counter are usually small and don't meet the necessary requirements to be listed on an exchange.

The OTC market is sometimes called the pink sheets, because prices for stock in that market were recorded on pink pieces of paper. You'll hear about the over the counter bulletin board (OTCBB), an electronic quotation system providing information about OTC stocks. Brokers use the Internet or phones to negotiate directly with one another for trading.

Because stock traded over the counter is considered to be a less reliable investment than if traded on a stock exchange, most investors avoid them, and most companies that are serious about creating capital by selling stock strive to get listed on an exchange.

Understanding Indexes

If you're driving home from work and have the radio on, or you tune in to the evening news on the TV or check it out on the Internet, you're almost sure to hear a report of how the markets performed that day. The reports might be accompanied by upbeat music if the markets fared well, or by slow, not-very-happy tunes if they performed poorly.

So, what are the measures of how the stock market did on any particular day? How do we get a sense of whether it was a good day or a bad day? The gauges of stock market activity are called *indexes* (also referred to as indices), which measure sections of the stock market. You've probably heard of the big guys: the Dow Jones Industrial Average, the NASDAQ indexes, and the Standard & Poor's 500. All of these are indexes, and they all gauge the general movement of the stock market.

> **DEFINITION**
>
> A stock market **index** is a group of securities that collectively is used to measure changes in the market. Different indexes employ different methods for doing so, but all are designed to track price movements of one or more sectors of the market.

Types of Indexes

There are many types of stock market indexes, and they work in different ways. It's best to consider several indexes rather than just one in order to get a truer reading of market performance. Some indexes include a global representation of stocks, while others are far more specific, such as the Tel Aviv Technology Index or the Space Foundation Index. General categorizations of indexes are as follows:

- **Broad-base index.** This represents the performance of the entire market, not a segment of the market. That doesn't mean that any index, of which the Dow Jones Industrial Average, Standard & Poor's 500, and Japanese Nikkei 225 are a few, considers the stock of every company listed on the stock market. They do, however, represent all of the different types of stock listed in the particular index. Some indexes, however, such as the Dow Jones Wilshire 5000 Total Stock Market Index, do represent the stocks of nearly every publicly traded U.S. company.

- **Industry index.** An industry index, or a sector index, measures only one segment of the stock market, such as oil or technology stocks. If you're concerned about your Apple stock, you'd want to look at an index like the NASDAQ, which concentrates on technology and related sectors. Other indexes track stocks related to transportation, biotechnology, precious metals, entertainment, and other sectors.

- **Performance-based index.** This type of index takes into account not only the performance of stocks, but the dividends and other cash that the companies that issued various stocks have paid to shareholders.

- **Price-weighted index.** A price-weighted index considers each stock in proportion to its price per share. This means that the performance of higher-priced stocks has more impact on the index than that of lower-priced stocks. If the index contained two stocks, one with a price per share of $2 and the other $10—five times as much as the first—the $10 stock is weighted five times higher than the $2 stock, and has much more bearing on the performance of the index. The Dow Jones Industrial Average is an example of a price-weighted index.

- **Capitalization-weighted index.** Also known as a market value weighted index, the stocks of companies with the most market value, or market capitalization, figure more heavily than the stocks of companies with less market value. The Standard & Poor's 500, NASDAQ, and Wilshire Total Market Index are cap-weighted indexes.

How to Use the Indexes

Stock market indexes can seem confusing, but they have the very practical purpose of providing a quick snapshot of market performance, either overall or by sector. Remember that a broad-base index will give you a better picture of the entire market and of the overall economy than an industry index, which focuses on just one area of the overall market.

Indexes provide a means for comparing how your portfolio is doing in relationship to the performance of the market. If your overall returns are higher than the overall returns of the stocks listed on the Dow Jones Industrial Average, for example, you can say that you "outperformed the Dow." People in the financial industry love to tell clients that their investments have consistently outperformed one or more of the major indexes.

Remember, however, that stock indexes are not an exact science, and you shouldn't depend on them as a sole measure of how the market or a market segment is doing. Indexes are just one way to measure the movement of the stock market.

TAKING STOCK

If the overall market, or a segment of the market, is doing well, it's worth looking into modeling your investments after those represented on an index. If the technology industry is thriving, for instance, you might consider setting up a portfolio based on a technology index, such as the Cleantech Index. If you want a broad-based portfolio, you can look into investing in index mutual funds or exchange traded funds (ETFs), which provide a basketful of stocks that match a particular index.

Indexes to Watch

The Dow Jones Industrial Average, Standard & Poor's 500, and NASDAQ are the most frequently cited financial indexes, but hardly the only ones. A quick Internet search will reveal hundreds of indexes used around the world, many of which are specific to one market segment or the stock of a particular country.

The Dow

The Dow Jones Industrial Average, popularly known as simply "the Dow," is the oldest stock market index, the brainchild of Charles Dow in 1896. When Mr. Dow started his index at the end of the nineteenth century, he considered only 12 stocks. The number of stocks jumped to 30 in the late 1920s, and has remained the same ever since.

The 30 stocks listed are all those of big, well-known companies, and the index is price weighted, meaning that stocks of higher value carry more weight in the index than those of lesser value. Although the Dow is well respected and has been around for more than a century, it is often criticized because it only considers 30 companies from a field of thousands.

And, critics say, even though the Dow purports to be an industrial average, it contains a significant number of nonindustrial stocks. In addition, it's a price-weighted index, which considers each stock in proportion to its price per share, meaning that the performance of higher-priced stocks has more impact on the index than that of lower-priced stocks.

Dow Jones & Co. has introduced the Dow Jones U.S. Total Stock Market Index, a capitalization-based index, in response to those criticisms. Because most investors don't rely solely on the Dow as a measure of the market, however, the Dow Jones Industrial Average continues to be considered an important index.

SHARE THIS

We talk about the Dow Jones Industrial Average or the NASDAQ Composite Index or the Standard & Poor's 500, but each of these companies—Dow Jones, NASDAQ, and Standard & Poor's—has other indexes as well. Dow Jones, for example, also lists the Dow Jones Utilities Average and the Dow Jones Transportation Average. Standard & Poor's also has the S&P Global 1200 and the S&P Timber and Forestry Index. In addition to the NASDAQ Composite Index and NASDAQ 100, NASDAQ offers a health-care index and a financial index, among many others.

Standard & Poor's 500

Published since 1957, the Standard & Poor's 500—known as the S&P 500—is regarded as the best indicator of the performance of the stock of the country's largest companies. It includes 500 of the biggest companies in the leading industries of the U.S. economy. Companies included in the S&P 500 Index trade on either the New York Stock Exchange or NASDAQ.

The S&P 500 is important because it serves as an indicator of the overall U.S. economy. Many mutual funds, ETFs, pension funds, and others are designed to model the performance of the S&P, investing in the stocks included in the index. It is made up almost exclusively of U.S. firms, although it includes a very few foreign firms.

The S&P 500 is a capitalization-weighted index in which the stocks of companies with the most market value, or market capitalization, figure more heavily than the stocks of companies with less market value. This differentiates it from the Dow.

NASDAQ

The two best-known NASDAQ indexes are the NASDAQ 100 Index and the NASDAQ Composite Index. As the names suggest, the 100 Index includes 100 of the largest companies included on the NASDAQ Stock Market. The NASDAQ Composite Index is a broad-base index measuring all domestic and international stocks on the NASDAQ Stock Market. It includes more than 3,000 stocks.

Both of these indexes are calculated using market capitalization, thereby representing each security proportionately to the value of the company it represents. The NASDAQ Composite Index concentrates primarily on technology industries, which have a large representation on the NASDAQ market.

International Indexes

Stock market indexes are not confined to the United States, and investors here can learn a lot about the markets in other countries by keeping an eye on their market indexes. This is important in a global marketplace, since what happens in one country directly affects the markets and economies of others.

Some international indexes to check out include the following:

- **MSCI EAFE.** This index measures the market performance of 21 developed markets outside the United States and Canada. The EAFE acronym stands for Europe, Australasia, and the Far East. It is maintained by MSCI Barra, a provider of investment decision support tools.

- **S&P/ASX 200.** Initiated in 2000, the S&P/ASX 200 is a stock market index of Australian stocks listed on the Australian Securities Exchange from Standard & Poor's.

- **S&P/TSX Composite Index.** Established in 2002 by Standard & Poor's and the Toronto Stock Exchange, the S&P/TSX replaced the Toronto Stock Exchange 300. The index includes 300 Canadian stocks in 14 subgroups, designed to represent the Canadian equity market.

- **Hang Seng.** With 45 of the largest companies listed representing about 60 percent of capitalization of the Hong Kong Stock Exchange, the Hang Seng is the main indicator of overall market performance in Hong Kong.

- **Bombay Sensex.** This is the most popular of Indian stock indexes, tracking stock that trades on the Bombay Stock Exchange.

- **FTSE 100.** This British index includes the 100 largest companies in Great Britain.

- **Nikkei.** This Japanese index is similar to the Dow, tracking stocks that trade on the Tokyo Stock Exchange.

Don't Forget the Little Guys

While the big three—the Dow, S&P 500, and NASDAQ—get most of the attention in the United States, don't forget that there are many smaller indexes that can provide valuable information about the market or a particular aspect of the market.

Remember to check indexes that pertain to a certain industry, or those that track the movement of stock of smaller companies. While Dow Jones and Standard & Poor's turn out the most popular indexes, stock exchanges, including the New York Stock Exchange and the American Stock Exchange, also offer indexes.

The Least You Need to Know

- Stock is purchased and sold in a giant market.
- Companies issue various types of stock to generate capital.
- Owning stock gives you ownership in a company.
- If the stock you own increases in value, you can sell it for more than the purchase price, but if it decreases in value, you'll experience a loss if you sell.
- Stock indexes are used to track movement of stock.

A Look Back at the Stock Market

In This Chapter

- The stock market's long history
- A snapshot of the Great Depression
- Rise and fall: bull and bear markets
- A tried-and-true investment strategy

The stock market is of much current concern, but it is by no means a modern concept. Companies and individuals have been buying and selling stock for centuries. Currency and commerce have been traced back to 3000 B.C.E., making it no surprise that by the 1600s the practice of issuing and trading stock was underway.

In this chapter, you'll get an historical overview of the stock market, intended to provide some perspective on its purpose, value, ups and downs, quirks, and peculiarities. We'll take a look at the circumstances surrounding the Great Depression of the 1930s, and some of the notable bull and bear markets that have occurred since then.

A Brief History of the Stock Market

Historians tell us that the oldest known stock certificate is dated … get ready for this … 1606, and was issued by a Dutch company that was looking to get involved with the spice trade in India and the Far East. This particular Dutch company, called Vereinigte Oostindische Compaignie, was not the only player in the game; other companies in the shipping and price trade business also were issuing and trading stock. As the British Royal Navy became increasingly influential in the late 1700s and early 1800s, the center of trade and commerce, along with the trading of securities, moved to England.

It's Nothing New

When English colonists came to America and began establishing commerce, it was a natural practice to sell and trade stock. Progressives saw the need for the new nation to develop a strong economy along with a strong military, and businesses began in earnest.

Much of the credit for America's modern banking system is given to Alexander Hamilton, who was, among many other things, the first U.S. Secretary of the Treasury under President George Washington. Hamilton, historians relate, favored the trading of government debt securities and was indeed an early proponent of the stock market.

Back then, traders met outside on the corner of Wall Street and Broad Street in New York, which, as you history buffs know, was the nation's capital early on in America's history. The corner trading was reportedly unorganized and often became unruly, leading a group of two dozen stockbrokers in the late 1700s to form the New York Stock and Exchange Board, later known as the New York Stock Exchange. The other exchanges, some of which you read about in Chapter 1, followed.

SHARE THIS

An historical account of Alexander Hamilton's career reveals that during the summer of 1791 stock prices were skyrocketing due to irresponsible speculation within the market. Investors were borrowing money from banks to buy up government securities and stock. Hamilton, then Secretary of the Treasury, warned against the practice, but it continued and in February 1792 the market crashed. Just a little history to point out that the ups and downs of the stock market have been occurring since its beginnings in America.

The Stock Market and the Industrial Revolution

Growth of the stock market was fueled by the Industrial Revolution in America. As the country became industrialized in the early 1800s and transportation and communication improved, new companies were starting up and looking for investors. Money was moving freely and people were optimistic about the future.

The New York Stock Exchange flourished, and stocks that weren't considered to be worthy of trade on that exchange were sold on the curbs of New York City streets. This "curb trading" evolved into the American Stock Exchange.

The Industrial Revolution resulted in innovation, jobs, and prosperity. The Chicago World's Fair in 1893 was held to bring attention to a bright future for America, due largely to the technology and science that had fueled the great rise in industry.

By the early 1900s, automobiles were beginning to be produced on assembly lines, workers' wages were increasing, and consumers were buying like never before. They bought clothing produced in America's mills and factories, durable goods for their homes, and cars. Companies continued to grow and expand, and stock was trading quickly to keep up with the boom.

By the early 1920s, people with no prior investing experience were looking to get into the stock market. Increasing wages resulted in workers having extra money to put into savings or to invest in the market. Industry was booming, and many new investors thought the market was an easy way to get rich. Their willingness to buy a company's stock drove up prices.

Banks had lowered interest rates, making it easier for people to borrow money. That meant that money was available, and some people borrowed money to invest in the market or real estate markets that also turned out to be speculative, such as those in Florida. With few regulations to keep them in check, companies offered more and more common stock for sale. Investors continued to buy, confident that they'd make huge gains with which to pay back their bank loans and enjoy the profits.

Those early and middle years of the 1920s were indeed a time of perceived prosperity in the United States. The total value of stocks more than quadrupled between 1920 and 1929, and a feeling of invulnerability gripped the nation.

SHARE THIS

Americans elected Herbert Hoover in 1928, confident that the economy would continue to grow and their personal fortunes would continue to increase. During his acceptance speech after being nominated as the Republican Party's presidential candidate, Hoover said, "We in American today are nearer to the final triumph over poverty than ever before in the history of any land. The poorhouse is vanishing from among us." As you know, the market crashed the following year, marking the beginning of years of misery.

How the Great Depression Happened

This growth of the stock market was, of course, unsustainable. Stock prices began fluctuating in the second half of 1929 and, in October of that year, the great stock market crash occurred, with people selling their stocks in unprecedented numbers, at whatever price they could get for their shares. Over the course of two weeks, more than $30 billion vanished from the American economy, about the same amount that it had cost to finance World War I.

Because the stock market had become such an important indicator of economic health, its collapse resulted in panic and a great loss of confidence among the American public. By 1932, banks had begun to fail as depositors rushed to withdraw their money, many only to find out that their savings were gone.

Between 1929 and 1932, the value of the stock market fell by 90 percent and wages decreased by 60 percent. The Depression continued until the end of the 1930s, and when it ended, despite increased government regulation of banking and securities exchange, economic conditions remained tenuous during the years of World War II.

Bull and Bear Markets

The stock market tends to move in a particular direction—either upward or downward—over a period of time. These shifts are called trends, and when you look back over the history of the market you can easily see those trends.

Prior to its spectacular collapse in October 1929, the market had been experiencing an upward trend. When that happens, the market is referred to as a *bull market*, and investors get to enjoy a period of rising stock prices. A bull market is the opposite of a *bear market*, during which time stock prices fall.

DEFINITION

A **bull market** is a period of positive movement within the stock market, during which time stock prices rise. A **bear market** is a period of time during which stock prices remain flat or fall. Bull and bear markets can occur across the stock market, or within a particular sector of the market.

Bull and bear markets can last for varying amounts of time. When they last for a long time, they're referred to as secular markets. A trend that lasts for a medium amount of time is called a primary trend, and a short-term trend is known as a secondary trend.

When the Depression ended, the stock market continued as a bear market for many more years. Generally, economic conditions were improving throughout most segments of society, but the market remained flat until the middle of the 1950s. Since then, it's been up and down for varying lengths of time.

A bull market ensued once the stock market finally pulled out of its slump in 1954, lasting until about 1966. Along came another bear market, and it was a secular bear, lasting for about 16 years. A bull market followed, lasting from about 1982 to 2000.

SHARE THIS

Nobody really knows for sure where the bull and bear symbols come from as they relate to the stock market. A common theory is that markets were named bull and bear based on the way in which each animal fights. A bull thrusts its horns upward when on the attack, while a bear swats downward to dissuade an enemy.

It's important to understand, however, that within long-term bull or bear markets, short-term cycles often occur. These are called cyclical market trends, and they mean that there could be little bull markets within secular bear markets. These can last anywhere from a couple of hours to a couple of years or more, and can provide some bright spots for investors in a down market.

Bull and bear markets are easy to identify in hindsight, and it's good to understand strategies that can benefit you in either market. Still, each type of market carries some risk, which you'll learn more about in Chapter 5.

The Dot-Com Bust of the Early 2000s

Toward the end of the twentieth century, the attention of investors turned to the technology industry. Companies such as Nortel, Cisco, Oracle, JDS Uniphase, and Corning were the darlings of the investor crowd, as Americans embraced almost anything that was technology related.

Of particular interest to investors were Internet-based businesses such as Amazon, eBay, HotJobs, and Monster. As investors readily purchased the stock of these companies at highly inflated prices, hundreds of other Internet-based businesses followed, with their stock values also artificially inflated by technology-crazy investors. The dot-com bubble was, of course, unsustainable, and burst in 2000, causing many investors huge losses and starting a long and ongoing secular bear market.

The Current Big Bear Market

Unfortunately, the bear market that started with the bust of the dot-com market continues as of the writing of this book, meaning that it has lasted for a decade. And, although the market is currently experiencing an upturn, having finally reached pre-2009 valuations, when it will fully recover is anyone's guess. Ben Bernanke, chairman of the U.S. Federal Reserve, has termed the economy as "unusually uncertain," a sentiment that has been echoed by other economists and left investors feeling wary and confused.

With the unemployment rate hovering at around 9 percent as of this writing, millions more people working but still struggling financially, and employers cautious about hiring, consumer confidence—although it appears to be improving—is still low. This causes people to pull in the reins financially. They put off buying anything except for what they absolutely need because of concerns about jobs and money, and this has the effect of slowing down economic recovery even further.

In addition to unemployment blues, the housing market remains weak, and banks are still reluctant to lend money to individuals and many small businesses. As a result, individuals can't spend and small businesses can't hire, contributing to this cycle of economic downturn.

Economists have noted that investors appear to be starting to anticipate an economic turnaround because they are buying small company stocks. Historically, this is an indicator of economic improvement because investors believe that those are the companies that will benefit most from an improved economy.

Even when the economy does begin to turn around and investor confidence increases, it's likely to take a long time before the market can make up the ground it has lost. Following the Great Depression, it took about 25 years—a quarter of a century—for the market to fully recover and reach a new closing high. Let's keep our fingers (and toes) crossed that the markets will recover much quicker this time around. When that will occur, however, is difficult to say.

CRASH!

During a significant economic downturn, it's easy to get cold feet or become overly emotional about your portfolio. There are a lot of doom-and-gloom scenarios floating around, and, depending on what they read or who they listen to, many investors may be tempted to cut their losses and sell some stock, or even get out of the market altogether. In most cases, however, that's not a smart decision. If your stock has already decreased in value, you have no chance of making up your losses if you exit the market. In a difficult economy it's more important than ever to remain calm and as unemotional as possible regarding your investments.

Still the Best Way to Invest Your Money

Historically, stock market returns have averaged about 10 percent per year. Returns from investing in the stock market usually outperform returns from other investments, which historically have returned between 5 and 7 percent. There are, however, periods of time during which other investment vehicles will outperform stocks.

Other investment vehicles include cash, such as that you'd keep in savings accounts, money market funds, or certificates of deposit (CDs). Cash investments are useful when you're saving for your next car, your first home, or holding funds for emergencies. They typically do not, however, yield much interest, so you're not earning much on your investment.

Short-term and long-term bonds are a type of investment in which you loan money to a company in return for two interest payments each year until the bond matures. The value of the bond can fluctuate depending on interest rates, but this fluctuation in value is inconsequential because when the bond matures, you get your initial investment back. Several investments, including bonds and gold, outperformed the broad stock market during the bear market at the end of the first decade of the 2000s, and the market nearing the end of 2010 was not rushing to any record highs.

Another type of investment vehicle is real estate, but it is usually such a large portion of an investor's portfolio that it doesn't lend itself to diversification. The return on real estate is a hedge against inflation, but is expensive to hold and expensive to sell, and usually is not compared to stock market investing.

The stock market shouldn't be considered as a get-rich-quick scheme. Sure, you can pick and choose stocks that go up in value quickly. But, as you will learn later in this book, investing takes time and a bit of work, and the stomach to sit tight when the going gets tough.

Investing in good quality stocks has and will continue to produce positive returns over time. Although stock market investors see ups and downs in their portfolios, the U.S. and world economies are vast. When the Dow Jones Industrial Average fell to 666 mid-day in March 2009, investors fled from the market. Since then, the market has almost doubled.

The stock market provides cash flow via dividends, growth over time, and tax advantages in that appreciation in a stock held for more than one year has a different treatment for taxes than ordinary income. And taxes do not need to be paid on a holding until the stock is sold.

The Least You Need to Know

- Stock has been a recognized security for hundreds of years.
- The Great Depression followed a period of soaring stock prices.
- Bull markets are favorable for investors; bear markets are not.
- Economic trends are difficult to predict while in progress.
- With higher returns than other investment vehicles, historically, the stock market is the best place to invest your money.

Are Stocks Right for You?

In This Chapter

- Assessing your financial situation
- Preparing for an emergency
- How's your job security?
- Evaluating your 401(k)
- Why the stock market isn't for everyone

To everything there is a season, and that certainly pertains to your financial situation. You might be just starting out financially, having landed your first job that pays a decent salary, and wondering if you should be thinking about a 401(k) or other type of retirement account. You might still be paying back student loans, or you might have a son or daughter getting ready to begin college.

Maybe you've started thinking about when you'd like to retire, or you're trying to figure out how to pay off some credit card debt. You might be looking to buy your first home, sell your house, or buy a vacation home. You might already be thinking about downsizing and looking into buying a condo.

The stage of your financial life should be a factor in deciding whether stock market investing makes sense for you. In this chapter, we'll have a look at your finances and decide whether you're ready to jump into the market or, perhaps, need to take care of some other things first.

Taking Stock of Your Personal Finances

So, what exactly are your personal finances? What does that mean? Simply put, personal finances are everything financial, as it applies to you. It's where you're going to get the money to pay the tax bill, how much you'll need to spend for groceries this month, whether or not you'll be able to save enough for a vacation, how much money you'll be able to save from your next paycheck, and the smartest thing to do with that money.

Your personal finances dictate whether you should buy a new car, move to a bigger (or perhaps smaller) house, apply for another credit card (or perhaps get rid of the cards you have), look for a higher-paying job or a second job, put more money into retirement accounts, adjust the insurance you have, or think about investing in the stock market.

SHARE THIS

It's true that certain people seem to have a more natural affinity toward finance than others. It's said that Warren Buffet, a famed investor and one of the richest people in the world, visited New York City when he was 10 years old and made a point of visiting the New York Stock Exchange. At about the same time, he bought his first shares of stock for himself and his sister.

We tend to make assumptions about a person's finances based on age, but that's a mistake. Some 20-somethings have a better grip on their personal finances than others in their 40s or 50s. We know a woman who by the time she was 30 had saved and invested more than $200,000 from her job as a server in a popular restaurant where she'd worked since her early 20s. On the other hand, some people who should be starting to think about retirement can't because they've got tons of credit card debt.

Personal finance is about planning and implementing financial goals, and should be of concern for everyone. Unfortunately, many people remain uninformed about personal finance for a long time and are detrimentally affected by that.

A big first step in getting and keeping your personal finances on track is to take a good hard look at what you've got, what you need, and what you owe. When you've got those questions answered, you can start to figure out what monies you have for investing or other purposes. Let's get started.

What Do You Have?

Financial advisors get to learn a lot about their clients' finances as they assess the clients' situations and come up with plans to move them ahead. If you're just starting to think about investing in the stock market, though, chances are that you don't have a financial advisor, or maybe have just started to work with one.

If that's the case, it's worth your time to sit down and figure out exactly what you have. Do you have savings accounts or checking accounts? Maybe you've started a money market account or have some certificates of deposit (CDs). You might even have an account someplace you've forgotten about, or some saving bonds you were given when you were a child.

If you've been working for a while, you may have started an individual retirement account (IRA) or have a 401(k) retirement savings plan. All of these accounts, regardless of their type or value, are assets.

The salary you get for the job you do is also an asset, as is any personal property you own, such as a car, a diamond ring, or a bunch of electronic equipment. Real estate also counts as an asset.

If you don't have a good handle on the value of your assets, take a little time to complete the following worksheet. It will allow you to see what you have, which you need to know in order to figure out your *net worth*. Understanding your net worth will help you to determine whether you're ready to start investing in the stock market, or if you've got other business that needs to be attended to first.

DEFINITION

Your **net worth** is the number you get when you add up all your financial assets and then subtract all your financial liabilities.

Net Worth Worksheet

Assets:

Bonds $_____

Cash accounts $_____

Certificates of deposit $_____

Mutual funds $_____

Savings bonds $_____

Stocks $_____

Tax refunds $_____

Treasury bills $_____

Cash-value life insurance $_____

Other _____ $_____

Other _____ $_____

Other _____ $_____

Assets subtotal $_____

Personal Property:

Business(es) $_____

Car(s) $_____

Other vehicles $_____

Jewelry $_____

Electronic equipment $_____

Other _____ $_____

Other _____ $_____

Other _____ $_____

Personal property subtotal $_____

Real Estate:

Mortgage(s) owned $_____

Residence $_____

Income property $_____

Vacation home $_____

Other _____ $_____

Other _____ $_____

Other _____ $_____

Real estate subtotal $_____

Retirement:

Annuities $_____

IRAs $_____

Keogh accounts $_____

Pensions $_____

Other _____ $_____

Other _____ $_____

Other _____ $_____

Retirement subtotal $_____

TOTAL $_____

What Do You Need?

"What do you need" may be one of the most subjective questions ever asked. What do you need? A house? A car? Groceries? Money for your kids' shoes? Love? A new iPad? A cruise?

If you checked off "love," try *The Complete Idiot's Guide to the Chemistry of Love, The Complete Idiot's Guide to the Perfect Marriage,* or *The Complete Idiot's Guide to Finding Mr. Right.* If you've checked off any of the other choices, continue reading this book.

The point, of course, is that need is different from want, and the definition of need and want varies from individual to individual. We all need a place to live, food, a method of getting from one place to another, clothes to wear, and a means of supporting those who are dependent on us. To be successful in a financial sense (at least for the purposes of this book) we need money to pay for these necessities, and also for things like taxes, insurance, to pay back loans, and so forth.

> **TAKING STOCK**
>
> Sit down and make a list of everything you need from a financial perspective. Put the list aside for a while, and then go back to it and think about what you've written. You just might discover some wants masquerading as needs that would allow you to cut down on some of your spending.

Beyond those really essential needs, however, the distinction between need and want can blur. You need clothes, but you don't need top-brand clothing. You need exercise, but you don't need to belong to an expensive gym. You need dinner, but it doesn't have to be in a restaurant. If you're looking to free up some money for stock market investing, examining and evaluating your needs (and wants) is a great place to start. If you don't have a budget, consider making one and sticking to it. The National Foundation for Credit Counseling offers a good, free budget worksheet online at www.nfcc.org/financialeducation/monthlyincome.cfm.

What Do You Want?

Once you've determined what you need, have some fun making a wish list. What do you want? Maybe you've been living in apartments for the past 10 years and want nothing more than to be able to buy a home. Maybe that car that was so cool when you graduated from college is starting to sputter a bit and not looking so good anymore, and you're wishing for a new car.

Or maybe you're at the stage of life where you're thinking about starting a family, or you would like to set up an education fund for a child you already have. Maybe you want to be able to save enough money for a big, extended family vacation to Europe, or to make a significant contribution to a charity or other institution.

We all want things—a new jacket, a nice dinner at a restaurant to celebrate a birthday, a pretty piece of jewelry—but those are short-term wants. Long-term or planned wants, like those mentioned in the earlier worksheet, carry more legitimacy because they are intentional wants that will affect your life or the lives of your loved ones.

When assessing your financial situation, don't discount your thoughtful, long-term wants. They may not affect your current financial position, but they will factor in as you move down the financial highway.

What Do You Owe?

Most of us owe money to someone for something. It might be college loans, a car loan, a mortgage, child support, or credit card debt. Hopefully, what you owe doesn't exceed what you have, and, hopefully, what you earn allows you to take care of your debts and have some money left over. If neither of those scenarios applies to you, you definitely should not be thinking about investing in the stock market, but focusing on how to simply get your finances on track.

The Complete Idiot's Guide to Personal Finance in Your 20s & 30s, Fourth Edition, or *The Complete Idiot's Guide to Personal Finance in Your 40s & 50s* would be a good place to start if you're terribly in debt and not able to save any money. You could also check out *The Complete Idiot's Guide to Getting Out of Debt* or *The Complete Idiot's Guide to Boosting Your Financial IQ,* both by Ken Clark; these and other books are listed in Appendix B.

The money that you owe is called liabilities. Take some time and fill out the following worksheet, listing your liabilities.

Once you've totaled up your liabilities the best you can, subtract your total liabilities from your total assets. The remainder is your net worth, and that will help you to determine if you're ready to begin investing in the stock market. Record that number here:

Net worth: $_____

While there are no firm rules concerning when you should begin stock market investing, it clearly doesn't make sense to invest in one place when you're losing money in another area of your personal finances.

Liabilities Worksheet

Current Liabilities:

Alimony $_____

Child support $_____

Personal loan(s) $_____

Other _____ $_____

Other _____ $_____

Other _____ $_____

Current liabilities subtotal $_____

Installment Liabilities:

Bank loan(s) $_____

Car loan(s) $_____

College loan(s) $_____

Credit card bills $_____

Furniture loan(s) $_____

Appliances loan(s) $_____

Home improvement $_____

Life insurance loan(s) $_____

Pension plan loan(s) $_____

Other _____ $_____

Other _____ $_____

Other _____ $_____

Installment liabilities subtotal $_____

Real Estate Liabilities:

Residence (include second mortgage/line of credit) $_____

Income property $_____

Vacation home	$_____
Other _____	$_____
Other _____	$_____
Other _____	$_____
Real estate liabilities subtotal	$_____
Taxes:	
Capital gains tax	$_____
Income tax	$_____
Property tax	$_____
Other _____	$_____
Other _____	$_____
Other _____	$_____
Taxes subtotal	$_____
TOTAL	$_____

Are You Prepared for an Emergency?

Before you begin investing in the stock market, you'll need to have an emergency fund in place. Such a fund is essential in the event that something unexpected occurs, such as a job loss, illness, or accident.

TAKING STOCK

If you can, have money automatically debited biweekly or monthly from a checking or savings account into a special fund designated as emergency money. That would assure that the money gets to its proper place and help you avoid the temptation to use it for other purposes.

It's recommended that you have money equivalent to three to six months salary set aside in a safe place such as a savings or money market account, where it's easily available should you need it.

A big danger of not having an emergency fund is the temptation to use credit cards to pay for expenses you can no longer afford. Sure, you can live for months on credit cards in difficult financial times by paying only the minimum required balance, but before you know it you'll owe a whole lot of money and it could take a long time before you get back on your feet.

How Secure Is Your Job?

It's unfortunate that, at the time this book is being written, the national unemployment rate is just a little under 10 percent, meaning, of course, that 1 out of every 10 people is out of work. And, as you read in Chapter 2, nobody is too sure of when hiring might pick up and put people back to work.

If your job situation is uncertain, it's especially important to make sure you have an emergency fund set aside. You also should be trying to save as much money as you can (of course, lack of spending is one of the reasons cited for a continuing sluggish economy) so that you have a cushion if job loss should occur.

If you should lose your job, it's important to try to remain as calm as possible. Some people immediately panic and take financial action that turns out to be extremely problematic—even disastrous—in the future. Don't run up credit card debt, cash out a pension plan or 401(k) plan, declare bankruptcy, sell property, or take any other rash actions. Before you do anything that affects your finances, take some time and get some sound advice. Look to your former employer for help. Ask if some sort of financial counseling is available. The company should have someone available to help you with matters involving your 401(k) or pension plan and your insurance coverage. Ask whether you're entitled to any severance pay, sick leave pay, or vacation pay. Is career counseling available, or might you get money for retraining or education? If you are a union member, contact your union steward for more information.

Certainly, if you think your job is on shaky ground, now is not the time to consider stock market investing. Finish reading this book and wait for better economic times. When the situation improves, you'll be ready to jump into the market.

How's Your 401(k) Looking?

Since they were introduced in 1982 as a means for employers to save money they'd previously been putting into pension plans, 401(k) plans have become the darlings of retirement savings options. Pension plans, traditionally, were plans in which employers would set aside money at no cost to the employee, to be redeemed by the employee after a specified number of years of service. Some companies still offer pension plans, but they've become a rare breed. The exception is public pension plans, such as those for teachers and government workers, which have become widely contested and are being looked at carefully to determine the economic impact they're having on communities, municipalities, and states.

TAKING STOCK

If your employer provides a match, either partial or total, for a 401(k) contribution, make sure that you invest at least to that match. If the company will contribute 50 percent of the first 6 percent you invest, then be sure you invest at least 6 percent. To not do so is giving up "free" money.

With a 401(k), employees contribute a portion of their paychecks to a company investment plan until they leave the company (either voluntarily or involuntarily) or retire. If you're lucky, your employer contributes a portion of what you do, and if you're really lucky, will match your contribution dollar for dollar. If you leave the company, the money can be left where it is or rolled over into another retirement account. It's also possible to withdraw funds from a 401(k) prior to retiring, but that usually involves penalties and income tax liability for taking the money early.

Before you begin putting money into the stock market, you should have a good start on your 401(k) or another type of retirement account. Many people invest in the stock market with hopes of accumulating a nice nest egg for retirement, but, as you read in Chapter 1, it's not a sure bet.

That's not to say that 401(k)s are completely safe, either, because they may be tied into the stock market and subject to the same sorts of fluctuations. Because your assets are diversified, however, and they are long-term investment vehicles, they are considered to be more secure than investing in individual stocks. The same rules apply to 401(k) investing as to stock market investing, and, again, the key is diversification. See Chapter 4 for more on saving for retirement.

The Stock Market Is Not for Everyone

Over the past few decades, as pensions have dried up and Americans have become more responsible for funding their retirements, more and more people have invested in stocks, either directly or through mutual funds. Currently, roughly half of all American households own stock.

But while millions of Americans invest in the stock market, it's not for everyone. Let's take a minute to review circumstances under which you should not be considering getting into the stock market:

- **You earn less than you owe and spend.** If your income is not greater than what you need for expenses and to pay bills and debt, you should be figuring out how to cut expenses or boost your income.

- **You have significant debt, especially at high interest rates.** If you have a $10,000 credit card balance (or even a $5,000 balance) at a high percent interest rate, any extra money you have should be going to pay down your balance. If you've got money stashed away in a low-interest paying savings account someplace, consider using some of it to pay your credit card debt. It doesn't make sense to pay 18 percent on credit card debt while you have money earning 2 percent in a savings account.

- **You don't have an emergency fund.** If you put your money into the market without first establishing an emergency fund, what happens if you find yourself in an emergency situation? You'll probably need to sell your stock, even if it's not a good time to do so. Be sure you have cash stashed in a safe, interest-bearing account, such as a savings account or money market fund. You won't earn much interest, but your money will be there if and when you need it.

- **Your financial situation is looking uncertain for the future.** If your job is insecure, you're experiencing health problems, or you're anticipating a divorce or other situation that could negatively affect your finances, you should preserve cash and income and put off entering the stock market.

- **You haven't yet started a retirement savings account.** Stock market investing should begin once you've established another, reliable means of saving for retirement, such as a 401(k) plan or IRA.

- **You anticipate impending cash commitments.** These can be expenses such as money needed to pay college tuition, a planned medical procedure that will require a contribution from you, or a trip to which you've already committed and made a down payment.

If you conclude that investing in the stock market isn't a good financial move for you at this time, don't get discouraged. Most financial situations can be improved if you're willing to be disciplined and forego unnecessary expenses. You also could look at increasing your income by working more hours or picking up a part-time job.

Don't count yourself out as a candidate for the stock market just because this might not be the best time for you to get started. Take a hard look at your personal finances, and decide whether stocks are right for you.

The Least You Need to Know

- It's important to assess your financial situation, including your assets and liabilities, before deciding whether to buy stock.
- An emergency fund should be a required piece of your financial plan.
- If there's a possibility you could lose your job, consider postponing a stock market investment.
- Make sure your retirement fund is in place and you're making steady contributions to it before buying stock.
- If your financial situation isn't where it should be, consider postponing stock investing until the situation is stronger.

Defining Your Goals and Time Frame

In This Chapter

- Knowing what you're investing for
- Understanding investment time frames
- Considering tax consequences
- Investments that make sense for you

Stock market investing isn't something you do because you're bored and investing seems more interesting than playing online Solitaire. Nor is it an activity that you should jump into without careful preparation.

Investing in the stock market should be a purposeful activity, carried out with clear financial goals in mind. In order for it to be so, you'll need to identify your goals and figure out what sorts of investments make sense in order for you to meet them.

In this chapter, we'll look at some common financial goals, the time frames necessary to achieve those goals, and tax regulations that could affect different types of investments. Once you understand those topics, you'll have a better idea of what type of investments make the most sense for working toward your financial goals.

What Are You Investing For?

We can't predict what our future holds, but we certainly can plan for what we hope it holds. As you formulate financial goals, you'll need to look into the future and identify just what it is you anticipate needing money for, and how much you think you'll need. Once you've done that, you can figure out when you'll need the money to fund particular events.

When you've identified what you'll need to pay for, estimated how much you'll need to pay for it, and have a time line in place regarding when you'll need to have the money, you can begin selecting the investment vehicles that make the most sense for you. Let's start by looking at some of the most common reasons people invest their money, either in stocks or something else.

Retirement

Building savings for retirement is one of the most common reasons that people invest in the stock market. With an average life expectancy in the United States of 77.9 years, according to the Centers for Disease Control and Prevention, and an average retirement age of 62, according to the U.S. Census Bureau, the average length of time spent in retirement is 18 years. Eighteen years is a pretty compelling reason to have some money available for when you're no longer working, don't you think?

The mistake many people make is waiting to start saving for retirement. When you're 22 or 23 with your first "real" job, chances are you're stretched a little thin with paying for a place to live, repaying college loans, making car payments, and handling other expenses. Besides, who can think about retirement when you're just starting out?

CRASH!

Despite the many opportunities available for retirement investing, 43 percent of American workers report having less than $10,000 in retirement savings, according to the Employee Benefit Research Institute's 2010 retirement confidence survey. That percentage increased from 39 percent the previous year.

By the time many people do start to think about getting some retirement savings together, they've lost years of opportunity to invest even small amounts that would have had the potential to result in significant savings. Of course, stocks aren't the only option for retirement investments, but many people do invest in the stock market, often in addition to other options, such as 401(k)s and individual retirement accounts. If you've already got some retirement savings and are thinking about adding stocks to your portfolio, give yourself a pat on the back.

College Education

Everyone knows that the cost of a college education has skyrocketed during the past decades, meaning that investing for your kids' education is a really smart idea. The College Board, a not-for-profit organization based in New York City that offers resources and tools for connecting students with colleges and universities, tells us that tuition at American colleges and universities has increased faster than inflation for the past 30 years, with the average tuition between the 1979–1980 school year and the 2009–2010 school year increasing more than 175 percent for private schools and more than 220 percent for public colleges and universities.

This means that parents need to be more aggressive—not to mention creative—about saving for their kids' education. There are some relatively new college savings vehicles out there and, while they offer some tax advantages, socking large amounts of money into Education Savings Accounts (ESAs) or Section 529 plans (also known as qualified state tuition plans) can decrease your child's chances of qualifying for financial aid. Whether or not the savings will affect financial aid depends on who is designated as the custodian for the accounts. Ask the investment firm that guides you with these accounts to set up the accounts to your child's best advantage.

If you have any hopes of qualifying for federal or state financial aid (and don't think you need to be impoverished in order to do so), it's generally best to minimize money saved in accounts in your child's name, which decreases the chance for aid, and do your homework before investing in ESAs or Section 529 plans. *The Complete Idiot's Guide to Paying for College* by Ken Clark is a good resource if you're looking at making the most of your dollars. (See Appendix B for more information.)

> **CRASH!**
>
> Something to keep in mind when trying to set goals for college funds is the increasing number of new fees being levied at many colleges and universities, in addition to those for tuition, room and board, and textbooks. Many schools now charge technology fees, library fees, orientation fees, student activity fees, parking fees, and other pesky costs that add significantly to overall educational costs.

Investing carefully in stocks and bonds, beginning when your child is young, may be your best shot at maximizing college savings. The trick is in achieving the proper allocations of stocks and bonds, with greater emphasis on stocks when your child is young, and moving more toward bonds as the college years get closer.

Down Payment on a Home

Investing in stocks in order to generate a down payment on a home can be tricky because it's generally a shorter time period than investing for retirement, although many people have been successful in doing so. However, because your time frame is compressed, you'll need to pay close attention to how your investment is allocated, keep an eye on risk factors, and be prepared to be nimble about making changes, should that become necessary.

Creating Wealth

Maybe your financial goal (or at least one of your goals) for stock market investing is just to grow your money and create wealth for yourself and your heirs. If so, you find yourself in a good position, assuming that you've already planned for other, more immediate goals and have met them or are on your way to meeting them.

Wealth creation is a long-term investment, meaning that you're able to tolerate more risk than you could with a short-term investment. Wealth occurs by building net worth through capital (assets). Most wealthy people don't have a lot of cash lying around. They own stocks, real estate, bonds, and other investments. And remember that "wealth" is a relative word. To some people, wealth is a comfortable retirement. To others, it's multiple homes, a private jet, and millions of dollars to leave to heirs. Truly rich people understand that one can be wealthy by simply having enough.

Fun Money

If you've achieved all your other financial goals, you may just be looking to invest in the stock market because you enjoy it and are looking to generate some fun money. This may be an even more enviable position than investing for wealth creation, which sounds far more serious than investing for fun money. As with any sort of investment, however, buying stocks to generate extra funds for vacations, a second home, or whatever should not be taken lightly or entered into inadvisably.

When Will You Need the Money?

Once you've identified your financial goals, you'll need to give some thought about the time frame in which you'll need the money you've invested. Money that you're going to need in three years should not be invested the same way as money you won't need for 20 years. Investing in the stock market is not without risk, a topic you'll learn much more about in Chapter 5.

Some stocks, however, are riskier than others. So if you're investing money that you're going to need in the short term, you can't afford to take a lot of risks with it because you need to be able to depend on having the money when you need it.

TAKING STOCK

If you're still in your 20s, you've got a huge investing advantage. Consider this. If you start investing $2,000 a year when you're 25 and you earn 8 percent interest, when you hit 65 you'll have something in the neighborhood of $585,000. If you wait until you're 35 to begin investing the same amount at the same yield, you'll have about a quarter of a million dollars—not nearly as good, but much better than if you wait until you're 45, when you'd end up with just $99,000.

If you're not going to need the money you're investing for 30 or 35 years, however, you can mix it up a little more, combining some higher-risk investments with some less risky ones. That's because if you lose money with a risky stock, it has time to recover and make up for the loss.

Long-Term Investing

There are varying schools of thought on what constitutes long-term investing, but it is usually defined as an investment that you'll keep for longer than three years. If started early on, retirement funds are long-term investments. A college education fund can be a long-term investment, depending on how long before it's needed that it is started, as can a home down payment fund.

Long-term investing has many advantages, and offers the best opportunities for achieving your financial goals. The real beauty of long-term investing lies in *compounding*. With compounding, the interest you earn gets added onto the money you've invested, earning you more interest, which in turn gets added to what you've invested.

DEFINITION

Compounding is a mathematic formula that involves adding interest earned on an investment to the principal and any previous interest. This, of course, increases the principal, allowing you to earn more interest. Compounding is a beautiful benefit of long-term investing.

For example, if you invest $100 at 5 percent interest, you'll have $128 after five years. If you leave that money alone and it's compounded over 15 years, it becomes $208, meaning you've more than doubled your initial investment. In another 10 years, 25 years after your initial investment, that $100 will be worth $339. And while you may not get too excited about $339, think about what your account would look like if you'd invested $1,000 or $5,000. That's why it's so important to get started early when you're saving for retirement or other long-term goals.

Another advantage of long-term investing, especially for those who have diversified portfolios, is that it affords you time in which to make up losses. When you invest in the stock market, there are years you'll earn more than you expected to, and other years in which you'll wonder why you bothered. Investing for long periods allows you to recoup money lost.

A possible complication when you invest for the long term could occur if you find that you need the money you've invested for an unanticipated event, and your investment is in a down period at that time. You could be forced to cash in your investment for less than your purchase cost.

Short-Term Investing

Short-term investing is usually defined as an investment that you'll keep for less than three years. Some short-term investments are for as little as a couple of months.

Short-term investments usually have low risks and low yields, depending on the type of investment you make. Despite that, they're an important portion of your total portfolio, including your long-term investments, because they fund financial needs that crop up.

You might consider buying short-term investments to generate funds for a down payment, a vacation, or a business investment. However, unless you are very sure of what you're doing, investing short term in stocks is very risky business, and you just might find yourself broke and out of luck if you depend on it to fund short-term goals. We are fans of the stock market, but other, less risky investments such as treasury bills, certificates of deposit, or money market accounts also have their place within your total investment portfolio.

Considering Possible Tax Implications

Tax implications also figure into your investment goals and time frame. One reason that people like retirement accounts so much is because they offer really significant tax advantages.

For instance, funds put into a 401(k) plan are both pre-tax money and tax-deferred money, providing a double win for investors. Contributions to a 401(k) plan are taken out of an employee's salary before the salary is taxed for federal income taxes. That means that the employee owes less current income tax. Plus, because the money contributed is also tax deferred, the employee doesn't have to pay any tax on it or the money it earns until he or she withdraws it. Other types of retirement savings programs, such as individual retirement accounts (IRAs), also offer tax advantages. Chapter 22 discusses tax considerations in depth.

SHARE THIS

Tax Freedom Day, the first day of the year on which Americans stop working to pay off their federal, state, and local tax obligations and begin working for themselves, was April 9 in 2010, more than two weeks earlier than it was in 2007. That's according to the Tax Foundation, a Washington, D.C.–based watchdog group. The recession, income tax cuts, and the repeal of certain taxes were cited as reasons for the earlier pay-off date. Still, according to the Tax Foundation, Americans pay more in taxes than they spend on food, clothing, and shelter combined.

Money earned in other types of investments, however, including stock market investments, is subject to taxes—some of which can significantly cut into your earnings. Profits made on a stock market investment are called capital gains. Losses from a stock market investment are called capital losses.

Short-Term Gains and Losses

Investments held for less than one year are considered for tax purposes as short-term investments. Short-term gains and losses are netted against each other, meaning that losses offset gains, and the other way around.

If you end up with a short-term gain, it will be taxed at the same rate as your regular income tax rate. For example, if you're in the 28 percent tax bracket, 28 percent of those short-term gains will go to the federal government, and tax will also be due to your state. So instead of coming out $5,000 ahead on your initial investment, you'll get to keep only $3,600 or less.

If you lose money on another investment, however, you can use the loss to offset your gain. So if you lose $2,000 on your initial investment, you'd have to pay the 28 percent tax on only $3,000 instead of $5,000.

Long-Term Gains and Losses

Investments held for more than one year are, for tax purposes, long-term investments, with long-term gains and losses. Long-term gains and losses can also be netted against one another, but it's done differently than with short-term gains and losses.

If you're in a 15 percent tax bracket, net long-term gains are taxed at 10 percent. If you purchased the asset after January 1, 2001, and held the asset for more than five years, the 10 percent capital gains tax falls even farther to 8 percent.

If you're in a 25 percent or higher tax bracket, your long-term capital gains are taxed at 15 percent. If you purchased the asset after January 1, 2001, and have held it for more than five years, the capital gains tax liability would have fallen from 15 percent to 10 percent. The taxes you avoid paying on long-term gains add up, making it desirable to hang on to your investments for longer than a year.

Another tax aspect to consider is that once you've figured out long- and short-term gains and losses, you can deduct short-term losses from long-term gains, or long-term losses from short-term gains.

You're probably getting the feeling, and correctly so, that taxes can be confusing. You'll read more about taxes in Chapter 22, but if you're feeling overwhelmed, consider consulting a tax professional to keep you on track.

Income Tax on Dividends

Most dividends, money paid to stockholders of companies that realize profits and vote to share them with investors, are considered income and may be taxed at an investor's regular income tax rate. You can assume that any dividends you receive are considered ordinary, or taxable, dividends, unless the corporation distributing them tells you differently.

SHARE THIS

Whether or not to extend the Bush tax cuts beyond the end of 2010 was a hotly debated topic when this book was written. If the tax cuts were repealed, some dividends would again be taxed at an investor's rate of income tax instead of the lower rate of qualified dividends.

Dividends that are not taxed as ordinary income are called qualified dividends and they're taxed at a lower rate, typically not higher than 15 percent. Qualified dividends, which were established as part of the Bush administration's tax cuts, include most dividends earned through mutual funds. Requirements concerning the length of time stock has been held also factor into whether dividends qualify as qualified dividends.

While it's important to keep tax implications in mind, you should never decide to buy or sell stock solely on the basis of tax considerations. Taxes are just one part of the bigger, overall investment picture.

Putting It All Together

When determining what kinds of investments make the most sense for you, you should consider your investment goals, your time frame, and tax considerations. Factors such as your risk tolerance, your ability to remain unemotional about your investments, and how much time you plan to invest in your investments also will play a role in what and how you buy.

Generally, long-term investing in the stock market is considered to be much safer than short-term, so if you want to invest but are going to need the money you're investing within a short period of time, understand that your risk of losing the money is much higher than it would be if you were investing for the long haul.

Beginning investors usually do well to sit down with a broker or financial consultant to discuss their goals and investment opportunities before jumping into the stock market. Having a clear understanding of your investment goals, however, and knowing when you'll need to have money available to meet those goals, will help you decide which investments make the most sense.

The Least You Need to Know

- Whether it's saving for retirement, a child's education, or something else, every investor has his or her own goals and reasons for investing.
- Long-term investing offers many advantages, including compounding.
- Short-term investing is generally considered more risky than long-term, but can be an important part of your total portfolio.
- Capital gains and losses can offset one another and affect your taxes.
- Dividends may or may not be taxed as regular income.
- Consider all the factors, such as your risk tolerance and your ability to remain unemotional about your investments, before deciding how to invest.

What Kind of Investor Are You?

This part explores your personal investing style, and what kind of investment vehicle makes the most sense for you. You learn about various kinds of investment risk, and get a sense of the amount of risk you're willing to take with your money. You also assess how much time you're willing and able to spend researching stocks and keeping up with your portfolio, as that will affect the type of investments that make the most sense for you.

While stocks are exciting and make sense for a lot of investors, some people are better off buying mutual funds or exchange traded funds (ETFs), or a combination of those types of investments. We also explore the differences between investing and trading, take a look at day trading, and provide tips on building a stock portfolio that is sufficiently diversified. That's important in keeping your investment as safe as possible.

Assessing Your Investing Style

In This Chapter

- Determining risk tolerance
- Understanding investment risk
- Limiting your risk with asset allocation
- How often to monitor your investments
- Determining your level of involvement

As is the case with many activities, there are different styles of investing. Some investors are gung-ho, reading stock reports like other people read spy thrillers, tracking the market from opening until closing, analyzing their portfolios on a daily basis, and checking with their brokers frequently. Others prefer to stand back and watch from a distance, depending on their brokers to steer them through, and hoping that the ups and downs will eventually result in gains and they'll reap the rewards of the stock market.

In this chapter, we'll look at some different styles of investing. As we do, try to figure out where you best fit in, as your style of investing will affect the types of stock you buy and other factors.

What's Your Risk Tolerance?

Some investors tolerate or even welcome high risk, while others shy away from it, willing to accept lower returns for the ability to sleep at night. It's very important to understand that in the stock market risk and reward are always linked. Higher-risk investments have the capacity to yield higher reward than lower-risk investments. It's that simple. Your job is to figure out how much risk you're willing to tolerate, and then match that with the investment.

The characteristics of *risk tolerance* and *time willingness* are instrumental in determining your investing style. Risk tolerance is simply how much risk an investor is willing to assume. It is usually based on factors such as your time horizon, or how much time you can allot to investing before you'll need to start collecting on your investments. Younger investors tend to be more risk tolerant than older investors—although, of course, there are exceptions. Time willingness is how much time the investor is willing or able to devote to the investing process and tending to investments.

DEFINITION

Risk tolerance is the level of risk an investor is willing to take as it applies to his or her investment portfolio. **Time willingness,** as it applies to stock market investing, is the amount of time an investor is willing to put into managing and monitoring his or her investments.

When you think about it, people tolerate different levels of risk in many different situations, including driving, sporting endeavors, and lifestyle choices. Some people are just more naturally cautious than others, and that includes investors. Some researchers believe that genetics at least partially determines how different people invest their money.

Researchers at Claremont-McKenna College in California believe that genetics help to determine how much tolerance for risk people have, including with their investments. Two professors studied the investment records of almost 35,000 identical twins in Sweden, and found that their investment styles regarding risk were eerily similar, even if they hadn't been raised in the same households.

Generally, we lump investors into three categories: high risk, moderate risk, and conservative or low risk. Let's take a look at some of the characteristics of each of these types.

High-Risk Investors

Many people are inadvertent high-risk investors because they aren't sufficiently prepared when they enter the stock market and therefore make unnecessary mistakes that put their investments at risk.

Others, however, are intentionally risky with their investments. A check on the web will turn up all sorts of groups and opportunities for high-risk investors. Some investors seek out high-risk stock, willing to gamble on big returns. Often they act on tips and buy and sell stock quickly in order to realize profits. While this is called high-risk investing, it really is speculation, and generally not a good idea. If you are interested in a higher-risk investment, make sure to commit only a small portion of your holdings. Five to 7 percent of a portfolio in high-risk investments is all an investor should consider until his wealth is enough to sustain him through retirement.

There are many different definitions for a high-risk investor, but it's generally considered to be someone who can live with losing one quarter of his or her investment portfolio within a year's time.

Angel investors are individuals or groups that seek out promising startup businesses and invest in them, betting on high returns as the company grows. These high-risk investors are great news for entrepreneurs as it's estimated they contribute between $20 million and $50 million a year to young businesses—with a lot of stipulations, of course.

Moderate-Risk Investors

Moderate-risk investors are those who are willing to include some riskier stocks in their portfolios, but make sure that they're balanced by conservative investments. A moderate-risk investor is generally defined as someone who can stand the thought of losing 15 percent of his or her portfolio in a year.

 TAKING STOCK

You can test your risk tolerance with some quick online quizzes such as one from Kiplinger at www.kiplinger.com/tools/riskfind.html or one from MSN Money at http://moneycentral.msn.com/investor/calcs/n_riskq/main.asp.

Conservative Investors

Conservative investors, like all investors, want to see their net worth increase, but they want to do that without risking any of their principal. That's a perfectly sensible ambition but can be limiting in that, without assuming any risk, you limit the rate of return you can expect.

Conservative investors, also known as risk-averse investors, often look to park their money in places other than the stock market. They might employ money market accounts or buy government bonds. Those who do jump into the stock market typically buy the stock of old, established companies.

Investing Can Be a Risky Business

You already know that investing in the stock market involves risk. There is no fool-proof formula that can guarantee you'll never lose any money. The trick is to minimize your risk, and there are various means for doing that.

When you invest in the market, you're exposing yourself to two very general types of risk (and lots of other kinds of risk that you'll read about in a bit). The first is the risk that your investment will decrease in value—that's called investment risk. The second is personal risk, and that is how a decrease in your investment would affect you and your life.

If you don't need the money you've invested, it doesn't really matter if your investment portfolio loses half its value. It might be annoying, but it would have little or no effect on your life. If, on the other hand, your plans for buying a seaside cottage in which to spend your retirement years goes down the tubes along with your investment portfolio, that's big trouble as a result of personal risk.

Now let's take a look at some of the types of risk that can affect the stock market—and your portfolio. Some types of risk affect the entire market, and they're called systematic risks. Risk that affects only a certain portion of the market, such as a particular business or industry, is called unsystematic risk.

Business Risk

Business risk is easy to understand. It's all about how the company in which you've invested is managed. Does it have a marketable product and a good management team that knows how to get that product to market? Is the business profitable? Will the market for its product continue to grow? If the answer to any of these questions is "no," the chances of your investment giving you a good return are not all that great. You minimize business risk by being diligent about investigating a business before you buy its stock. You'll read all about how to do that in Part 3.

CRASH!

Some but not all investment risk can be insured against. You can buy insurance on a rental property to protect yourself in the event that it burns down, for instance. You can't, however, buy insurance to protect you if your stock values take a nosedive.

Financial Risk

Financial risk is directly linked to business risk, since the way in which a business is managed directly affects its financial situation. Financial risk is the risk that your investment will lose value because the company loses money, or worse yet, goes bankrupt.

A great example of financial risk was seen in September 2008, when the giant financial company Lehman Brothers filed for bankruptcy, sending share prices tumbling more than 95 percent. Lehman shareholders who had felt good about investing in a huge, established firm experienced financial risk firsthand, with major losses for many.

Looking back, we can see there were many indications that Lehman Brothers was in serious trouble, although it worked hard to avoid the appearance of that reality. Again, it's not only important to research a company before you buy its stock, but to keep up with the goings on of the company once you own it.

Interest Rate Risk

Interest rate risk is the risk that the value of an investment will change due to a shift in interest rates. Generally, interest rate risk affects bonds more than stocks, because when interest rates rise, bond prices fall. When interest rates fall, however, bond prices rise.

Stock investments, while less dramatically affected, are not immune to interest rate risk. Dividend-paying stocks may be drastically affected by rising interest rates. Rising interest rates have negatively affected stock prices in the past, and there's no guarantee that, if we experience a significant rise in rates in the future, they won't be negatively impacted again. If a company has a high level of debt and has to pay more interest on that debt, its profitability will decrease. High interest rates can also hinder a company's plans for expansion, thereby limiting its growth.

Changes in interest rates tend to affect some industries more than others. Generally, real estate, the financial industry, and utilities are affected most by interest rates, as rates both rise and fall. When you're thinking about buying stock, keep an eye on what's going on with interest rates and consider how the company you're considering might be affected if rates are changing.

Market Risk

Market risk reflects the tendency for stock to move with the market. You frequently hear people talking about the market as though it's one giant stock, when, in fact, it's millions of stockholders holding millions and millions of shares of stock. And, as you read in Chapter 1, the value of stock always comes back to supply and demand. If demand for a stock you own increases, its price will rise. If nobody wants it, the price will go down. Thus, the market, and segments within the market, rise and fall in value.

Market risk is not easy to control, but diversifying your portfolio through asset allocation can help. You'll read more about that later in the chapter.

Purchasing Power Risk

Purchasing power risk is the risk that inflation has on the value of your holding. If you earn 8 percent a year on a $10,000 investment, you'd earn $8,000 over 10 years, plus the value of your original investment. If high inflation occurs during that 10-year period, however, your $18,000 (due to the time value of money) will be worth considerably less than the value of $18,000 at the time you made the investment. Inflation is a negative factor in that it causes buyers to purchase in the present because they fear the purchase will only be more expensive tomorrow. On the other hand, deflation prevents the consumer from buying in the present because he believes the item will be "on sale," or cheaper tomorrow.

Industry Risk

Some businesses and industries are subject to risks that are unique or inherent to them. The airline industry, for instance, is subject to the risk of plane crashes, which definitely affects its bottom line. The food industry is subject to product recalls, such as the massive 2010 egg recall because of salmonella concerns. The oil industry faces risk in the form of leaks that result in environmental disasters (think BP), and so on. You can minimize exposure to industry risk by considering the likelihood of risk before investing.

Uncontrollable Risk

Some of the risks we've just discussed are more controllable than others. Business risk, for example, is easier to control than market risk. If a company is not performing well, the board of directors can make changes in management and policy. A declining market due to generalized anxiety over the economy, however, is harder to control.

Some risks are uncontrollable. A natural disaster that destroys a company or affects an entire industry is an uncontrollable risk. Acts of terrorism can affect the market in general, as we saw after 9/11, and certain industries such as the airline industry in particular. These risks are difficult or impossible to anticipate, but again, having a diversified portfolio and remaining alert and nimble in how you respond to such events can make it more likely that your portfolio will survive.

Asset Allocation Makes a Difference

Asset allocation is simply the process of deciding where to invest your money. Most financial advisors will tell you it's better to have your investments divided between different families of assets. That way, if one aspect of your portfolio is doing poorly, another part can keep you afloat until the ailing portion recovers.

In a healthy portfolio, funds are divided between investment vehicles such as stocks, bonds, real estate, precious metals, treasury securities, and cash. Although this book concentrates on stock market investing, I'd never advise that every dollar you have to invest should be tied up in the stock market.

Having your money spread out across a variety of investment vehicles helps to protect your investment, even if one aspect of it suffers. Stocks and bonds are the classic example of the benefits of asset allocation. That's because, when bond yields are low, investors get fed up and start buying stocks. The influx of buyers into the stock market causes stock prices to rise. When the stock market gets into trouble, investors seek out the security of the bond market and give it a boost, as evidenced by the historic influx of money into bond mutual funds in 2010.

Your goal should also be *diversification* within the stock market. You shouldn't put all your money into stocks from one company, or even one industry, no matter how well you understand a sector of the market. The fact that you've been working in the health-care industry for 20 years in no way guarantees you'll do well financially by investing all your money in health care–related stock. If all your money is tied up in oil stocks and somebody comes up with a new technology for a great car that runs on oxygen and costs $500, you're going to be really sorry you didn't diversify your portfolio.

DEFINITION

Asset allocation is the process of assigning your investment funds to different families of assets, using your financial objectives and risk tolerance as guides. The goal of asset allocation is diversification. A portfolio that contains investments in a variety of investment vehicles is said to be a **diversified** portfolio.

Many investors found out the hard way in the early 2000s that it wasn't a good idea to invest all their money in Internet and technology stock. A great deal of money was lost when the dotcom bubble burst in 2000. It's recommended that your investments include stock of companies in at least four or five different industries.

Along the same lines, if you simply love a particular company and have all your money invested in its stock, you're going to be very unhappy if that company should fail. Most advisers recommend that you invest no more than 10 percent of your money in any one company.

Monitoring Your Investments

Some people love to check up on their investments, while others pretty much ignore them until a statement shows up in the mail or online. The amount of attention you give to your investment portfolio is another piece in determining your investment style.

Of course, some people have more time to spend monitoring the ups and downs of the stock market than others, and some people are simply more interested in what's going on than others. You should decide what makes sense for you in terms of time spent monitoring your investments, and what your comfort level is. Some investors are perfectly comfortable going for weeks without checking in, while others feel the need to view their accounts every day.

Checking In Daily

If the market is volatile, keeping a close eye on your investment portfolio can be a full-time job—not to mention a wild ride. Let's face it: obsessing over your portfolio during a bear market can be downright depressing. It's not easy to watch your net worth decreasing, month after month. On the other hand, it's darned exciting to watch your Apple stock shoot up by 8 percentage points in one day!

People who are in the stock market with the intention of buying and selling stocks on a very short-term basis must pay much greater attention to it than investors who are in for the long haul and willing to wait through the highs and lows in hopes of substantial returns down the road. Sometimes, though, investors with no thought of daily trading feel the need to keep up to date with every move their portfolio makes.

A risk of that daily or near daily scrutiny of your stock portfolio is that you're more likely to feel compelled to buy or sell in reaction to what you see occurring, even if you didn't intend to. Many of us have a difficult time remaining calm and not reacting to market fluctuations. On the other hand, keeping a close eye on your portfolio gives you a better chance of catching any unauthorized trades or mistakes that might have occurred.

If you invest online, you can have alerts tied to your account to notify you when one of your stocks hits a 52-week high or drops 8 or 10 percent below the purchase price. Alerts can advise you of company statements or news about one of your stocks. This kind of information is helpful and can be exciting, but can also be distressful in a down market.

You wouldn't have invested in a particular company if you felt that you were going to lose money. After a few years, investors forget their fear of a market decline. The psychology of investing for most people is that they abhor a loss of 10 percent much more than they enjoy a gain of 20 percent. That's because they consider that a gain is a given. You wouldn't (at least you shouldn't) invest in a stock if you didn't anticipate that it was going to go up, so when it does, it's what you expected.

CRASH!

Mental health experts have studied the effect of economic recession on investors and concluded that resulting stress can lead to conditions ranging from addiction problems to domestic violence. Resist the urge to check your financial portfolio several times a day if you find it to be extremely troubling and a drain on your energy. Do what you can to manage it, get help when you need it, and find something else to do while you wait for the economy to improve.

See You Next Month

The flip side to obsessively checking on a portfolio is ignoring it, or just glancing at statements as they come in. At the very least, you should examine monthly statements to make sure there is no activity that you haven't authorized, and that any activity you have authorized has been recorded.

There's a good middle ground between feeling that you have to track every movement of your portfolio and ignoring it to the point where it's irresponsible. You'll need to determine where that middle ground is for you.

How Involved Do You Want to Be?

How involved you want to be in the day-to-day management of your investment portfolio is up to you. You could opt for a full-service broker or discretionary investment advisor who will help you oversee your accounts and take much of that task off your hands. Or you can do it yourself, putting in as much time as you deem necessary.

It's important to understand, however, that you should expect the process of preparing to enter the stock market to be somewhat time-consuming. You'll have to learn the language of the market, figure out how to read market reports, research companies before you buy stock, learn to read financial reports, and address other issues associated with investing. And once you're in the market, you'll need to take time to keep up with financial news, stay abreast of general market conditions, and maintain an understanding of general economic conditions.

That's not to say that by the time you buy your first stock you'll be an expert, and you should expect to keep learning and expanding your knowledge over the years as you track your investments and adjust them as your lifestyle changes. Wall Street seems to come up with new products and investments almost daily, and it's likely that some of them may be right for you. Some people set aside an hour or two a week to review their portfolios and research companies that they've heard or read about and think they might be interested in their stock. Others check in with their brokers on a monthly basis to discuss their accounts.

Your level of involvement in your investment portfolio is a personal decision, but keep in mind that it's your money invested and, ultimately, you're responsible for whether or not your investments are successful.

The Least You Need to Know

- Investors have varying levels of risk tolerance: high, moderate, and conservative.
- Stock market investing is inherently risky, but higher risk correlates to higher returns.
- Spreading your money out across a variety of investment vehicles helps to protect your investment.
- Consider how much time your lifestyle allows you to spend monitoring your investments; it will affect your investing style.

Trading vs. Investing

In This Chapter

- How trading differs from investing
- How day trading works
- Understanding speculation
- Short-term and long-term investing
- Assessing the risks of short-term trading
- Short-term trading know-how

Many people consider stock trading and stock investing to be the same thing, but they are not. They occur in the same manner, and similar research may be used when determining what to buy, but the intent of trading and investing varies greatly. Both investors and traders operate with the intention of generating returns, but the expectations of how those returns will be realized vary greatly.

In this chapter, you'll learn about the differences between trading and investing, and we'll explore the fascinating life of a day trader. We'll look at some of the rewards and risks associated with trading, including speculating, which, as far as we are concerned, is never a good idea.

At the end of the chapter, you should be geared up to learn how to become a stock market investor. Trading has its place, and some people have done very well by it. For the great majority of people, however, investing is the smarter route.

The Difference Between Investing and Trading

Investing is a long-term process based on the study of fundamentals such as a company's earnings, sales, debt, and industry outlook. Fundamentals are what investors look at to determine the outlook for a company and how its stock will perform in the future, and you'll be learning much about them in later chapters. The study of fundamentals regarding a company is called *fundamental analysis.*

An investor, at least a smart investor, makes an informed decision to purchase the stock of a particular company, and, because he's done his homework, he can be fairly confident that, over time, his investment will increase and he'll realize some returns. That means he doesn't get overly excited if the value of his stock increases or decreases, and he doesn't feel the need to micromanage his portfolio. He doesn't lie awake at night wondering if he can make up tomorrow what he lost today, or if he might lose tomorrow what he earned today.

Trading, on the other hand, is a quick succession of buying and selling of stock, based not so much on fundamentals as on what the market is doing at any given time. A trader has an immediate, or at least a short-term, goal of appreciation of capital. That means that stock must be watched closely, so that it can be acquired or sold to meet that goal. It's sometimes said that a day trader concentrates on the view as to the next price movement of a stock. He or she certainly isn't looking at the overall market, or even at the particulars of an individual company.

You'll read more about income taxes in Chapter 22, but you should know that short-term trading has its disadvantages. Under the wash-sale rule, an investor can't deduct a loss on his tax return if he buys the stock back within 30 days.

While investors tend to rely on fundamental analysis, most traders lean more toward the use of *technical analysis,* which is a method of evaluating stocks by looking at statistics based on market activity such as volume or pricing. Technical analysis involves the use of charts and other tools to spot patterns, which are considered predictors of future activity.

DEFINITION

Fundamental analysis is the process of researching a stock by studying the business prospects and earnings power of the company offering the stock in order to determine the financial health of the company. **Technical analysis** relies on charts and other tools that identify patterns regarding price and volume, and are believed to signal the direction in which stocks will move in the future.

Traders often will look for something expected to happen that could cause the price of a stock to rise or fall, such as an earnings report or the announcement of a buyout or merger. They are poised to jump on the stock if the news is good, or sell if it isn't, moving quickly in and out of the market in order to make a quick gain.

Understanding Day Trading

Traders who buy and sell securities within a single day are called day traders. Some people work at day trading as a profession, while others are amateur day traders who trade with their own funds or on behalf of someone else.

Day traders have been the subject of a lot of controversy, and often are painted as greedy and reckless speculators looking to get rich quick. While that description might apply to some, day trading is a legitimate business, and some people do it very well and have made lots of money in it. Many others have not done as well. So, who are these day traders, and how do they operate?

CRASH!

Internet addictions are becoming an increasingly widespread problem, and online trading is ranked as the second-highest addictive behavior, right after pornography. Compulsive online traders tend to be young males who are big risk takers and trade with money borrowed from a brokerage. This is a serious and real problem that can have disastrous results. If you think that you or someone you know may have an online trading problem, you can get more information from this article from Smart Money. It's online at www.smartmoney.com/investing/stocks/online-trading-addiction-the-warning-signs-9917/#ixzz11hj4Jylr.

Being a successful trader, as you can imagine, requires a lot of study, and a sound understanding of market trends and the events that cause stock prices to move up and down. Most day traders are well educated and have significant resources, both of which are necessary qualities for success. Day traders also must have steady nerves and great focus, as they have to act quickly as opportunities arise. Day traders share the goal of buying low and selling high with other investors; it's just that they do so in minutes or hours instead of months or years.

It Can Be a Full-Time Job

Among professional day traders, some work on their own and some work for financial institutions. Those who work for financial institutions, called institutional day traders, have access to lots of fancy analytical and trading software, support teams to help with research or news analysis, trading tools, and lots of money.

Those who work on their own often don't have the advantage of state-of-the-art equipment, but they do have access to a very large number of Internet resources, such as day trading platforms and sources for news that could affect the market. Most day traders employ direct access trading systems, which use trading software and high-speed computer links to stock exchanges. Direct access trading systems allow day traders to execute trades almost instantaneously, with confirmations immediately displayed on their screens.

TAKING STOCK

Despite what you read and hear about the benefits of day trading, statistics show that only about 11 percent of all day traders are successful over time.

Successful day traders make money by making numerous trades throughout the day. That allows them to maximize profits through volume trading. Day traders might make 30 trades or more during one day, generally selling everything before the end of the day to avoid overnight price fluctuations.

Initially, day traders buy part of a position, some shares, and then if a stock continues or begins to move higher, they add a little more to the position. If a stock moves up a certain percentage or dollar amount, the shares are sold. Shares are sold immediately if the shares go down. A small loss can turn into a large loss quickly, so day traders sell quickly to keep losses at a minimum.

Do You Have the Stomach for It?

Day trading is not for the faint of heart. While the Internet is loaded with success stories from defenders of the practice, it's also got tons of tales of woe, like the schoolteacher who became so addicted to day trading that he eventually lost his job because he couldn't stop trading during classes, or the young man who one day realized he owed more than a quarter of a million dollars in taxes—money he didn't have.

Speaking of taxes, a problem with day trading is that, as you read in Chapter 4, gains on investments held for less than a year are taxed at the same rate as your regular income tax rate. So in day trading, big gains result in big tax bills, and that's been the downfall of some traders, like the young man mentioned previously, who didn't reserve enough of the gains to pay them.

While best left to the pros, an increasing number of amateurs are testing their hand in day trading, sometimes to the detriment of their careers and relationships. The U.S. Securities and Exchange Commission warns that "day trading is extremely risky and can result in substantial financial losses in a very short period of time," and advises people who are trading or considering day trading to read its publication, "Day Trading: Your Dollars at Risk." If you're thinking about trying your hand at day trading, you can check it out at www.sec.gov/investor/pubs/daytips.

Even if trading is profitable, it tends to be more expensive than holding stock for a period of time. An investor incurs expense through brokerage fees both when he buys and sells shares of stock. Even at deep discount brokerage charges of $7.95 or $8.95 per trade, these charges add up if you trade often.

We would never advise anyone to begin day trading, and particularly not someone at your current level of investing knowledge. Consider that legendary investors like Warren Buffet are proponents of intentional, long-term investing, not day trading.

Beware of Speculation

Speculation occurs when someone chooses stock based on the expectation that its value will increase rapidly and can be sold at a higher price than for what it was purchased. Speculation is not based on knowledge of fundamentals or underlying value or the industry futures or any of the factors that investors consider before buying stock. It's a guessing game, and it's risky.

> **DEFINITION**
>
> **Speculation** is the act of purchasing stock or another investment with the expectation that its value will increase and it can be sold for more than the purchase price.

So, you ask, doesn't everybody buy stock with the expectation that its value will increase and they can sell it at a higher price? Well, yes. Certainly, that's the point of investing money. You want to select a stock that, because of its inherent value, will increase in value and result in returns. Speculation, however, doesn't pay much attention to the inherent value of a stock; its concern is only that the stock will increase in value as other speculators buy it and force up the price.

Some consider speculation to be just a form of gambling, and in some ways it is. But in other ways it's different, because speculators (at least the smart ones) buy what they buy based on information. Of course, there are speculators who buy based on a tip overheard at a cocktail party, but many speculators are financially savvy and their speculation is based on informed decisions, just not the sort of informed decisions that investors use as a basis for buying and selling stock.

If you feel the need to trade speculative stocks, allocate a very small portion of your portfolio to this very risky activity—no more than 1 or 2 percent. And if you lose that money, don't take any additional from your current portfolio. Save up more money before you begin again.

Speculation occurs at all levels and in all areas of finance. People speculate with stocks, bonds, currencies, real estate, collectibles, and other entities. Speculation is a controversial topic among economists, some of whom claim it's valuable to financial markets, and others who say it increases volatility and can wreak havoc if it goes unchecked. One thing is for certain: speculation is not investing, and it shouldn't be used as a substitute for informed purchasing of long-term investments.

Long Term vs. Short Term

You read a little bit about short-term and long-term investing in Chapter 4, so you know that, for our purposes, a short-term investment is one you keep for less than three years, and a long-term investment is one you keep for more than three years.

Stock market investing is generally a long-term endeavor. History tells us, without a doubt, that the stock market is a good place to park your money if you plan to keep it there for a long time. Positive years in the market far outweigh negative ones, and if you're willing to ride out the negative years you will be successful.

Short-term investments sometimes are necessary because you'll need the money in a short period of time. The stock market, however, is not a good choice for investing for the short term.

The market has its highs and lows, but as a whole, there are more up years than down years, as shown in the following table. Investors who are willing to ride out difficult periods most likely will realize a return over time and will benefit from long-term investing.

Annual Return for the S&P 500 from 1975–2010

Year	Return	Year	Return
1975	37.2%	1993	10.0%
1976	23.8%	1994	1.3%
1977	–7.2%	1995	37.4%
1978	6.6%	1996	23.1%
1979	18.4%	1997	33.4%
1980	32.4%	1998	28.6%
1981	–4.9%	1999	21.0%
1982	21.4%	2000	–9.1%
1983	22.5%	2001	–11.90%
1984	6.3%	2002	–22.1%
1985	32.2%	2003	28.7%
1986	18.5%	2004	10.9%
1987	5.2%	2005	4.9%
1988	16.8%	2006	15.9%
1989	31.5%	2007	5.5%
1990	–3.2%	2008	–37.0%
1991	30.5%	2009	26.5%
1992	7.7%	2010	15.1%

Source: www.standard&poors.com

With only seven of the years between 1975 and 2010 resulting in losses in the annual returns of the Standard & Poor's (S&P) 500, it's easy to see that long-term investing, although sometimes nerve-wracking, is a sound strategy.

Risks of Short-Term Trading

You'll notice that this section is about short-term *trading*, as opposed to short-term investing in the stock market. As you've just read, short-term investing and the stock market are not compatible, and you should consider other investment vehicles, such as a money market fund, short-term bond, or certificate of deposit if you're looking for a short-term investment. The stock market is not a place to be if you are going to need the funds within a short time frame. That's because if you're looking at a short-term investment, it probably means that you have a target date for when you'll need the money you're investing. There's just no way to accurately predict where the market will be at your target date and, therefore, no way to assure your investment will be there for you. As tempting as it might be to think you can jump into the market and trade your way to big returns, it's not realistic, particularly at the level of investing knowledge you currently find yourself.

Successful Short-Term Trading

Chances are that you've heard or read about someone who's made a killing from short-term trading. Again, though, it's a risky business. If you do decide to jump into short-term trading, consider the following advice.

Technical analysis, which most short-term traders rely upon, includes looking at *moving averages*, which are the average price of a stock over time. Moving averages are used to measure the general trend of a certain stock, and they're normally measured over 10, 20, 30, 50, 100, and 200 days. Stocks that stay above the average would be considered healthy, while those that fall below would not.

The price movement of the stock relative to its moving average is often used as a buy/ sell indicator. If a stock price crosses a moving average line from above, it's considered a bad sign and an indicator to get rid of the stock. A rising stock price that crosses a moving average line from below, however, is a good sign, and a signal to buy.

Technical analysis also relies on relative strength indicators (RSIs), which compare the amount of recent gains to recent losses in order to figure out whether a stock is either overbought or oversold. The RSI ranges from 0 to 100. A stock is considered to be overbought when it reaches the 70 level. This is an indication that the stock may be selling for more than it's worth and a signal for a trader to sell it. A stock that reaches 30 on the RSI chart is considered to be oversold and a candidate for becoming undervalued. Traders look for oversold stock.

Traders also use technical analysis to recognize market trends, which are simply either upward or downward drifts of the market. As you read in Chapter 2, a downward market trend is called a bear market, and an upward trend a bull market. Traders buy more stock in a bull market than in a bear market.

If you're going to trade on a short-term basis, it's important to control your risk to the greatest extent possible. One step in doing that is to employ stop orders and limit orders, which you'll learn more about in Chapter 16. Basically, you decide at what price point you will buy or sell a stock and place a brokerage order indicating that. That way, if the price of your stock drops below a certain level, it will automatically be sold, limiting your loss. If it increases, you'll realize a profit by selling the stock.

If you look at stock market performance over the past 50 or 60 years, you would notice that most of the gains have occurred between November and April, and the period between May and October tends to be flat. Certainly there have been exceptions, and this doesn't mean that you should limit your investments to the months between November and April, but it's something to keep in mind if you're looking at short-term trading.

Conventional Wall Street wisdom advises investors to "sell in May and go away," suggesting that it's a good idea to sell your stock in May and sit out the market until fall comes around. A big proponent of this axiom is Jeffrey A. Hirsch, the editor of the *Stock Trader's Almanac*, a yearly report of stock market data, statistics, and trends collected from over the past 100-plus years. Hirsch claims that data collected between 1950 and 2008 indicate that the Dow Jones Industrial Average gained an average of 7.3 percent for the November-through-April periods of those years, and only 0.4 percent during the May-through-October periods. This phenomenon is attributed to the theory that vacation season begins in May and investors are more interested in hitting the beach than trading stock. Reduced trading tends to pull down or hold down markets, and the prices of securities fall.

Successful short-term traders generally are knowledgeable and experienced, with a thorough understanding of how the market works. There is a lot more involved with short-term trading than what you've read here, and if you're thinking about getting involved in it, you'll need to learn much more about it if you hope to be successful.

The Least You Need to Know

- Investing is an intentional and long-term process based on research that reveals important information about a company, while trading is a quick succession of buying and selling of stock, largely based on the movements of the market.

- Although some day traders have been highly successful and made lots of money, many more have lost assets in this risky practice.

- Speculation, which is buying stock with the expectation that its value will increase rapidly and the stock will be able to be sold at a big profit, is closer to gambling than investing.

- The stock market is generally not a smart short-term investment vehicle because short term does not provide opportunity to gain a return over time.

- Prepare wisely for short-term trading by understanding and employing aspects of technical analysis.

Finding the Right Kind of Stock

In This Chapter

- Figuring out how much to invest
- Understanding the value of stock
- Low-priced versus high-priced stock
- Deciding between growth and value
- Understanding income stock
- Socially responsible investing

So, you want to buy some stock. But what kind? And how much? How many shares will you be able to afford? Do you have to buy a certain number of shares, or can you get just a few? How do you know what's the right type of stock for your portfolio?

The point of investing in the stock market is to find solid stock that is a good value, and that will increase in value over time. Buying stock isn't too much different than buying anything else. If you try on two pairs of jeans, both of which are of equal quality and fit, but one pair costs $60 and the other pair costs $40, you'd probably conclude that the $40 pair of jeans is a better value.

The same is true with a stock. For all sorts of reasons, stock prices can be all over the place, and some stock is overvalued, which means you'd end up paying more than necessary. In this chapter, you'll learn about different types of stock, and how some stock might make more sense for you than others. In this chapter, we're going to consider how to get stock that's a good value, and that has the potential for good performance down the road.

How Much Can You Invest?

Chapter 3 included a discussion about personal finance and whether or not it's a good idea for you to consider investing in the stock market. If you've gotten this far, we're assuming that you have some investment money that isn't needed for other purposes. With that assumption in mind, let's look at how much money you'll need to have to invest in the stock market.

The amount you'll need to get started depends on how you're going to invest. If you're going to use a *broker*, it will depend on the type of broker you get. You'll learn a lot more about the role of brokers in Chapter 15, but basically, there are three types—full-service, discount, and online—and they offer different levels of services and fees. Full-service brokers usually require a minimum investment, some as high as $100,000. Others, however, require much less, so if you're interested in a full-service broker, be sure to inquire about what is required. Discount and online brokers often require a lower minimum investment, and some have no minimum requirement.

DEFINITION

A **broker** is a person who is registered to act as your agent when you buy or sell stock. Brokers charge a commission for their services. Depending on the level of service you purchase, brokers also may offer advice and stock tips. The word "broker" also refers to a brokerage firm. You might, however, say that J.P. Morgan is your broker.

Many financial people will recommend that you have a minimum of $1,000 with which to buy stock. Many discount and online brokers, however, require only $500 to start, and some, such as ShareBuilder, have no minimum requirement. However, you may be limited to certain products, such as mutual funds, if you have only a minimum amount to invest. Be sure to do your homework regarding fees before choosing a broker. A broker might require a low minimum opening balance, but charge you if your account goes below a certain level. The fees might not seem like much, but they add up and, when you're just starting out, can chisel away at your account.

Basically, you'll need to have as much as the minimum investment requirement if you choose a broker that has one, or you can decide on your own how much you want to invest. Remember that you'll pay some sort of fee to buy stock, so if you're planning on buying just a little bit, it might be better to wait until you can buy more at one time. Remember also that you'll do best in the market if you keep on investing, even if it's a small amount.

Understanding the Cost of Stock

Stock prices are always changing, due to supply and demand. If lots of people want to buy a particular stock, the price goes up because the demand exceeds the supply. On the other hand, if everybody is trying to get rid of a particular stock, the price goes down because the supply exceeds the demand. It's the same premise as the auction house, where if only one person wants to buy the painting, he'll get it for less than if 10 people were bidding on it.

It's important to understand that you can buy stock for $50 a share, or you can buy stock for $2 a share. While $2 a share sounds cheap, it's not a bargain if the company selling it doesn't have any earning prospects. If you buy 100 shares of $2 stock from a company that goes bankrupt the next day, you're out $200. However, if you buy four shares of $50 stock from a company with tremendous earning prospects, your $200 will show you a nice return.

Many brokers aren't permitted to purchase shares under $5 per share for you, particularly if you are a new investor. That's because a price that low is often a signal that the company is in distress. So, while price is certainly a consideration when you're buying stock, you should never buy solely based on price. Most investors use valuation ratios that compare the price of a stock to the results of the company offering it. The most common ratios are:

- **Price-to-earnings (P/E)** is the current price of the stock divided by the earnings per share. This ratio indicates whether the market considers a stock to be overly priced or not, and lets you compare a stock's market price to the earnings per share. P/E is calculated over a 12-month period, and it's the most widely used valuation tool, particularly when used to compare companies within an industry.

- **Price-to-sales (P/S)** is the company's current stock price divided by its sales for the last 12 months. It's mainly used for comparing similar companies because P/S ratios can fluctuate dramatically from industry to industry. It's not as widely used as the P/E ratio, and it's not considered as valuable because it doesn't consider a company's expenses or debt. It is used to determine whether a firm's sales are increasing.

- **Price-to-book (P/B)** is also known as book value, and it's the value of the assets of a company, minus the liabilities. A P/B ratio divides the company's stock price by its book value per share. It gives you the value of the company, if liquidated. If the P/B ratio is low, it could mean that the stock is under-valued, which would make it an attractive buy. It also could indicate a big problem with the company.

You'll learn more in Part 3 about determining the value of a stock. For now, remember that you can only understand the value of a stock if you recognize the value of the company offering it.

Apple at $280 a Share

For many beginning investors, stock in a company such as Apple is unaffordable. And, as we just mentioned, your decision to buy a stock should never be based solely on price, either low or high. A particular stock isn't necessarily a good one to buy even if the price is high. Remember that stock is sold at a high price because it's in high demand. That doesn't always mean, however, that it's a good investment.

SHARE THIS

A classic example of a company whose stock took a spectacular nosedive is Lehman Brothers, the giant investment banker that declared bankruptcy in September 2008, sending its stock crashing from a record high in February 2007 at $86.18 per share to a current value (as of this writing) of 4¢ per share. Investors who bought the stock without conducting good research on the state of the company were the biggest losers when the company failed.

When a share of a company's stock is priced at more than $100 or $200 or $500 or $1,000 a share, you would, with good reason, expect that it's a great company and you'd be very well off to own some of its stock. And often that's the case. Without doing your homework, however, you could sock every cent of your investment fund into a company experiencing serious problems, despite the fact that its stock was still selling at a high price.

Your Regional Bank at $20 a Share

Shares of stock of your regional bank for $20 each could be a great buy, or not. Again, that depends on the strength of the institution. You'll learn about how to research a company in Part 3 of this book, and it's important to remember that you should learn about every company, and the industry that company is in, if you plan to buy its stock.

Stock of a company you know can be a good investment, for the very reason that you know the company. You understand how it works, and you can keep an eye on how it's doing. You'll know when the bank opens additional branches that it's growing. Or you'll know it's in trouble when you hear your friends complaining about its lousy service, see branches shutting down, or hear that employees are being laid off.

Buying reasonably priced shares of stock of a company that's poised to take off is what every investor hopes for. The trick is being able to predict what those companies are.

Buying Lots of Low-Priced Stock

Some people, often those who enjoy trading, like to load up on low-priced stock. Beginning investors who want to own stock but don't want to risk a lot of money as they learn the ins and outs of the market also sometimes will buy low-priced stocks, which often are referred to as penny stocks.

Understand, however, that penny stocks do not represent all low-priced stock. Penny stocks usually sell on the over the counter (OTC) market, which trades the shares of the smallest and least established companies. They are considered to be a risky investment, and it's not a good idea to fill up your portfolio with them. Even though you don't pay a lot for penny stocks, their volatile nature can result in significant losses. Some people swear they've become rich from trading penny stocks, but we'd argue that these situations are few and far between.

CRASH!

Penny stock scams are common, so be careful if you're tempted to buy them. An unethical investor buys up tons of a company's penny stock, sends out a "hot tip" about how great it is, and waits for the price to increase as others rush to buy it. He dumps his shares at a big gain before the demand disappears, leaving others sitting with a bunch of worthless stock. The Internet makes these scams easier and more prevalent, so buyer beware!

Low-priced stocks issued by legitimate companies can also be found on the New York Stock Exchange and other major exchanges. If you do your homework, you can find plenty of stocks in your price range, without putting your money greatly in jeopardy.

An example of a low-priced stock at the time this book was written is Wendy's—the fast-food restaurant that was purchased in 2008 by Triarc Companies, a holding company that at the time of purchase also owned Arby's. Wendy's had been having lots of problems since 2002, when its founder, Dave Thomas, died.

Triarc, however, is known for smart decisions in the food industry and for its ability to bring struggling companies back around. And if you watch TV, you'll know that Wendy's has a couple of major campaigns going on, including a new line of fancy salads and an offering of $4.99 combo meals. These could be indicators that Wendy's is turning the corner after a rough time. A little more research would show you that the restaurant chain is on track for meeting financial goals established for the end of 2011, and that it's sitting on a lot of cash, which is a good thing.

And with Wendy's stock currently selling at a little less than $5 a share, it's affordable for lots of investors. This isn't to say you should run out and buy a bunch of stock in Wendy's, but it gives you an idea of how, if you're looking to purchase inexpensive stock, you can minimize your risk by doing your homework and making decisions based on good information, not "hot tips" from friends or the Internet. There's nothing wrong with owning lots of low-priced stock, as long as you buy it for the right reasons.

Buying a Little Bit of High-Priced Stock

As this book was being written, there were about 45 U.S. stocks priced at higher than $100 a share. The highest-priced stock was that of Berkshire Hathaway, priced at $125,000 a share for Class A. For most investors, of course, that's an impossible buy. And some financial folks will tell you that Berkshire stock can't possibly go any higher. However, some financial folks said that same thing 20 years ago, when the stock was trading for just under $6,000 a share.

A little bit of high-priced stock can make a nice addition to your investment portfolio, but you should determine that the stock is a good value before buying.

At the time this book was written, Google stock had fallen more than one third from its all-time high. So, you might figure, the company is a losing proposition because its growth has slowed and stock values decreased. A bit more research, however, will show you that Google is on track to expand in several areas, including increasing its advertising revenues and launching a tablet computer to compete with Apple's iPad. Some analysts predict that Google's stock will be back up over $700 per share in the next 12 months. If that's so, the current $550 price per share looks very attractive. You should note, however, that expectations are extremely high for companies like Apple and Google, and investors sometimes turn on them if they don't perform as well as investors feel they should. If that happens, it could result in a sell-off, meaning that stock values would drop.

If you don't have much money to begin investing with, very high-priced stocks probably will be out of your price range. Remember that even $10,000 is considered small potatoes when it comes to stock investing. And even with that amount, you'd probably have to purchase in odd lots, which is fewer than 100 shares of stock, because you don't want to put all your money into one stock. One hundred or more shares of stock is called a *round lot*.

DEFINITION

Shares of stock are usually sold in groups of 100, which are called **round lots.**

There's nothing wrong with buying odd lots of stock. The trick is to make sure you have enough money to properly diversify your stock purchases. If you're buying expensive stock with a little bit of money, you might not be able to do that. In that case, it's better to buy a more diversified collection of less expensive stock (which you've carefully researched and approved, of course) or invest in a mutual fund, which invests your money in a diversified group of securities.

Growth vs. Value Investing

Stocks can be divided into two categories: *growth stocks* and *value stocks*. As you know, there are other kinds of stocks as well, but for now let's consider these two kinds, and the reasons that investors buy them.

DEFINITION

Growth stock is stock that's growing at a faster rate than that of the overall market. **Value stock** is stock selling at a price considered to be less than normal valuation.

Some people consider growth stocks and value stocks to be completely different animals, but actually, there can be a lot of overlap. Growth stocks can actually morph into value stocks, as we've seen with pharmaceutical companies. Conversely, value stocks can become the new growth stocks, as we've seen recently with companies that deal in commodities, such as oil companies. Generally, growth investors look at how fast a company has been growing instead of how closely the price of its stock reflects the company's value. Value investors use fundamental analysis to identify stocks that are undervalued.

The trick, then, is to find growth stocks in companies that are strong and have qualities that will help them to continue to grow and assure that the price of stock will reflect the value of the company. Let's have a closer look at these two types of stocks.

What Are Growth Stocks?

A growth stock is the stock of a firm that's expected to experience increases that are higher than average in revenue and earnings. These firms tend to retain most of their earnings for reinvestment (research and development within the firm), meaning they don't pay dividends, or pay small dividends.

Growth stocks often sell at relatively high P/E ratios, and are subject to wide swings in pricing. Investors who buy growth stocks generally are looking for capital appreciation and long-term capital growth. Growth stock is considered to be more volatile than value stock, but it has a better chance for growth in the short term. Examples of growth stocks include Lowes, eBay, and Starbucks.

What Are Value Stocks?

A value stock is a stock with a price that's considered below normal, based on valuation measures common to the market. An investor will look at the underlying financial health of the company, and, using tools such as P/E ratios, return on equity, growth perspectives, and other factors, make a determination concerning the valuation of the stock.

Investors who buy value stock tend to hang on to it for relatively long periods of time, and believe it will result in returns down the road. It might take a while for a value stock to be recognized as such, meaning that your investment may take time to increase in value. Historically, however, a value stock carries less risk than a growth stock and its growth tends to continue for a longer time. Examples of value stocks include McDonald's, Proctor & Gamble, and Verizon.

Which Make Sense for You?

Whether you buy growth stock, value stock, or a combination of the two, depends on your investment style, which considers factors such as your time frame, risk tolerance, and how much time you plan to invest in your investments. Most financial types would recommend that your portfolio contain both growth and value stocks, as it's important for diversification, as you read in Chapter 5, and will learn much more about in Chapter 10.

Income Investing

Income investing is when you buy stock that has a relatively high dividend yield, a major consideration for older investors. That's called income stock, and it typically is that of a firm that has stable earnings and dividends and operates in a mature industry. Critics of income investing say it's defensive investing and too conservative, but defensive and conservative no doubt sound great to an older investor who receives dividend income to supplement Social Security and any other income.

CRASH!

From a tax standpoint, in most states dividend payments are taxed at the same rate as wages. If you're in a high tax bracket you may have to say bye-bye to a significant portion of your dividend income, as federal tax cuts limiting dividend income taxes are set to expire.

Income investing is recommended for investors who are looking for security. Historically, income stocks have outperformed other investments over time, and with less price fluctuation. Income investing is particularly effective when dividends are reinvested. Income investing isn't flashy or exciting like growth investing, but there's probably a place for it in your portfolio.

Just remember that income stock, like any stock, is subject to the ups and downs of the market, and there are no guarantees that you'll end up receiving big dividends. Also, income stocks can be affected by rising interest rates because investors tend to move into other types of investments, causing the prices for income stocks to fall.

Understanding Dividends

You learned in Chapter 1 that dividends are payments companies make to investors who hold shares of their common stock. Dividends occur because these very large and established firms are no longer rapidly growing and expanding, meaning they don't need to reinvest as much of their earnings back into themselves. The earnings that aren't being plowed back into the company can be divided up among shareholders instead, as a means of providing a return on their investments.

Companies within certain industries are more likely to pay out dividends to shareholders than those in other industries. Utility companies, energy sectors, and financial institutions have traditionally, although not always, come through with dividends. Of course, many financial institutions were hard hit by the recession that started in 2008, affecting their ability to reward investors, and companies within other industries were forced to decrease dividends as well.

Dividends generally are paid four times a year. For an investor to receive this dividend, you have to own the shares on the record date. For instance, J.P. Morgan's dividend was declared on September 9 to owners of stock held on October 6. If you bought shares on October 7, you would have missed the dividend. If you bought the shares on October 5, you would have received the dividend. When you buy is important if the company pays a healthy dividend.

Johnson & Johnson is a good example of a company that pays dividends to stockholders. In fact, Johnson & Johnson increased the rate of its dividend payment every year for more than 40 years, beginning in the 1960s. The dividend yield on an initial investment grew by about 12 percent annually, resulting in great annual returns.

SHARE THIS

Technology companies traditionally have not paid dividends because they were too busy investing earnings back into themselves to fund their growth. Many of the large tech companies, however, have accumulated huge stashes of cash, and the pressure is on them to start handing out dividends. Microsoft Corp. started paying quarterly dividends in 2003 and increased them in September 2010. Cisco Systems, Inc. is set to pay its first-ever dividends to investors in 2011.

Identifying Income Stocks

Income from stocks sounds great, but it isn't just about locating companies that pay the highest dividends and buying their stock. As when purchasing any type of stock, you'd want to make sure the company offering it is sound. And you should consider the dividend yield, which you get by dividing the total annual dividend per share by the price of a share. That number reveals what percentage of the stock's current market price the dividend represents, and allows you to see how it stacks up against the average dividend yield.

The average dividend yield for companies within the Standard & Poor's (S&P) 500 is between 2 and 3 percent, but most investors look for companies with higher yields. You can find out what sort of dividends a company pays by visiting the Yahoo! Finance website (http://finance.yahoo.com) or other financial websites (see Appendix B). The last declared dividend amount and the yield are usually listed near the current price of stock.

When looking to identify income stocks, you should also look at the underlying company's past dividend policy. If there's just been a big increase in dividends, analyze whether the company may have been overly generous and likely to find out it can't continue distributing dividends at that rate.

Remember that the longer a company's been paying out dividends, the more likely it is to continue doing so. Look for those that have been doing so for at least five years, and check to see which companies offer dividend reinvestment plans (DRIPs), which allow you to reinvest dividends to buy additional shares of the company's stock.

Also, if a dividend yield is too good to be true, check out the recent performance of the stock. Ten percent is too high in today's economy, so if a stock is paying a 10 percent dividend, it most likely recently plummeted in value. Dividends, unfortunately, can be cut.

Choosing the Right Ones

Picking income stocks entails the same degree of methodical analysis as picking any other type of stock, and you should never invest solely because you'd get dividends. Although many reliable, well-established companies pay out dividends, the payment of dividends does not automatically mean that a company is a good one.

A few companies that experts have recommended as good income investments are listed in the following table. Remember that the list, which includes the company's name, website, exchange on which it's listed, and its ticker symbol, is just suggestions of companies you can research in order to draw your own conclusion as to whether it's a good investment.

Company Name	Website	Exchange	Ticker Symbol
AT&T, Inc.	www.att.com	NYSE	T
Coca-Cola	www.coca-cola.com	NYSE	KO
H.J. Heinz	www.heinz.com	NYSE	HNZ
Johnson & Johnson	www.jnj.com	NYSE	JNJ
Kraft Foods	www.kraft.com	NYSE	KFT
Southern Co.	www.southernco.com	NYSE	SO
Verizon Comm.	www.verizon.com	NYSE	VZ
Wells Fargo	www.wellsfargo.com	NYSE	WFC

Investing with a Cause

Some investors invest in particular industries or buy stock from companies because they like what they stand for. Conversely, some investors won't invest in companies because they don't like what they stand for. This broad-based approach to investing, often referred to as *socially responsible investing*, has been in play for years, as groups have either supported or rejected certain industries or businesses. Investors who engage in socially responsible investing typically are concerned with environmental factors, social justice, and corporate governance.

DEFINITION

Socially responsible investing is the practice of investing in companies and industries that represent the social and political preferences of the investor. Conversely, the investor would not buy stock in companies or industries that did not represent, or went against, those interests.

Investing in companies associated with the green industry is attracting a lot of attention from socially responsible investors. They are looking to invest in companies involved in improving environmental conditions, lessening environmental impact, and providing new technologies in the areas of alternative and renewable energy. Some of these same socially responsible investors are boycotting investment in BP in light of the massive oil spill in the Gulf of Mexico in 2010. Over the years, socially responsible investors have balked at investing in companies that manufacture guns, cigarettes, war materials, alcohol, and baby formula exported to poor countries where it would be diluted and misused.

Whether or not you're interested in socially responsible investing is entirely up to you. Remember, though, that while standing up for social causes is necessary and admirable, to do so at risk of your financial future isn't responsible. Make sure you conduct the same research you would with any other sort of investment, and never invest in a company just because you're admiring of its purpose or product.

The Least You Need to Know

- Regardless of how much you have to invest, you want to look for the best stock value for your money.
- Financial tools are available to determine stock value, and you should fully utilize them before deciding what to buy.
- Growth and value stocks are not mutually exclusive, in that one sometimes evolves into the other.
- Income stocks can provide security for investors through dividends.
- All stock choices should be systematically thought out, using techniques and tools that analyze and assess their values.
- You can practice socially responsible investing by either supporting or rejecting the stock of certain businesses and industries.

Understanding Mutual Funds

In This Chapter

- Defining mutual funds
- Why mutual funds are great
- Why mutual funds aren't always so great
- Different kinds of mutual funds
- How to buy and sell mutual funds
- Are mutual funds right for you?

We hear a lot about mutual funds and tend to think of them as a fairly recent innovation, but they're not. Just as stocks have been in play for hundreds of years, so have mutual funds. The idea of combining assets for investment purposes—the idea behind mutual funds—has been traced to the Netherlands during the 1700s. A type of mutual fund was introduced in Boston during the late 1890s, but it bore little resemblance to what we think of as mutual funds today. The first modern mutual fund was established in Boston in 1924, and the Wellington Fund, the first mutual fund to include stocks and bonds, was introduced in 1928.

The popularity of mutual funds grew, and they expanded wildly during the bull markets of the 1980s and 1990s. Then came the burst of the tech bubble, and some scandals involving mutual funds in the early 2000s, causing mutual funds to lose some of their luster. However, at the end of the first decade of the twenty-first century, the mutual fund industry is growing, with trillions of dollars invested. There are more than 10,000 mutual funds established in the United States, and thousands and thousands more elsewhere.

In this chapter, we'll look at exactly what mutual funds are and why they're so popular, as well as the downsides associated with them. If you're wondering why a book about stock market investing contains a chapter about mutual funds, remember that mutual funds are big baskets of stocks, bonds, and other assets, and they affect the performance of the overall stock market.

What Are Mutual Funds?

So, what are these things called *mutual funds?* Mutual funds are investments that pool the money of many people and invest it in stocks, bonds, and other assets. Each investor owns shares that represent a percentage of all the holdings in the fund. When you invest money in a mutual fund, your little portion becomes part of a great deal of money, as most mutual funds are valued at a billion dollars or more.

Your money, along with that of everyone who has contributed to the fund, is managed by a *fund manager* (also called a portfolio manager) and a team of researchers, who are responsible for figuring out the best places to invest all that cash. During the golden years of the mutual fund in the 1980s and 1990s, managers such as Peter Lynch, Michael Price, and Max Heine were regarded as rock stars, at least within financial circles.

DEFINITION

Mutual funds are collections of stocks, bonds, and other assets purchased with money from many investors. They are managed by a **fund manager** and a team that researches the market and recommends how to invest the money.

Because mutual funds may contain both stocks and bonds, they can be ownership or lending investments, and in some cases both. When you purchase stock, you own the stock and you have an ownership investment. When you buy bonds, however, you purchase a lending instrument in which you loan your money with the understanding that you'll get it back, with interest, after a specified amount of time.

You can think of a mutual fund as a pie. When you invest in one, you get a slice of the pie. If your investment increases in value, the slice gets bigger. If it decreases, the size of the slice gets smaller.

Why Investors Love Them

Mutual funds are nothing new, but they've experienced a great surge in popularity during the past 20 or 30 years. Not everyone likes mutual funds, of course. Many people would rather purchase individual stocks or otherwise invest their money.

What you have to realize is that there are all different types of mutual funds designed to serve different objectives. Just as with stocks, you can choose mutual funds that are geared toward growth, or safety, or income. The beauty of mutual funds for many people is that they don't have to be responsible for choosing the investments that make up the funds they buy into. Also, it often makes more sense for someone without a lot of investment money to start out with mutual funds rather than stocks because of lower risk. Mutual funds are most likely a portion of your 401(k) plan at work. A single mutual fund may contain more securities than you could ever afford to buy on your own. Let's have a closer look at some of the reasons investors like mutual funds.

Affordable and Portable

You don't need a whole lot of money to get started in mutual funds, and it doesn't cost much out of pocket to buy mutual fund shares. If you purchase a no-load fund (more about that a little later in the chapter), you don't need to pay a sales charge to buy the fund. The cost of buying and selling shares or stocks and bonds within mutual funds is generally much lower than standard brokerage. That's because fund managers buy or sell so many shares of a security at one time and buy and sell so often.

Once you're in a mutual fund family, you can direct almost any amount of money to where you want it. If you determine you're going to need some money in a short amount of time, for instance, you could direct funds to a money market mutual fund, which offers short-term securities. If you're into a mutual fund for the long haul, you could invest in funds that rely more heavily on stocks. And you can contribute regularly to mutual funds by having money taken directly from a paycheck or bank account. Mutual funds also allow you to reinvest dividends and capital gains payouts, which in the long term can significantly increase your total return.

Check out the following mutual fund companies if you're looking for funds that don't require a lot of money to open or to be contributed each month. They all received a high rating from Morningstar Mutual Funds, a mutual fund report published bimonthly by Morningstar Inc., Chicago.

- American Funds at www.americanfunds.com
- Fidelity Funds at www.fidelity.com
- Oakmark Funds at www.oakmark.com
- T. Rowe Price at www.troweprice.com
- Vanguard at www.vanguard.com

You Get Help from the Pros

Mutual funds are managed by fund managers, who, along with teams of researchers, are paid to analyze investments. The good news for many people is that means they don't have to assume that task. You'll still need to research different types of mutual funds and consider which is best for you, based on factors such as the anticipated length of your investment, risk tolerance, your age, and your investment objectives, but you don't need to research every stock, bond, and other asset contained within the fund.

SHARE THIS

When you take your car to be serviced, you want to be sure the mechanic who works on it has good credentials and experience. The same applies to the managers who choose investments for and oversee the mutual funds in which you're invested. Fortunately, most fund managers are top-of-the-line financial types with degrees from the best business schools and plenty of experience. A mutual fund company cannot risk hiring an inexperienced manager.

If you're invested with a mutual fund company such as one of those listed above, you can call or e-mail with questions regarding your account. Most companies don't charge for that type of service, although you'll want to make sure you're clear about that. This is helpful when you're seeking advice about your investments or thinking about making some changes to your portfolio.

When you own a mutual fund, you receive reports that list its holdings. These reports, which may be distributed quarterly or semi-annually depending on the investment company, are also available online for anyone to review. Reviewing the holdings of mutual fund companies is fun, and a good starting point to get an idea of what's out there.

The reports break down the investments within the mutual fund by sector, and then report the individual holdings with the amounts paid for the shares and the current market value, as of quarter end. So if you are interested in purchasing a biotech stock, for instance, you would take a look at the most recent statement from The Growth Fund of America. It's interesting reading.

Mutual fund companies have customer service representatives who will talk to you about your risk tolerance, and some mutual fund families provide online tools to guide you into an allocation you're comfortable with.

Lower Risk

Mutual funds are considered to carry less risk than a financial portfolio that contains all stocks because they are available as a diversified collection of assets. Mutual funds carry almost no risk of going bankrupt, due to their diversification and other factors. The money you invest in a mutual fund is protected by the legal structure of the fund, which is set up as a particular type of trust, with its assets protected against potential improper or illegal acts by the sponsors or managers of the fund. It can be difficult to plan that diversification on your own, which is why people look to mutual funds to help achieve it.

With that said, however, you need to be aware of diversification within your portfolio of mutual funds. You'll read more about the different types of mutual funds later in the chapter, but you should be sure that you have a mix of funds representing various types of investment vehicles. Owning five funds invested only in technology stocks is not diversification.

While most mutual funds invest in at least 50 different securities and some in more than 100, providing a good degree of diversification, there are some that are narrowly invested in stock of a particular country or industry. These might be good funds, but you then would need to diversify in other ways. If all or most of the securities in a mutual fund were invested in the oil industry, for example, and oil stocks lost their value due to turmoil in the Middle East, you would want to be sure that you were also invested in securities representing other industries in order to shield your losses.

The Downside to Mutual Funds

Every type of investment has advantages and drawbacks, and mutual funds are no different. Critics cite disadvantages of mutual funds including excessive fees, the possibility of management abuses, tax issues, lack of liquidity, the ability to buy or sell only at the end of the day, and transfer difficulties.

As with any type of investment, it's up to you to do your homework before you invest, and decide whether the advantages outweigh the disadvantages. Mutual funds are better investments for some people than for others, and investors of different levels and circumstances will be affected differently by the pluses and minuses that pertain to them.

Costs and Expenses

Costs and fees can vary dramatically from mutual fund to mutual fund, so it's important that you make sure you know what fees apply and compare them to other funds.

TAKING STOCK

You can compare the fees and costs of up to three mutual funds using the Financial Industry Regulatory Authority's mutual fund expense analyzer. The tool estimates the values of funds and informs you of how the fees will affect your investment. It also lets you look up applicable fees and see if there are any available discounts. It's online at http://apps.finra.org/fundanalyzer/1/fa.aspx.

The first fee to look out for is the sales load, which is a sales commission on your transactions. Mutual funds come in two types, load and no-load. *Load funds* are those with shares that are sold at a price that includes a sales charge. The charge typically ranges from 4 percent to more than 6 percent of the net amount invested. This means that load funds are sold at a price exceeding their net asset value, but they are redeemed at their net asset value. That costs you money. *No-load funds*, on the other hand, are sold without sales charges. They sell directly to customers at net asset value.

DEFINITION

Load funds are mutual funds that pay sales commissions to a broker when bought or sold. **No-load funds** are mutual funds sold without sales charges.

You can avoid paying these loads, or commissions, by choosing no-load funds available from companies that sell directly to clients, without the benefit of a broker. Examples of these companies include Janus, Oakmark, Vanguard, and T. Rowe Price. If your mutual fund has a load, know how much it is, and how you will pay it. Fund loads should be reviewed by your fund's salesperson and stated in information from the company.

Load funds can have front-end loads, deferred sales charges, or back-end loads. Front-end loads, as the name suggests, are paid up front. If you have a 6 percent front load, you'll pay 6 percent of every dollar invested as a fee. That means that $60 of your $1,000 investment goes to the broker and only $940 is invested. You have to earn back what is paid to your broker before you begin to make any return on your investment.

Deferred sales charges permit the load to be postponed, and the fee gradually declines over a period of years until it is down to zero. So with a 6 percent deferred sales charge, you'd pay 6 percent if you sold your investment in the first year, 5 percent in the second year, and so on, until the seventh year, when you could withdraw all the funds without a fee.

A back-end load means you pay a set fee upon the sale of the mutual fund, usually 1 or 2 percent.

Other fees include operating expenses, which pay the costs of running a fund, such as salaries, supplies, and marketing. You don't see these fees, but you're paying them and they affect your investment. Mutual funds tend to be transparent about some of the fees they charge, but not as forthcoming about others. Do your homework and read all information carefully to get an accurate portrayal of the fees involved with your investment.

Possibility of Management Abuses

Despite the safeguards mentioned earlier that are in place to protect your investment, mutual funds can be subject to mismanagement and malfeasance. The Securities and Exchange Commission (SEC) and state regulatory agencies regularly investigate complaints about fund management, which sometimes results in legal action.

You can find out which investment firms and managers have been the source of complaints or regulatory action at BrokerCheck, a website established and maintained by the Financial Industry Regulatory Authority, Inc. It's online at www.finra.org/Investors/ToolsCalculators/BrokerCheck/index.htm.

Where Is My Money, Anyway?

Another potential downside to mutual funds is that you may not have a clear view of exactly where your money is. A mutual fund report, for instance, might tell you that the net assets of the fund are $3.5 billion, and it contains 862 stocks. Of the 862 stocks, however, the report lists only the 10 that constitute the largest holdings.

So you know about the 10 biggest stocks, but that leaves 852 that you haven't heard about. To be fair, you can get a complete listing of all 862 holdings and find out exactly how much is invested in each one, but how many people are going to take time to do that?

If you want to know exactly where your money is in mutual funds, you'll need to commit to devoting a fair amount of time to finding out. Otherwise, you'll need to learn to trust the fund manager and turn your mind to other matters.

You're Not Calling the Shots

For those of us who like to be totally in control of our money, mutual funds can be a bit troublesome. When you invest in a mutual fund, you're agreeing to pay someone else to determine exactly where your money should be invested. You, of course, get to see what the fund holds, but only at the end of the quarter.

Sure, you get to pick the type of fund and gauge it to your personal goals and requirements, but it's not like buying stock, which gives you the ability to buy exactly what and how much you want. You're dependent on the fund manager's expertise in choosing the assets that make up the fund.

CRASH!

Mutual funds can be more difficult to research than stocks because they don't offer opportunity to compare the price-to-earnings (P/E) ratio, sales growth, and earnings per share. You can easily see the total net value of the fund, but you don't have the benefit of fundamental analysis.

Limited Access for Buying and Selling

The inability to sell shares of a mutual fund at any time of the day is problematic for some investors, who prefer the flexibility of being able to buy and sell as the markets fluctuate.

It's frustrating if you have the idea that the market is going to have one of those 2 percent up days in the index, because while you can call and buy shares in the fund, the sale will only go through at the end of the day. At that point, everything is more expensive. Also, you can only sell at the end of the day after the market has sold off 2 percent. The lesson here is that mutual funds are not meant to be traded quickly.

Different Types of Mutual Funds

In addition to load funds and no-load funds, which were discussed earlier, there are different types and categories of mutual funds. Here is a rundown of what you might encounter:

- **Index funds.** These are mutual funds that track the performance of a market index, such as the Dow Jones Industrial Average or the Standard & Poor's (S&P) 500, by buying and holding all or some of the securities in the index. Index funds don't require active management and there is low turnover of assets within the portfolio, making it easier to contain costs.

- **Active funds.** Active mutual funds are those that try to outperform average returns of the financial markets, employing managers who conduct extensive research when choosing securities to buy and sell. Active funds are more costly, due to the hands-on administration.

- **Stock funds.** Stock funds, as the name implies, are those that invest in stocks. There are different types of stock funds, some involving more risk than others. Stock funds can contain stock of only U.S. companies, only foreign companies, a combination of the two, or only a particular industry.

- **Bond funds.** Mutual funds that invest in bonds. Normally less risky than stock funds, some provide tax advantages. Bond funds contain many bonds, usually set up to mature periodically.

- **Balanced funds.** These are funds that contain both stock and bond investments and are a great place for someone to invest a child's account for college, their 401(k) funds, and newly invested money.

- **Money market funds.** These are funds in which the value of your original investment doesn't change. They are usually considered short-term investment vehicles. They're not too different from a savings account, although you usually can get higher yields. Money market mutual funds, although not FDIC insured, are considered to be the safest type of mutual fund.

- **Open-end mutual funds.** These are funds with no size limit and no limit to the number of shares they can hold. They continue to grow as long as investors continue to invest.

- **Closed-end mutual funds.** Closed-end funds contain a limited number of shares, which are sold like stocks and bonds.

- **Unit Investment Trusts (UITs).** UITs are wide-ranging investments created by the investment companies that sell them. Unlike most mutual funds, which are open ended, UITs have start and end dates. When the fund matures, the trust is liquidated and the money is divided among investors, who can choose to reinvest if they wish. The assets in UITs are professionally selected and the portfolios are monitored, but the funds are generally unmanaged, as once the assets are selected, they remain unchanged until the trust matures. UITs have somewhat fallen out of favor, but some are still available.

As you can see, mutual funds are not a one-size-fits-all investment. While most people consider them easier to manage than an all-stock portfolio, they still require some time and attention.

Buying and Selling Mutual Funds

Let's say that you've decided you want to invest in some mutual funds, and, during a conversation at a family dinner, your sister-in-law was particularly enthusiastic about an international fund she'd just invested in. Now, you would never invest in a mutual fund on the recommendation of one person without doing some homework yourself, but you know that your sister-in-law spends a lot of time researching her investments, and she's actually done pretty well with them. So you decide you want to check out the same international fund.

Basically, there are two ways to do that. You can contact a stockbroker or mutual fund firm—some of the big ones are Charles Schwab, Vanguard, Fidelity, Merrill Lynch, T. Rowe Price, and TD Ameritrade—and inquire about the fund. If you already have a brokerage account, you can purchase mutual funds through it.

Or you can go directly to the mutual fund in which you're interested and get the report, which usually comes in the form of a *prospectus*, from the fund's website. The prospectus will include an overview of the fund, price and performance figures, minimum investment requirements, risk potential, the portfolio composition, and the expense ratio. You should pay close attention to the mutual fund's historic rate of performance, and consider the risk factor. A good fund should provide a favorable rate of return that reflects its risk potential. We also recommend that you consult Morningstar, a company that reviews mutual funds and provides outstanding, independent information.

DEFINITION

A **prospectus** is a legal document that outlines details about an investment that's offered for sale to the public. The Securities and Exchange Commission (SEC) requires that a prospectus be filed for every investment offering.

Brokerage houses and mutual fund companies such as T. Rowe Price and Vanguard serve as custodians for the mutual funds they offer and manage. And some of these firms are set up so they can hold not only their own mutual funds, but the funds of other firms as well. For example, Charles Schwab has the capability of holding more than 5,000 mutual funds. This means that you could decide to buy the T. Rowe Price Capital Appreciation Fund through Charles Schwab, or directly from T. Rowe Price.

Brokerage firms that offer access to a variety of mutual funds from different fund families are sometimes referred to as "fund supermarkets."

TAKING STOCK

In the interest of consolidation and ease, it's a good idea to house all of your mutual funds within a custodial firm that can hold all your investments, not just one mutual fund family.

Once you've decided on a mutual fund, you can do pretty much everything online, including getting the initial application at the mutual fund company or brokerage house, making payments, and receiving confirmation. Be sure to print out and save confirmations for your records. Keep an eye on the fund, and always check your statement to make sure any transactions appear correctly. Your statement will keep you informed about the value of the fund, but you can also access that information online between statements.

If you are unhappy with a mutual fund in which you're invested, you can cash it in and reinvest your money in another investment vehicle. Common reasons that investors sell off mutual funds include the following.

- A fund's manager changes.
- A fund consistently underperforms.
- There is a change in the strategy of the fund.

However, don't be tempted to sell off mutual funds until you've thoroughly considered the pros and cons of doing so. You don't want to hang on to a fund that's inherently not a good one, but selling a mutual fund will subject you to fees and taxes.

Deciding if Mutual Funds Make Sense for You

Once you've gathered a good deal of information about mutual funds and learned something about them, take a few minutes to think about your investing goals and objectives. Chances are, because mutual funds are so varied, you'll be able to find some that make sense for your investment portfolio. If you're saving for retirement, you might consider a stock fund. If you're not too adverse to risk, you might consider a growth stock fund.

Your investing personality also will help you decide whether or not mutual funds are a good investment vehicle for you. If you're a hands-on investor, you might be happier investing directly in the stock market. If you don't enjoy analyzing stock and companies, mutual funds might be more your cup of tea.

You can find a lot of information about any mutual fund from a source like Morningstar or S&P. There are books about mutual funds and hundreds of online sources for information (see Appendix B for a sampling). Read and learn enough until you feel you can make a sound decision. But remember, a mutual fund isn't a guarantee that you won't lose money.

The Least You Need to Know

- Mutual funds are collections of stocks, bonds, and assets, purchased with money from a pool of investors.
- Advantages of mutual funds include affordability, ease, and security.

- Disadvantages of mutual funds can include hefty fees, the potential for mismanagement, and lack of control.

- There are various types of mutual funds, each with types of securities that reflect particular investing goals.

- You can research and purchase mutual funds through a broker or directly from the mutual fund itself.

- Buying and selling mutual funds can be performed online, and you can track your funds through the fund's website.

Exchange Traded Funds

In This Chapter

- Defining exchange traded funds (ETFs)
- Advantages of ETFs
- Disadvantages of ETFs
- How to buy and sell ETFs
- Deciding if ETFs are right for you

As you read in the last chapter, we sometimes think of mutual funds as a rather new innovation, only to learn they're not new at all. Exchange traded funds (ETFs), on the other hand, which share characteristics of both stocks and mutual funds, really are a relatively recent addition to the financial stage.

In this chapter, we'll learn what ETFs are, how long they've been around, and how they came to be so popular. If you don't know much about ETFs, be prepared to learn, both in this chapter and from other aspects of your financial education. Many financial people are crazy about ETFs, and they've recently enjoyed a surge in popularity, indicating they'll become increasingly important. Currently, they hold about 5 percent of all the assets within the mutual fund industry.

What Are Exchange Traded Funds?

An *exchange traded fund* (*ETF*) is a collection of assets that tracks an index; a commodity; or a basket of assets, such as an index fund. Although ETFs share similarities with mutual funds, they trade like stocks on a stock exchange. That means that, unlike mutual funds, the price of ETFs fluctuates throughout the day as they are bought and sold.

DEFINITION

An **exchange traded fund (ETF)** is an investment fund that trades on a stock exchange. Comprised of a collection of assets, most ETFs track an index, such as the Standard & Poor's 500.

You learned in Chapter 8 that an index mutual fund is a mutual fund that tracks the performance of a market index by buying and holding all or some of the securities of the index. An ETF also generally tracks a major market index, making it similar to an index fund.

So an ETF is similar to a mutual fund in that it is a collection of assets and it tracks a market index, but unlike a mutual fund, it trades like a stock on a stock exchange, and its price fluctuates throughout the day.

ETFs have only been traded in the United States since 1993. They resulted from something called Index Participation Shares, a product that tracked the securities of the Standard & Poor's (S&P) 500 and was traded on the American and Philadelphia stock exchanges. Index Participation Shares were popular, but they didn't last long because a lawsuit shut them down. A similar product, the Toronto Index Participation Shares, soon followed, and trading on the Toronto Stock Exchange became widely popular.

The American Stock Exchange, noting the popularity of these products, worked to design a product that would meet the regulations of the U.S. Securities and Exchange Commission (SEC) and could be marketed in the United States. Two executives of the stock exchange, Nathan Most and Steven Bloom, in 1993 developed Standard & Poor's Depositary Receipts, the first ETFs traded in the United States. The product became known as SPDRs or "Spiders," and soon was the largest ETF in the world.

SHARE THIS

The credit for the first ETFs goes to Nathan Most and Steven Bloom, who were in charge of new product development for the American Stock Exchange in the early 1990s. Remember that we had a bull market in the 1990s and investors were eager to try something new, thereby putting pressure on executives to develop new investment products.

As you can imagine, alternatives to Spiders soon cropped up, and in subsequent years the financial world and investors said hello to World Equity Benchmark Shares, known as "WEBS," and later renamed iShares MSCI Index Fund Shares; "Sector

Spiders," which track the nine different sectors of the S&P 500; "Dow Diamonds," which track the Dow Jones Industrial Average; and "Cubes," which track the movement of the NASDAQ 100.

While ETFs became popular with a small group of investors, most individual investors didn't know much about them during the early years. In 2000, however, Barclays Global Investors, a major global financial services provider, got into the game and pitched a campaign to make long-term investors aware of the relatively new investment vehicle. It sold off iShares to Blackrock Financial in order to bolster capital early in 2000, and within five years surpassed all the competition.

While the basis of ETFs has remained the same, they've been modified to track progressively more specific sets of asset classes, including sectors, industries, bonds, commodities, and futures.

Why Investors Love Them

It's clear that many investors are enamored with ETFs, which have been on the financial landscape for only 20 years, as opposed to their much better established stock, bond, and mutual fund counterparts.

It was reported in May 2010 that, worldwide, ETFs listed on world stock markets had a value of $1.08 trillion. The report, compiled by Blackrock Financial Group, the company that issues iShares ETFs, revealed there are about 2,130 ETF products listed on 42 stock exchanges worldwide. At the end of March 2010, 814 ETF products from 29 providers were available in the United States, with more expected to be available soon.

Basically, investors report that they like ETFs because they're affordable due to low minimum buy-in requirements and low fees, they provide diversity within investment portfolios, and they're flexible in that they can be bought and sold during the day like stock. Let's have a closer look at each of those ETF advantages.

Affordable

Those who want to get into the market but don't have big bucks to invest have been enthusiastic about ETFs, which can be purchased in small amounts for less than $1,000, compared to some mutual funds that have high starting balance requirements.

Because ETFs are index based (at least most of them are, but in light of the SEC approval for active ETF funds, make sure you check that before buying), they don't require active management. As a result, ETFs generally have low *expense ratios*, which keep fees low. You figure out an expense ratio by dividing the cost of a fund's operating expenses by the average dollar value of its assets. Operating expenses are deducted from the fund's assets, thereby lowering the return to its investors.

DEFINITION

An **expense ratio** is the cost to an investment company to operate a fund. It's calculated by dividing the cost of a fund's operating expenses by the average dollar value of its assets. The greater the operating costs, the lower the value of the fund's assets will be.

ETFs that track the major indexes, like the S&P 500, are particularly likely to be able to keep fees low. Those that track more obscure indexes might charge higher fees, but ETF fees tend to be lower than those associated with mutual funds.

Although you'll run into capital gains taxes on earnings, as with most types of investments, the way ETFs are structured makes them less subject to big capital gains because they generally have a low turnover of assets. That's a help to you when it's time to pay Uncle Sam.

Diversification

Like mutual funds, ETFs can offer a great means of diversification for your portfolio. Because of the way they're designed, there are ETFs that represent all segments of the market. ETFs can give you exposure to foreign and global markets and virtually every industry and market sector.

You can buy ETFs that get you invested in energy, water, precious metals, or food markets. One ETF, the iShares MSCI-Australia fund, invests you only in Australian companies. The original U.S. ETF, the Spiders fund, which is still very popular, tracks the S&P 500 and makes you a shareholder in large U.S. companies.

SHARE THIS

Investment analysts report that participation in socially responsible ETFs has risen significantly during the past several years. These funds, such as the First Trust NASDAQ Clean Edge Green Energy fund, the iShares KLD Select Social Index fund, and the iShares S&P Global Clean Energy Index fund, invest in companies that support environmental, social justice, or other causes. Faith-based funds are also gaining in popularity.

As you can see, when added to other investments, ETFs can provide valuable diversification.

Range of Options

You can easily call your broker and buy some ETFs (after careful research and consideration, of course) and then let them sit, as many investors do with mutual funds. Because they're easy to buy, however, they're also easy to sell, which means some people trade ETFs like stocks.

We recommend ETFs for long-term or mid-range investing, not as trading vehicles. However, if for some reason you'd need to sell them in order to buy something else or for another reason, you have that option.

The Downside to Exchange Traded Funds

You probably saw this coming, right? As with every investment, where there's an upside, there's going to be a downside. The biggest complaint that investors seem to have regarding ETFs is that they have to be purchased through a broker. Having to pay brokerage commissions can devalue your investment, especially if your investment is small. An $8 or $10 trading fee can put a big dent in a $100 or $150 investment in an ETF. That's why investors often are warned against trading ETFs like they would stocks, even though they're set up for that. Let's look at a couple of other complaints about ETFs.

Lower Fees, but Fees Nonetheless

Few things in life are free, and service on your ETFs is no exception. They're mostly low, but you will encounter service fees on your ETF accounts.

As you read a bit earlier, ETFs typically have low management fees because they're index based and most of the work is done by computers. They don't require a lot of well-educated, experienced, and highly paid financial types to sit around analyzing them. For that reason, they have low expense ratios, which keeps fees low.

What you should do if you're looking to buy ETFs, though, is to compare fees on funds issued by different companies. That's where you'll see a difference between fees. Then, you can go to an information source such as Morningstar, research the different funds, and decide whether the higher fees one company may charge over another are worth it.

Understanding Net Asset Values of ETFs

A matter of concern in recent years is that ETFs have often traded either above or below the net asset values of the holdings they contain. A net asset value is simply the ETFs' per-share value. This happens because, like stock, the price of an ETF depends on how many people want to buy it—a simple case of supply and demand. The combined value of the holdings within the fund largely determines the demand for the fund, but other factors can also affect market prices. That means that ETFs sometimes trade at more or less than their net asset values.

This is worrisome because of the possibility that an investor who for some reason must quickly sell ETFs will find that the value of his funds is below the net asset value of its holdings. There are mechanisms in place to keep the values even, and they normally work. If you decide to invest in ETFs, however, this would be something to ask your broker about.

Buying and Selling ETFs

ETFs are like mutual funds in that they're collections of assets, not a single commodity like a stock or a bond. However, if you want to buy ETFs, you do so through a stock exchange where they trade, just as you would buy a stock. That means that you need a brokerage account, and will have to select a brokerage firm if you don't already have one.

As long as you're willing to research before you buy and sell investments and keep an eye on your accounts and statements, a discount broker most likely will serve your purposes quite nicely. Some reputable discount brokers include the following:

- ShareBuilder
- TD Ameritrade
- Scottrade
- E*Trade
- Fidelity
- Charles Schwab
- TradeKing
- Firstrade

- WallStreet-E

- OptionsXpress

- Zecco

- WellsTrade

- Just2Trade

- Muriel Seibert

To learn more about these and other brokers, check out SmartMoney's annual broker survey at www.smartmoney.com/Investing/Economy/SmartMoneys-Annual-Broker-Survey-23119/. Click on "Table: Top Discount Brokers" to get rankings and information about each brokerage.

A positive aspect of ETFs—and one that is especially appealing to beginning investors—is that you don't need a lot of money to buy them. You can get started in ETFs for less than $1,000. Remember, though, that like stocks, if you trade ETFs, you'll have to pay a broker's commission. Heavy trading of ETFs can result in you paying a lot of money to the broker.

When you buy an ETF, you're actually buying it from a *secondary market*, which means you're purchasing it from other investors instead of underlying companies. Only "authorized participants"—which are usually big players like a pension fund or life insurance company that can trade huge quantities of securities—buy and sell shares of ETFs from fund managers. The rest of us, through a broker, buy and sell on this secondary market.

DEFINITION

A **secondary market** is one where investors buy stock or other assets from other investors—usually large, institutional investors—instead of from issuing companies. Secondary markets are common and include national exchanges, including NASDAQ and the New York Stock Exchange.

ETFs were designed to be index funds, meaning that they track the performances of a market index and don't require active management. In 2008, however, the SEC authorized the first actively managed ETFs, which are those that try to outperform average returns of the financial markets, employing managers who conduct extensive research when choosing securities to buy and sell. Active funds are more costly, which could raise fees on ETFs.

Deciding if Exchange Traded Funds Make Sense for You

Just as with any investment, you'll need to weigh the pros and cons regarding ETFs to decide whether they'd be a valuable addition to your portfolio. And if you decide you like ETFs and are going to invest, make sure that you look carefully at the holdings of each ETF you consider, just as you would with a mutual fund.

With all the interest in ETFs, there are more and more companies getting into the act. Some of the funds' names can be a little misleading, so be sure to do your homework to make sure that the First Trust NASDAQ Clean Edge Green Energy fund actually does contain assets that are in tune with your environmental sensibilities.

Also, be sure that the ETFs you purchase make sense financially. Perusing all the different ETFs available can be like a walk through the ice cream section of the grocery store for an investor—there's a flavor for everybody. Just because you like everything Australian, however, doesn't mean that the iShares MSCI Australia Index fund is a great addition to your portfolio.

TAKING STOCK

The number of holdings in an ETF portfolio varies dramatically, from hundreds to just a few. One Internet ETF, B2B Internet HOLDRs12/40, once included 20 holdings, but by 2010 had dropped to just 2. Always check out a fund to be sure of what you're actually buying.

One other word of caution involves diversification. Don't assume you're buying diversification for your portfolio just because you're buying an ETF. If you've already got a hefty supply of energy stock, for instance, avoid buying an ETF that contains more of the same. Remember that ETFs are representative of nearly every industry and market sector, and choose one that gets you into an area in which you don't already have holdings. Or play it safe and buy an ETF that tracks a major index, like the NASDAQ or S&P 500.

The Least You Need to Know

- ETFs are similar to mutual funds, but they can be traded throughout the day.
- Advantages of ETFs include their affordability, diversification, and flexibility.
- Disadvantages of ETFs are a lack of purchasing options, fees, and possible problems with selling.
- ETFs must be purchased and sold through a brokerage.
- ETFs should be carefully researched before you buy them to make sure they are a good option for you.

Diversifying Your Stock Portfolio

In This Chapter

- Why asset allocation is necessary
- Methods for diversifying your portfolio
- Finding the right mix of stock
- Knowing when to adjust your portfolio
- Avoiding over-diversification

Smart investors understand the importance of having a diversified portfolio. Simply put, this means that you avoid having all of your eggs in one basket. That way, if one basket drops and all the eggs break, you still have some more eggs to keep you going.

Often, a discussion about asset allocation and diversification would address having funds divided among investment vehicles such as stocks, bonds, real estate, precious metals, treasury securities, and cash. Although this book concentrates on stock market investing, we would never advise an investor, especially someone just getting started, that every dollar you have to invest should be tied up in the stock market. That's because having your money spread out across a variety of investment vehicles helps to protect your investment, even if one aspect of it suffers.

With that in mind, however, for the purposes of this chapter, our discussion will focus on diversifying your stock portfolio, not your total investment portfolio. Don't get confused and interpret that to mean that we're advising you to invest only in stocks—that is not the case. For now, however, we'll focus on the market and how you should think about allocating your assets within it.

The Importance of Asset Allocation

We introduced asset allocation in Chapter 5, so we'll just have a quick review here. Asset allocation is simply the process of deciding where to invest your money. Actually, that's a simple definition for a process that should involve systematic and considered placement of assets into investments that balance one another and provide some protection in the event of market volatility or other circumstances.

Since we're focusing on asset allocation among stocks, we'll be looking at how you can best achieve a healthy allocation of assets within your stock portfolio. This takes into account the amount of risk associated with particular stock and the amount of risk you're willing to assume, the amount of time you estimate you have before you'll need the money you've invested, your financial goals, and other factors.

> **CRASH!**
>
> You'll read time and time again about the dangers of emotional investing, but it can't be overstated. We knew a young investor who had saved $15,000 to get started in the stock market. Smart move, right? It was, until she decided to invest her entire nest egg in her boyfriend's startup enterprise, an Internet business selling stuffed animals. Needless to say, she wasn't happy when she lost her entire investment when the business went bankrupt. And in case you're wondering, the relationship did not survive.

Within the stock market, you should aspire to achieve diversification by acquiring different types of stock. You shouldn't consider putting all your money into stocks from one company, or even one industry. It's recommended, in fact, that your investments include stock of companies in at least four or five different industries.

Hopefully all investors learned from the sad tale of Enron employees, who during the early 2000s lost their life savings because they had all their money invested in energy trader Enron stock. The stock nosedived from a high of $80 per share to less than $1 a share within a year as the company collapsed.

Looking at Your Options

So how do you achieve diversification within the stock market? Taking a lesson from real life, you need to find assets that complement one another through a balancing act. Someone made a comparison in an article between the stock market and a street vendor's cart. The article pointed out that a street vendor's cart typically is loaded down with a variety of materials, ranging from umbrellas to sunglasses or sunscreen. While that might seem like an odd mix of products, upon closer scrutiny, it makes perfect sense.

The street vendor is out there every day, rain or shine. On rainy days he'll sell more umbrellas; on sunny days, he'll sell more sunglasses. Within the stock market are securities that range from downright dangerous to so safe that they're almost boring. Your job, just like the street vendor, is to find a mix of products so that you maintain the possibility of reward, while limiting the possibility that you'll lose all your money. So what factors should you consider when choosing stock? Let's have a look.

Understanding Stock Sectors

You'll learn more about sectors in Chapter 12, but for now, it's important to understand the concept of stock sectors in terms of diversifying your portfolio.

Stocks are classified into groups, called sectors. If you think about the stock market as a pie, each slice of pie would be a sector, representing different areas. The Standard & Poor's (S&P) Global Industry Classification System (GICS) is a common means of grouping stocks into sectors, and it includes the following:

- Consumer discretionary
- Consumer staples
- Energy
- Financials
- Health care
- Industrials
- Information technology
- Materials
- Telecom
- Utilities

All of the stocks held within the S&P 500 fall within one of these sectors, and each sector contains a certain percentage of the entire S&P 500 portfolio. The percentages range from 3 percent of all stocks within the telecom sector, to 18 percent in the financials sector.

TAKING STOCK

Recent research conducted by the Schwab Center for Financial Research found that matching the sector weightings of your portfolio with those of a benchmark like the S&P Global Industry Classification System (GICS) can reduce your risk by 25 percent without affecting average returns.

You can use the GICS as a guide to diversifying your portfolio by sector or, after conducting your own research, you can decide for yourself. If you only own a few stocks, of course, you can't be represented in every sector. It's important to understand, however, that stocks within the same sector tend to increase and decrease in value as a group, so you don't want all your eggs in one basket—or stocks in one sector. Remember that stocks within the same sector are varied and carry varied levels of risk. Within the software sector, for instance, you'd find both the software giant Oracle, and a fledgling software startup.

CRASH!

Don't limit your investments to companies within the industry you work in, even though it's within your comfort level to buy stock of companies you understand and are comfortable with. Also, remember that you can't afford to hang on to stock that might have been passed along to you by parents or grandparents if it's not sound and performing well.

U.S., International, and Global Stocks

Another consideration in asset allocation is to look at investing in stock held by companies outside of the United States. It's easy to understand that rapidly expanding economies hold opportunities for investors, but (you saw that coming, right?) there is also risk involved.

During the 1970s, the United States issued more stock than all other countries combined. As economic power shifted through the 1980s and 1990s, however, foreign countries began issuing more stock and becoming increasingly influential in international trading. Today, at least 60 percent of all stock is issued by countries other than the United States. And if you consider the rapidly growing economies of China and India, that percentage is likely to continue to rise.

SHARE THIS

International investing is buying stock of foreign companies that do not have corporate headquarters within the United States. Global investing is different because it includes stock of multinational corporations like Coca-Cola that are based in the United States.

While many advisors recommend investing in some international or global stock, most will limit that stock to no more than up to 20 percent of your total portfolio. Many advisors do not recommend foreign securities or markets for beginning or highly risk-adverse investors, as they do tend to be more volatile due to risks including foreign exchange risk, political instability, lack of regulation, and others.

Foreign exchange risk is also known as currency risk, and it refers to the value of foreign currency in relationship to the U.S. dollar. It's just like the exchange rate you look at when planning a trip to Europe or another location. If the value of the dollar rises on a foreign exchange market, the value of the foreign currency decreases. And when the value of the dollar drops, the value of the foreign currency increases.

This can affect stock prices and the value of dividends that a foreign company pays out to investors. If the dollar value increases in relationship to the currency of the company paying dividends, your dividends will be devalued when they're converted. Of course, this works the other way around, too. Another factor with foreign stock is that, once traded, it can take days or weeks for a transaction to settle, as the trades may need to be paid for in local currency.

Governments in some foreign countries are much less stable than the U.S. government, and political instability can wreak havoc with a country's economy and business investments. And it's important to understand that regulations regarding trading and business vary widely from country to country, meaning you can't assume that someone is looking out for the safety and integrity of your investments.

If you do consider purchasing international or global stock, it's best to do so through a U.S. brokerage firm through American depositary receipts (ADRs). Introduced in 1927, an ADR is a stock that trades in the United States but represents a specified number of shares in a foreign corporation. ADRs are sold on the American stock market like a regular stock and are issued in the United States by a bank or a brokerage firm. Your broker will need a clearing agreement with his or her counterpart in the foreign stock exchange. And once you own foreign securities, be prepared to keep a close eye on them and be ready to adjust your portfolio when necessary.

Emerging and Developing Markets

Emerging and developing markets are countries with expanding economies that are experiencing growth and industrialization. With the U.S. economy in a long bearish state, some economists are advising investors to look at countries like China, the Philippines, and Brazil, which they see as having the potential for great growth.

As with international investing, however, there is significant risk associated with emerging markets, so be careful and do not buy stock of companies in these places without conducting careful research and attaining a clear understanding of circumstances affecting the company and the country. While there are excellent companies based in emerging markets, some of which trade on U.S. exchanges, it's important to consider factors such as the political situations of these countries or events such as the recent devastating flooding in Malaysia and ongoing instability and violence in Mexico, both of which are identified as emerging markets.

Growth and Value Stock

The last method of diversifying your portfolio is dividing your investments between growth and value stock. You read a little about these types of stock in Chapter 7, but it's important to understand the role they play in diversification.

You'll recall that growth stock is the stock of a firm that's expected to experience increases that are higher than average in revenue and earnings. A value stock is a stock with a price that's considered below normal, based on valuation measures common to the market.

Value stock is considered to be a safer investment than growth stock, but growth stock, as its name implies, has more potential for growth and higher returns. Growth companies tend to hang on to most of their earnings for reinvestment, and that means that they pay little or no dividends. Investors who buy growth stock typically are looking for capital appreciation and long-term growth.

Those who invest in value stock usually plan to hang on to it for a relatively long period of time, banking on the hope that they'll realize future returns. Value investing is more of a "slow and steady wins the race" style of investing. Value stocks tend to do better in a down or flat market—as evidenced by the Consumer Staple sector holding its own during late 2008 and early 2009. Advisors generally steer younger investors toward a greater percentage of growth stock than they would recommend for older investors. Most portfolios, however, would benefit from some mix of the two. Currently, growth is the place to be in the market, with value taking a back seat.

Deciding whether to allocate heavier to growth or value depends on your comfort level, your risk factors, and whether the market is bullish or bearish.

Creating the Right Mix for You

When it comes right down to it, your stock portfolio is personal. Sure, you can get a financial advisor or planner to tell you where to put every investment dollar you have, and many people do that. The most successful investors, however, not to mention the ones who have the most fun with their investments, are those who take ownership of their investments, and, based on diligent research and study, make their own portfolio decisions.

That's not to say that you should invest based on emotion, or disregard time-tested and proven advice from experts. When you invest yourself in your investments, however, you learn more, you're more likely to pay attention to them, and, overall, you're more likely to be successful. Having said all that, let's look at factors that are important in finding the right allocations for your assets.

The Age Factor

Nearly all advisors will tell you that your portfolio, much like your choice of clothing, should become more conservative as you get older. This book focuses on stock market investing, but it wouldn't be fair to you to not mention other investments at this point. Basically, we talk about three groups of investments: stocks; bonds; and cash or cash equivalents, such as savings accounts, money market funds, and treasury bills.

Subtract your age from 100. The number you get is approximately the percentage of your investment funds that should be invested in stock. The rest of your funds should be invested in bonds and cash equivalents, such as money market funds. If you are 30, for example, it's appropriate for you to have 70 percent of your investment funds in stock. If you're 50, about half of your funds should be in stock. Few investors, if any, should put all of their money in stock.

TAKING STOCK

While you should move toward more conservative investments as you move closer to the time that you'll need to start cashing in your portfolio, some advisors warn against becoming too conservative too early. The Centers for Disease Prevention and Control puts the average life expectancy in the United States at 84, meaning that, if you retire at 64, you need to have some potential for growth in order to keep up with inflation.

For the purposes of stock investing, you'll need to consider how much time you have until you'll need to cash in on your investment. This can be a factor of age or circumstance. If you're investing for a down payment or college tuition fund, for instance, there's a specified time for when you'll need the money. To ensure that it's available, you'd want to have it invested conservatively.

Historically, an investor needs to have 40 percent of total investments in stocks in order to keep up with inflation. Although inflation hasn't been an important consideration these past few years, it most likely will in the years ahead.

The Lifestyle Factor

When it comes down to how the lifestyle factor affects your portfolio, it's pretty simple. If you can't afford to lose your investment, you should move your assets into more conservative holdings.

Take a good look at your lifestyle and consider what you want, what you have, and what you will need. How much money do you anticipate you'll need when you retire? If you work with a financial advisor, he or she should work with you to provide a financial plan. This would take into account factors such as any investments you might have, assets such as a home or condo, your current age, and the age at which you expect to retire. Other factors would include whether you anticipate having any income during retirement and how much money you anticipate you will need.

The advisor will use formulas to determine whether your level of finances is in line with your retirement goals. If it is, he or she can help you work out a plan to maintain that balance. If it isn't, you'll need to figure out how to save more for retirement, or plan to continue working past your planned retirement date. You also can access an online retirement calculator to help you figure out if you're on track.

There are lots of retirement calculators online, but we like the Bloomberg calculator at www.bloomberg.com/personal-finance/calculators/retirement or the MSN Money calculator at http://money.msn.com/retirement/retirement-calculator.aspx. How long is it until you plan to retire? We tend to use 65 as the typical retirement age, but maybe you're planning to retire at 55 or 60, instead. If so, you need to plan your asset allocation accordingly.

If you're determined that you'll have that beach house you've always wanted by the time you're 45, you're going to need some aggressive growth investments to move you toward your goal. College tuition funds should be allocated within relatively safe investment areas.

Adjusting Your Portfolio When Necessary

When thinking about the diversification of your portfolio, you will need to assess your lifestyle and the plans you have for your future, and then consider whether your portfolio contains a proper allocation of assets or perhaps should be adjusted. Beginning investors don't need to worry much about diversification, as you'll only have a few stocks in play. As you acquire more stock, however, the goal is to be sure it's spread around and to assess it periodically to make sure it remains properly allocated. Once you've established an allocation of assets that works for you, work at keeping the allocations aligned.

Some investors react to the market and change their asset allocations to match market trends and events, but that is not a sound investing strategy. In fact, it's a really bad idea. You should never chase after a stock segment or foreign stock just because it's hot at the time, but invest based on research and careful consideration. On the other hand, don't be tempted to hang on to stock in volatile industries, such as the airline industry.

TAKING STOCK

A tried-and-true investing strategy is to never have more than 10 percent of your total assets invested in any one stock. This can be challenging when you're just starting in the market, but it's a goal to strive for as rapidly as possible.

You can rebalance your portfolio either on an as-needed basis, or check it periodically on an ongoing basis, such as every six or nine months. Either way, your portfolio will remain most healthy if you adjust it only when it becomes out of balance, not because you're looking for more exciting investments or reacting to a tip or rumor.

Keeping Allocations Aligned

To keep your allocations aligned, you have to examine each of the categories we've discussed earlier in this chapter as factors for diversification, and then check your investment statements to be sure that you're on track.

Let's say, for instance, that you used the GICS to allocate your investments across sectors, and decided that you wanted 15 percent of your funds invested in companies in the health-care sector. If that sector has experienced a sudden surge, however, the value of your investments may have risen way beyond 15 percent of your total investments.

That means that, in order to rebalance your portfolio, you'd need to either sell some of your (winning) health-care stock and reinvest your profits in other sectors to even out the allocation, or come up with other money to invest in other sectors. If you make ongoing contributions to your portfolio, you can also change them so that more of the money goes to under-weighted asset categories to realign your allocations.

The same principle applies to the other categories you've read about. If the value of your international stock increases to 20 percent of your total portfolio, your allocations are out of alignment with the rule of investing no more than 10 percent in foreign securities and need to be realigned.

Knowing When to Ask for Help

If your portfolio becomes badly out of alignment and you don't know how to bring it back in, it's a good idea to look for some help. Call the brokerage firm you work with and ask for a consultation. Many of the discount brokers, such as Schwab or E-Trade, provide help at no charge to clients. Ask to schedule a meeting with a specialist and get an expert opinion on what you should do.

Some firms have electronic stock rebalancers that allow you to enter your holdings, set your allocations, and wait for the computer program to tell you how your stock should be adjusted to attain better diversification.

Beware of Over-Diversification

Diversification within your stock portfolio is desirable, but it's got to make sense. It's got to be achieved in a systematic, rational manner. Some investors, in their quest for diversification, end up with stock that makes little sense for them, purchased solely out of the desire to accomplish asset allocation and spread their investments around.

Most financial advisors recommend that your portfolio contain about 20 different stocks, and it's pretty conclusive that while increasing the number of stocks you own from 1 to 20 greatly reduces risk, increasing it from 20 to 100 does very little to further reduce risk. With whatever number of stocks you own, make sure that they are spread out over sector, country, growth potential, and other factors in a manner that makes sense.

The Least You Need to Know

- Asset allocation is necessary to achieve portfolio diversification and reduce your investment risk.
- Asset allocation can be achieved by considering various factors that ensure diversification.
- Time factors and lifestyle expectations are considerations when figuring how to allocate your assets.
- Your portfolio may require periodic adjustment to keep it properly aligned.
- It is possible, and not preferable, for a portfolio to become overly diversified.

Getting Started: One Step at a Time

In this part, you learn how to assess and understand financial, industry, economic, and political news that can affect a company's finances and the performance of its stock. Having a handle on this type of information will help you to make the best and safest stock selections. From reading a market report to getting sound information from radio, TV, and the Internet, you learn what it all means and where to look for reliable information.

You also find out what to look for when you begin researching companies and the industries in which they reside, and how to judge whether a company is heading toward a successful future by checking out its product, market share, size, management team, and other factors. You learn about balance sheets, earnings, cash flow, and debt—all the financial stuff that's crucial to the health of a company, and to you, as you look for companies in which to invest.

The Importance of Being Informed

In This Chapter

- Why you need good financial information
- Deciphering market reports
- Locating reliable information
- Using rating services
- Resources for reliable information

We live in an age of information overload, to be sure. Information of all kinds comes at us fast and unceasingly from a variety of sources. We're bombarded with news from around the world, commentary, gossip, infomercials, advertisements, and opinions regarding the most mundane of matters, accounts of the day-to-day activities of acquaintances, and the list goes on and on.

While too much information can be annoying, confusing, and distracting, information about the stock market, particularly about stocks you might be considering for your portfolio, is extremely important and absolutely necessary. Fortunately, there is a lot of information available, and it's easy to access. The trick, or course, is being able to discern which information is reliable, and which is best avoided.

In this chapter, you'll learn about market reports and other sources of reliable information that can help you to understand the stock market and make smart, informed choices about the stock you buy.

Let's Start at the Very Beginning

It's important not only to learn about a company whose stock you're interested in, but to scope out the bigger picture and learn about the industry it's in, overall market conditions, and other factors. To achieve this, you'll need a variety of information sources and the ability to understand them, as some financial news can seem complicated. A good starting point is to look at market reports, which are available both in print and online.

Market reports are useful in that they provide lots of information about the overall market and economy, which is valuable when you're trying to figure out what stocks to buy. Once you've purchased some stock, they keep you up to date with information relating to your particular holdings.

How to Read a Market Report

Market reports, which are simply compilations of news affecting either a particular market or the general stock market, contain a lot of information and can seem a little daunting. Once you get the hang of reading a report, however, it's easy. And you'll find that the reports become increasingly interesting after you've been in the market for a little while and start to observe trends and watch how events such as a political election or natural disaster can affect stock prices.

You can read market reports online or in a newspaper. The online version, of course, is able to provide more information than the newspaper version, which, depending on how much space your paper allocates, can be limited.

Topics Covered in a Market Report

The financial sections of newspapers generally will report on the major indexes, top stock and bond funds, which stocks were traded most actively the previous day, *story stocks*, and *stocks of local interest*. They also might include how the dollar compares to different currencies, whether durable goods orders have increased or decreased, some analysis, a stock market definition of the day, and other information. Remember, however, that the financial news in your morning paper is from the day prior.

> **DEFINITION**
>
> **Story stocks** are those whose value is based on something that's expected to happen or has happened, rather than a company's financials. **Stocks of local interest** are those of companies based within a newspaper's readership area or that otherwise have ties to the community.

A market report on an Internet site such as MSN Money, MarketWatch, CNNMoney, or Bloomberg, on the other hand, provides all of the same information as the newspaper version, but comes with the advantage of allowing you to check out any particular stock you want. All you have to do is enter the symbol or name of the stock you want to check, and you'll get information including the prices it closed at the previous day and opened at on the current day, the day's high and low, and much more. Let's have a look at some of the information you'll encounter on a market report and what it means:

- **Previous close.** The price at which the stock closed on the previous day of trading.

- **Open.** The price at which the stock opened on the current day of trading.

- **Day's high.** The highest price the stock achieved during the day.

- **Day's low.** The lowest price the stock achieved during the day.

- **Volume.** The total number of stocks traded.

- **Average Daily Trading Volume (ADTV).** The average number of shares traded in a day, a week, or a specified period of time (13 weeks or for a quarter is a statement time period). ADTV is a measure of liquidity. The higher the volume, the easier it is to sell a stock without affecting the price. Volume is also a measure of how easy it will be to buy and sell a stock. If a stock has more or less volume during a trading day, it's important to know the reason why, and to read any and all news you can about the company that day.

- **52-week low.** The lowest price the stock achieved during the past 52 weeks.

- **52-week high.** The highest price the stock achieved during the past 52 weeks.

- **Dividend.** The quarterly distribution of earnings paid for one share of stock. Dividends are either stated as a percentage or a dollar amount. If dividends are stated as a dollar amount, you need to multiply the number by four so you know how much you will receive if you hold the stock for a year.

- **Dividend yield.** The dividend expressed as a percent of stock price. It's important to compare this number with other companies within the sector and to the applicable index. If a stock has an 8 percent dividend and the average Standard & Poor's (S&P) stock yields 2.3 percent, you'll need to ask why the company's dividend is so high.

- **P/E ratio.** The ratio between the current stock price and the company's earnings per share. Usually reported for the prior four quarters of earnings, some estimates use projected or forwarded P/E. Measure of how expensive a stock compares to others in a sector.

Being able to access the wealth of information contained within an online market report is great, but for new investors it can result in information overload. The trick is to take some time to become familiar with market reports, and figure out which of the information is applicable to you and your portfolio. You also should pay attention to the overall strength of the market, price changes in the different indexes and industrial sectors, and current financial news, but don't drive yourself crazy by trying to digest every bit of information contained within the report. Your goal should be to get an overview of the stock market for the day and to check on the stocks you hold.

An expedient way of checking on your stocks is to keep an updated list of all that you own stored on your computer. Include the stock symbol, such as COST for Costco; IP for International Paper Company; SPLS for Staples, Inc.; or EBAY for eBay, Inc. That will allow you to quickly see how your stock is doing and get on with your day.

TAKING STOCK

Complete lists of stock symbols are available online, as well as lists of symbols for stocks listed on particular exchanges. Some sites offer search tools that allow you to look up symbols for companies you're interested in. MSN Money offers a good one at http://moneycentral.msn.com/investor/common/find.asp.

What Kind of Information Will You Need?

Before you go ahead and buy stock, you need to learn as much as you can about the company that issues it. You'll read a lot more about this in the chapters that follow, but, basically, you'll want to verify the following information:

- The company is on firm financial ground.
- It's either growing, or is well established and stable.
- It provides products and services that people want to buy.
- It's competitive with comparable companies.

- It's in an industry that's growing.

- The current economy can support the company.

- It has a management team that appears to be interested in enhancing share-holder value.

So where do you get this kind of information before you buy a company's stock? You already read about the value of market reports and the wealth of information they contain. You also should be looking at company sources of information, industry news sources, the stock exchanges on which the companies are listed, and other reliable sources.

Company Websites

The websites of public corporations almost always include a section for investors. Some of these are more sophisticated than others, but most will contain information about the company's stock and how to buy it, its sales figures and earnings, any major announcements affecting the company, company news, financial reports, and annual reports. All of this information is useful for investors and prospective investors, and certainly worth spending some time reading.

While the company site is a valuable resource, it will, of course, tend to present company news and statistics in a favorable light. You'll also want to check out some other sources of information, including industry sites and resources, stock exchange websites, and other websites that offer news and opinions about the company in which you're interested.

Industry News Sources

Maybe you drove a Ford Mustang when you were in high school, and you've been loyal to Ford ever since. When you started thinking about investing in the stock market, Ford seemed like a good fit. But you knew that the auto industry, including Ford, had encountered more than its share of problems during tough economic times, and you weren't sure where the company and the industry were heading.

A search of automotive industry news will turn up a variety of well-regarded publications such as "Automotive News," "Ward's Auto," and "Automotive Digest," all of which provide plenty of news about the condition of the automobile industry in general, and give you an idea of where Ford stands within the industry.

Look to publications such as the online version of The Detroit News, which carries extensive coverage of the auto industry and offers backlogs of articles from previous issues. There also are plenty of automotive trade magazines, many of which are available online.

CRASH!

As with Facebook, Twitter, or e-mail, reading market reports can become a bit addictive. It can be tempting to check in frequently to see what's happening in the market, so be prepared to establish some parameters for yourself. You might decide to check a market report during your lunch break and then again before you head for home, or wait until after dinner to see how the market closed. Don't let tracking your stocks become an obsession.

The Stock Exchange

Another source of information about a company is the stock exchange on which it's listed. Stock exchanges, particularly the major ones, want people to be informed about and comfortable with investing so that they'll do more of it. So if you're interested in learning more about Ford, you'll need to learn on which exchange or exchanges it's listed, and then pay a visit to the website.

A quick Internet search will tell you that Ford is traded on the New York and Pacific stock exchanges in the United States, and also on some exchanges in the United Kingdom, France, Germany, Belgium, and Switzerland.

A search for "Ford" on the New York Stock Exchange site (www.nyse.com) will yield not only information about the movement of Ford stock, but tons of press releases and financial information. The exchange's site also provides industry news and analysis, giving you lots of information (probably more than you want) about Ford's place within the auto industry, current events affecting the company, and major changes within the company.

Other Sources

Many websites are happy to provide all sorts of information about Ford or pretty much any other company, but you'll need to be selective about which ones you trust.

Many investors read publications such as *Investor Business Daily* or *The Wall Street Journal*. The newspapers and websites provide current financial and business news, but also list stocks, including charts, that the company likes and recommends.

Also look for business sites such as Hoovers.com, Yahoo! Finance, TheStreet.com, or BusinessWeek.com for current financial information about the company you're researching. Many of the business websites provide alerts, advising you when news comes out about a stock you are interested in. These alerts are a great way to receive up-to-the-minute information. Also, look online for current articles in reputable publications and periodicals, as they can provide valuable information.

> **CRASH!**
>
> Beware of blogs and websites that contain opinions and comments from consumers or unauthorized "journalists." While these types of sites as they relate to Ford might be valuable if you're considering whether to buy a Bronco or trade in your old Focus for a new model, it's quite likely that a website called ford-sucks.com (we're not making that up!) will offer little valuable information regarding the financial strength of the company.

Relying on Rating Services

Another information resource for investors and soon-to-be-investors is rating services. Companies that offer rating services, such as Morningstar, Value Line Investment Survey, Schwab Equity Ratings, Motley Fool's ratings, and S&P Outlook, do the research for you and rate stocks based on a variety of criteria. You can find out more about these companies, and how to access them, in Appendix B.

Although they vary in scope and content, most rating services provide overall ratings of various stocks, an overview of risk factors, reasons to buy or not buy a stock, expected returns, analyst opinions, top rated stocks within different industries, daily stock picks, and other features.

You can learn a little bit about the company and what it does, what sector of the market it resides in, the financial size of the company, and other factors. Some of the ratings are machine generated, while others result from human analysis.

Rating services can be fun to explore, and they contain some good information. They're quick and easy to use and can be a good supplement to your own research.

Some rating services are available for free, while others charge a fee for the information provided. Rating services, however, should never be a substitute for your own research before buying stock. Analysts and investment advisors use these ratings as a backup to their personal analysis. As an example, Morningstar's ratings are based on valuation of the firm, and their ratings are often more conservative than other rating agencies.

It's important that you understand the underlying factors that determine the soundness of a company and the value of its stock. While it's fine to use rating services as a backup, you should never base your decisions solely on their recommendations.

Resources to Get You Started

Following are some recommendations for websites, publications, and other sources of information that we consider to be reliable for financial news. You'll find lots more resources in Appendix B.

- The Internet is convenient to use and loaded with information. Stick to tried-and-true websites such as Bloomberg, MarketWatch, Motley Fool, USATODAY Money, Forbes, the SEC's EDGAR database, Morningstar, and Reuters, and avoid the sites that offer financial information along with products and services for sale.

- Magazine and newspapers are excellent sources of information. Look for classics like *The Wall Street Journal, Bloomberg Business News, Barrons,* or *Investor's Business Daily.*

- Company reports, such as annual reports, are good sources for learning about what's going on. Complement company-released information with news reports to be sure you're getting a balanced mix of information.

- Many people rely on radio and television for financial news, and with sources like Bloomberg Television and the Financial News Network, there's lots of information available. Television and radio reports can help you keep up with any major financial news and provide a real-time picture of how the market is performing.

Not All Information Is Accurate

As mentioned earlier, some information, including that obtained from websites, printed material, radio and TV reports, and people is more reliable than other information. Remember that financial news, like any other type of news, can be biased. Reporters and commentators have been known to distort information to reflect their own views or challenge previously stated information. And it sometimes happens that financial news is projected incorrectly.

Finances are not an exact science and, by necessity, financial information often is based on what has happened in the past. Even the best analysts make mistakes, so you shouldn't rely entirely on their opinions. Stick to sources you know to be reliable. Pay attention to reviews of websites and other sources of information, and avoid sources that are biased or have vested interests in financial news.

Avoiding the Chatter

We are living in interesting times of competing news sources, culture wars, and extremist views on just about every topic. It's extremely important that you are able to discern the message from the messenger, and discern news from opinion and chatter.

SHARE THIS

Pam Krueger, creator, co-host, and executive producer of *MoneyTrack* (a PBS television show about personal finance and investing) recently warned of the danger of financial advice overload, particularly for people who are worried about their investments or financial situations during a time of economic uncertainty. Krueger advised investors to not react to every piece of advice they hear, but to stay the course with what they know works and avoid making hasty and sometimes costly decisions.

There are some really good financial analysts out there, some of whom are very influential and can affect the popularity and value of stocks simply by revealing their views regarding them. There are also some analysts who like or dislike stock based on vested interests.

The bottom line is that you should sort through available information and make your own decisions concerning the stock you'll buy. It's great to listen and watch and read and learn, but at the end of the day you must be responsible for your own decisions. Investors who follow the herd are generally not the most successful.

The Least You Need to Know

- Having access to reliable information is vital to researching stock market opportunities.
- Market reports are a good starting point for obtaining a variety of financial and stock information.
- It's important to get an overview of news concerning both a company and the industry in which it resides.
- Stock rating services provide good supplemental information, but shouldn't be the sole source for your financial decisions.
- Learn to discern between fact and opinion contained in financial information.

Finding the Right Market

In This Chapter

- Macro and micro approaches to investing
- The pieces of top-down investing
- Looking at bottom-up investing
- Consumer price index and other key economic indicators
- Analyzing sectors and industries
- Narrowing your search for the right market

Buying stock is like sifting for gold. You start with a big pile of sand, or for this analogy stocks, and you begin sorting and sorting, sifting and sifting, until you're left with just the good stuff. There are thousands of stocks listed on the major stock exchanges, making it overwhelming when you start thinking about which to choose. As with sifting for gold, however, there are methods of sorting through the big pile and determining which ones you want to keep.

In this chapter, you'll be introduced to different methods of finding the right market in which to invest. Should all your stock be in national markets or international markets? In which stock sectors should you consider buying?

There are various means of determining where to invest your money, and much disagreement concerning the best way to do so. In this chapter, we're going to look at two very different methods of evaluating investments and finding the right markets. The first method, top-down investing, considers the big picture of the overall economy, while the second method, bottom-up investing, drills in on a particular company and studies what it does and how well it does it. Let's start by looking at top-down investing.

Looking at the Big Picture

Top-down investing does just what the name implies. You start by looking at the big picture and then narrowing down choices (think sifting gold) until you find the stock you like. This is sometimes called the macro view, and it entails focusing on *macroeconomics*, as opposed to *microeconomics*.

> **DEFINITION**
>
> **Macroeconomics** looks at what the economy is doing as a whole, considering past and current trends and shifts. **Microeconomics** focuses on specific issues that affect a particular company or industry.

A top-down investor begins by assessing the condition of the overall market. Are we in a bull market or a bear market? Is the economy strong or faltering? What's the unemployment rate?

Anyone who pays attention to the news, reads Facebook, and gets out of the house on a regular basis to talk to people probably has a general feel for the condition of the overall economy. What are people talking about? Do they seem worried or nervous about the economy? Are they spending money or pulling back?

Once you've answered those questions it's time to ask yourself another. Is this a good time to be investing in the stock market, or should you do something else with your investment funds and revisit the market when conditions have changed? Some investors look for down markets in which to invest, while others prefer to take a wait-and-see attitude. Again, your choice depends on your individual investing style and the factors that influence that style.

Starting at the Top

There are certain factors to consider when assessing the strength of the overall market. Understanding the overall market is important in helping you decide what investing strategies make sense.

The first thing to consider is cash flow, not as it pertains to a particular company, but to the market and economy in general. If the stock market as a whole is declining in value, that means that cash is leaving equities and the prices are likely to fall or continue to fall. If cash is flowing into the market, on the other hand, stock prices will rise as a result. You can easily determine what's occurring by reading and listening to daily stock reports.

Once you've looked at the overall market, assess the national and international economies. If money is coming into the U.S. economy, that's good for the stock market. If it's leaving the country, however, it's likely that domestic markets will decline. You can get that information by reading about gross domestic product and trade information released by the U.S. government. The Bureau of Economic Analysis provides this sort of information on its website at www.bea.gov. Another good source of economic, market, and technical statistics is Market Lab (http://online.barrons.com/mktlab), a feature of *Barrons* magazine.

Now that you have a feel for U.S. economic conditions, take a look at what's going on in the rest of the world. We are living in tumultuous times, with events around the world affecting both foreign markets and our own. While you want to be aware of investment opportunities offered by emerging economies in countries in Latin America and Asia, you also need to recognize when financial instability caused by war, unstable governments, natural disasters, or other factors simply makes a geographical area too risky in which to consider investing.

Checking Out Charts and Indicators

Once you've gotten a picture of overall economic conditions, you can look at how market prices have performed over a specified period of time. Compare the last 6, 12, or 18 months of market movement to a 10-year chart of the Standard & Poor's (S&P) 500 Index to determine whether the market is moving upward or downward.

You can also employ moving averages, which are tools that help determine the momentum of a stock by averaging its closing prices over a period of time. These types of charts and indicators can be used to evaluate both domestic and foreign markets and stock.

This type of analysis is called technical analysis. Technical analysis relies on charts that show the past movements of a stock's price and volume to predict trends and future movement of the stock. Technical analysis is considered to be the opposite of fundamental analysis, which considers a company's financial information to determine its value and whether or not the price of the stock reflects that value. If the stock sells for below the value of the company, it's a good investment. If its price is higher than the value of the company, it's not a good investment.

SHARE THIS

While investors have a wide range of opinions regarding technical and fundamental analysis, most experts agree that one is not better than the other—they're
simply different, and both have their advantages and disadvantages. Generally,
long-term investors employ fundamental analysis to a greater degree than short-
term investors, who tend to favor technical analysis.

You'll read a lot more about using fundamental analysis to assess a company's
financial strength in Chapter 14. Fundamental analysis, however, is an important part
of top-down investing because it can be used to determine the fundamentals of the
market as they're determined by stock ratios and other tools. There is of course much
more involved with both types of analysis, and many investors use both technical and
fundamental analysis when considering whether to buy a stock.

Adding in Cycles

Another step in top-down investing is to look at *market cycles* to help determine where
the market stands and where it might be headed. Market cycles are hard to identify
until after they've completed, but are considered to be useful tools for investors
trying to decide whether or not to buy a stock. All markets are cyclical, and investors
who pay attention can predict (to a point, at least) the length of time that current
conditions will exist and the future movement of a market. Most economists agree
that a typical market cycle occurs over about 48 months, or 4 years. In a typical cycle,
we'll experience a bear market that's in a downturn that lasts from 12 to 14 months,
before experiencing a period of expansion and recovery lasting for about 36 months.

DEFINITION

Market cycles are patterns of stock movement over time in a specific market
environment. They can be used to predict when a market will peak or hit a low
point, giving investors the opportunity to profit by trading stock within the
swings of the cycle.

To get an idea of cycles, simply check out an S&P 500 chart and identify where stock
prices have topped out. Look at the period of time between the highs, and compare
the movements with the current market position. If the time period between which
prices have topped out averages out to 2 years, for instance, and it's been only 6
months since the last time the stock price hit its high, you can figure the stock

probably has another 18 months or so before it peaks again. That would indicate it might be a good time to buy. You can also use this method to predict when a stock price will bottom out.

Adding It Up in Top-Down Investing

There's certainly a lot more involved with top-down investing than what you've read on these pages. The important thing to remember is that it takes a broad look at overall conditions, and then employs both technical and fundamental analysis to weed out potential stock.

Investors look to see if stock prices have bottomed out and are on the rise with, according to the stock's cycles, at least a year of upward movement remaining. They understand that market cycles tend to be indicators for broader economic cycles, usually leading the broader cycle by two to six months. They also look for favorable cash flow into the country and the stock market, and consider factors affecting both domestic and foreign markets that could result in volatility.

Smart investors, however, also anticipate change and don't expect markets to behave strictly according to their analysis. Markets are fluid and change quickly, and trends don't always point in the direction that we might expect.

What Is Bottom-Up Investing?

While top-down investors are scoping out worldwide economic conditions and looking at big-picture market movements, bottom-up investors are concerned primarily with numbers.

Bottom-up investors aren't overly concerned about macroeconomic factors because they're convinced that the right company can do well in any market environment. If a company has the right stuff, bottom-up investors insist, it will be just fine, regardless of what's occurring in the larger world.

TAKING STOCK

Some investors like to use stock screeners, which are tools that let you enter a set of criteria to weed out stocks and leave you with the ones that meet your requirements. You could specify, for instance, that you're interested only in NASDAQ stock, or technology stock, or stock of companies with a certain valuation. You can create your own stock screener, using your criteria or that suggested, by searching on a financial site such as MSN Money or Motley Fool (see Appendix B).

Because these investors focus on particular companies, they look carefully at factors such as potential market size, sales and earnings figures, balance sheet, cash flow, debt, the effectiveness of management, and market share. They'll examine factors that could affect the growth of the company and the company's business model, as well as its history.

They won't, however, consider industry or economic trends. Bottom-up investors aren't concerned about what industries or sectors are hot. They prefer to look at the credentials of a particular company, regardless of the type of industry.

Key Economic Indicators

You've read that when using top-down investing, it's important to gain a feel for the overall health of the economy and what might be affecting it. If you pay attention to economic news, you probably hear talk about consumer confidence, job growth, gross domestic product, retail sales, and earnings growth rates. All of these things (and there are lots more) are *economic indicators,* and when put together with other economic data, they serve as signals of the economy's current health and the direction in which it might be heading.

DEFINITION

An **economic indicator** is a piece of economic information used by investors to measure the overall strength of the economy and to predict opportunities for successful investments based on economic trends.

Economic indicators can include a huge variety of factors, and needn't be determined by economists. As we mentioned earlier, simply pay attention to get a feel for economic conditions. If four of your six closest friends have lost their jobs and moved back in with Mom and Dad, that's an economic indicator. If everywhere you look there are big new homes being built and the third upscale shopping mall in nine months is set to open in your area, those are economic indicators as well.

Fortunately, government agencies and nonprofit groups gather economic data and extract economic indicators, making it easy for the rest of us to follow up on what's going on with the economy. Some key economic indicators that are widely used as benchmarks include the consumer price index, unemployment rate, gross domestic product, the price of crude oil, retail sales, durable goods orders, reports released by the Institute for Supply Management, and the producer price index. These are by no means the only economic indicators, but they are key and heavily relied upon as clues regarding the general health of the economy. Economists and investors consider many, many factors in order to predict economic swings and cycles, as the economy is never an exact science. Let's look at each of these areas and why they're important indicators.

Consumer Price Index

The consumer price index (CPI) helps to measure increases or decreases associated with the cost of living by gauging the average price of a bundle of goods and services. These goods and services include transportation, medical care, and food. Large increases in the CPI during a short period of time point to inflation, while large decreases over a short period of time indicate deflation—both of which affect the overall health of the economy.

Unemployment Rate

The rate of unemployment is a strong indicator of the strength or weakness of the economy. The U.S. Bureau of Labor and Statistics releases unemployment figures every month. It's best to compare the numbers with those from the same month of the previous year instead of the previous month of the same year, as employment is affected by seasonal and other factors not directly related to the economy. Unemployment is a *lagging indicator*, as compared to a *leading indicator* or *coincident indicator*, because it doesn't become apparent until after the economy has already taken a downturn, and doesn't turn around until the economy is well into recovery.

> **DEFINITION**
>
> A **lagging indicator** is one that occurs after the economy changes, such as unemployment. A **leading indicator** is one that occurs before the economy changes, and is useful in signaling the forthcoming change. Stock market returns are an example of a leading indicator. A **coincident indicator** is one that moves along with the economy, such as the gross domestic product.

Gross Domestic Product

The gross domestic product (GDP) measures economic growth and is the primary measure of the health of the economy from quarter to quarter. The GDP measures the total output of the nation's goods and services.

Price of Crude Oil

The price of crude oil affects energy costs across a broad spectrum, and energy costs affect the general health of the economy. Economists and investors also look at oil inventories in refineries to get an idea of upcoming supply and demand. If inventories are high, oil prices will usually be lower. Oil prices are released weekly by the Energy Information Administration.

Retail Sales

A retail sales report for the previous month is released on or about the thirteenth of each month, and it's considered an important economic indicator. It includes sales reports from companies of all sizes, from Wal-Mart to the little corner boutique. If retail spending is up, it signals consumer confidence. A downturn in retail sales could indicate a pending recession.

Durable Goods Orders

Durable goods are defined as higher-priced capital goods with a useful life of three or more years. They include cars, airplanes, turbines, and semiconductor equipment. The number of durable goods purchased each month is another indicator of where the economy is headed. If a lot of durable goods have been ordered, the companies that make them can anticipate increases in sales and earnings, which also contributes to healthy consumer spending.

Institute for Supply Management's Reports

The Institute for Supply Management (ISM), a not-for-profit organization and the largest supply management organization in the world, releases reports on business each month indicating the level of economic activity in a wide range of both manufacturing and nonmanufacturing industries. Factors considered in the reports include new orders, employment, production, inventories, backlog of orders, exports, imports, and prices.

Producer Price Index

The producer price index (PPI) measures the average change over time in the selling prices received by domestic producers for the goods and services they output.

The index is released monthly by the U.S. Bureau of Labor Statistics, and is used to analyze sales and earnings trends within the wholesale and commodities markets and manufacturing industries.

Forecasting Future Success

In your effort to sift through that basketful of stocks and end up with one or more that you want to buy, you've considered both macro- and microeconomic factors. You've looked at the big picture and considered what's happening within global and national economies, and you've scoped out the condition of the overall market. You've also employed some charts and indicators and considered the significance of stock cycles.

Your job now is to put all of those things together to predict or look at how certain industries are doing, and to get a feel for sector strength. The next chapter details what to look for when assessing a company. For now, we're going to stick with the job of looking at industries and broader markets.

Predicting the success (or failure) of a market, industry, or sector isn't rocket science. A lot of what you need to consider is just common sense. First, let's take a look at factors that might affect the future of national markets.

Of National Markets

As mentioned earlier in this chapter, you can get a handle on general economic conditions by gauging whether money is moving into or out of securities, and coming into or going out of the United States.

To gauge the health of national markets, you'll need to check out daily volume, both of the market as a whole and for specific companies. Daily volume, also known as average daily trading volume (ADTV), is simply the average amount of individual stocks traded in a day's time, or within another specified time period. Daily volume indicates the liquidity of a stock or of the market. When volume is high, the stock or the market has high liquidity and can be easily traded. This means more people trade, and prices go up.

TAKING STOCK

TheStreet.com (www.thestreet.com), an online financial website, contains an extensive section on average daily trading volume, with news reports on stocks experiencing particularly high or low trading volume and the reasons why those highs and lows are occurring. It's interesting reading, and a good source for keeping up with breaking news and financial developments.

When ADTV is low, stock prices tend to go down, because nobody's buying. When there's a big jump in ADTV, it's usually a sign that some news has been released that's affecting the views of investors, either about a particular stock or the market as a whole. High daily volumes signal that the market is stable.

Another indicator of market health is whether investors are moving funds from equity mutual funds into bond funds or money market funds. If investors start pulling money out of the stock market and putting it into what they perceive are "safer" investments, you can expect the market to slow down and stock prices to fall.

Of Industries and Sectors

Many people use the words "industry" and "sector" interchangeably, but they are, in fact, different entities. An industry is a grouping of companies, while a sector is a grouping of industries that makes up a large segment of the economy.

A large economy contains multiple sectors, and each sector can contain many industries—sometimes hundreds. Examples of sectors within the U.S. economy include the following:

- Wholesale trade
- Retail trade
- Manufacturing
- Real estate, rental, and leasing
- Transportation
- Utilities
- Construction
- Educational services
- Information
- Health care

The businesses that fall within those sectors are then categorized as industries, or groups of industries. Industries within the transportation sector, for instance, include air transport, automotive, transportation services, motor freight, and gas.

When predicting the future of industries and sectors, you'll need to consider several factors. Some industries and sectors are more affected by changes in the economy than others. They are referred to as cyclical industries and sectors, as opposed to defensive industries and sectors, which are less affected by economic downturns.

Cyclical sectors include manufacturing, transportation, and construction—all of which are home to industries that produce goods people don't absolutely have to buy when the economy declines. Defensive sectors and industries are those that provide food, power, gas, water, and other things we consider to be necessary. Cyclical sectors and industries perform well in good economic times but drop off in down times, while defensive sectors and industries tend to remain more stable through good times and bad times.

Other considerations are whether an industry or sector is growing, if there is demand for its services or products, and if there are other factors affecting it. Your prediction should be based on what you read, statistics and reports, what experts are saying, what economic indicators reveal, and other factors.

Of International Markets

We live in a global economy, and getting familiar with international markets is an important piece of an investor's homework. When judging the future success of an international market, you would use much of the same criteria as when you're examining U.S. markets. You would need to look at ratings from Moody's, Standard & Poor's, or other reputable rating agencies to see if a market is considered to be a good investment. You'd also want to check out the economic and financial fundamentals.

In addition to those considerations, however, you need to take a look at the degree of economic and political risk associated with international markets. If a country is in debt and unable to pay off that debt, that's an economic risk to its markets.

CRASH!

Some investors are drawn to high stakes international markets, but that is by no means a good idea for a beginning investor. Changes in markets outside of the United States are often quite dramatic and occur quickly, giving investors little time to react. And with world economies becoming increasingly interrelated, volatility in one international market can quickly spread to another. If you're thinking about investing in an international market, you should ask someone at your brokerage firm for advice.

Political risk is risk that results from political movement within an international market that results in the market being inhospitable to foreign investors. Having said that, there are some excellent opportunities in foreign markets that aren't inhospitable to foreign investors, particularly in bullish economies such as those of China and India, both of which are expected to be dominant suppliers of manufactured goods. And due to lower labor and production costs, these countries are seen by manufacturers as opportunities for foreign expansion.

Narrowing Your Search

Regardless of how you choose to do so, as you spend time sifting through factors impacting the general economy and overall markets, you'll begin to be able to identify areas that appear to be stronger than others. This will be a result of all your research efforts, based on information you accumulate over time.

As this book is written, for instance, the housing market is in shambles with record numbers of foreclosures, decreasing home prices, and other problems. Experts identified more than 100 industries that have been affected by these housing problems, resulting in difficulties for a significant portion of the economy. Understanding how one problem area affects other areas will help you to narrow your search.

Once you're homed in on the sectors and industries you like, you begin the sifting process all over again as you start to look at the stock of individual companies. This might sound like too much work, but remember that there are all kinds of information available that can help you measure financial strength and predict how entire markets, sectors, industries, and other areas will do.

Combining Top-Down and Bottom-Up to Win

While some investors will consider using only top-down investing or bottom-up investing, many—perhaps even most—use a combination of the two. With tens of thousands of stocks for sale, you clearly have lots of choices. If you're willing to look, you can find industries and companies that satisfy the criteria used in both top-down and bottom-up investing, coming through with good numbers, strong management, and sound fundamentals to make both kinds of investors happy.

Many investors begin by employing a top-down approach, and then, once they've weeded out some candidates and come up with a list of prospective winners, use bottom-up criteria to further narrow their search and come up with the best of all the initial contenders.

In the end, you'll develop your own style of investing. It might be top-down, bottom-up, a combination of the two, or something else that's completely unique to you. As long as you understand what you're looking for, the fact that you find industries and companies you like is more important than how you find them.

The Least You Need to Know

- Top-down investing considers a broad economic spectrum, while bottom-up focuses strictly on a particular company.

- Economic indicators measure the overall strength of the economy and predict investment opportunities.

- Knowing what factors affect sectors and industries can help you identify those headed for economic success or downturn.

- Sifting through news, statistics, charts, indicators, and other information will narrow your search for the right markets.

- As long as you establish good search criteria there is no right or wrong way to research investment opportunities.

Look Closely Before You Buy

In This Chapter

- Getting informed about a company
- Identifying the product or service
- Who's buying the product?
- Assessing the company's life cycle
- Figuring the value of a company
- A look at who's running the show

Some people spend hours online before they book a hotel room, checking out features and amenities, rates, cancellation policies, and parking. They'll spend days comparing the qualities of different laptops before deciding which to buy, and weeks searching for the perfect vehicle before signing a sales agreement. But in some cases, these same seemingly meticulous folks jump feet first into the stock market, buying here and there with very little preparation and, as a result, ending up wondering why their stock doesn't perform the way they think it should.

Doing your homework before investing in the stock market is every bit as critical as consulting Consumer Reports or Edmunds before you buy a new car. Learning about the company in which you're thinking about investing is an integral part of the process of buying stock.

In this chapter, you'll learn about some of the more general things you need to find out about a company before you buy its stock, such as how long it's been around, how big it is, and what its management team looks like. In the next chapter, you'll learn how to get the scoop on the specifics of its finances. None of it is all that difficult, and you'll be glad that you took the time to learn.

Learning About a Company

The process of learning about a company by gathering and considering information pertaining to it is a pretty straightforward process, and, as you read in Chapter 11, there is plenty of information available to help you learn what you need to know. Once you've identified a company that interests you, either because you have personal experience with the company, you've read about it, or you've heard about it from someone else, it's time to dig in and see what you can discover about it.

Many experts advise that it's better to buy stock in a company that you understand than in one that you don't, and that's usually a very good idea. If your research leaves you scratching your head or wondering if what you're reading might actually be written in a different language, there's probably a better fit for your money and a company's stock.

You want to be able to understand not only the company in which your money is invested, but factors and situations that could affect the company either negatively or positively. Having a good grasp of exactly what the company you're investing in does, along with an understanding of how the industry or sector in which it belongs works, will be a huge help as you monitor the performance of your stock.

TAKING STOCK

It's important to remember that the stock of a company can be positively or negatively affected by factors over which the company has no control. A big oil spill, major storm, or other event could have a serious negative effect on a seafood business, for instance. While you're learning about a company, you also should consider factors that could affect it.

In addition to understanding what the company does, you'll need to do a little sleuthing to learn about its history. Is it a new company, or has it been around for a while, indicating stability? Taking that a step further, has it been around for so long that its product or service has become obsolete?

Another consideration is the size of the company you're looking at. Historically, the stock of big, established companies is considered to be less volatile than that of small companies. However, there sometimes is more opportunity for growth with stock of smaller companies.

Is the company providing a product or service that's exciting and cutting edge or indispensable? Are people talking about the company and what it does? What's its place in its industry? Who's in charge of the company?

Once you've gotten a handle on all the factors, and taken into consideration the financial factors discussed in the next chapter, you'll have a much better idea of how the stock you're considering will fit into your portfolio.

What's the Product or Service?

It's easy to identify the products and services provided by highly regarded companies such as Target Corporation, Starbucks, McCormick, and Ross Stores. It's likely that you've been to their stores or restaurants, or perused their products on the spice rack of the grocery store.

SHARE THIS

Headquartered in Maryland, McCormick & Co. is a global leader in the manufacture, processing, and distribution of spices. McCormick is known as a niche company, because it dominates one market segment of a larger industry, in this case the food and beverage industry. Niche companies can be good investments because they control their markets and often don't encounter as much competition as other companies within the larger industry.

If you're interested in learning more about Target and possibly buying some of its stock, visit a store and spend some time checking out what it has to offer. You'll see that Target sells clothing and household items and toys and phones and electronics and food and thousands of other items. You know that Starbucks sells coffee and yummy lattes and other related products; and that Ross Stores sell clothing and gift items; and that McCormick offers spices from around the world.

But what about other, also highly regarded companies like Praxair, Monsanto, or C.R. Bard? Most people aren't nearly as familiar with these names as the ones we just mentioned, and most people probably can't name their products or services. Fortunately, if you're interested in learning more about Praxair or C.R. Bard because you've been reading that they're good companies, it's easy to find out exactly what they do by turning to the sources you learned about in Chapter 11:

- Company website
- Industry news sources
- Stock exchange on which company is listed
- The Securities and Exchange Commission's EDGAR database
- Other reliable sources, such as business websites, magazines, or newspapers

By checking out some of these sources, you'll learn that C.R. Bard produces medical equipment. More specifically, it "designs, manufactures, packages, distributes, and sells medical, surgical, diagnostic, and patient care devices worldwide," according to Yahoo! Finance's business summary of the company.

C.R. Bard's website (www.crbard.com) provides a complete listing of its products, along with descriptions and a lot of other kinds of information. The New York Stock Exchange, on which C.R. Bard is listed, also will inform you about C.R. Bard's product line and provide other information. "Health Industry Today," a monthly industry publication, will also help you learn more about the company. You can access the publication, including back issues, online at www.accessmylibrary.com/archive/427795-health-industry-today.html.

Who's Buying It?

Once you've got a good understanding of a company's products and/or services, you should look to see who's buying them. A company may have a terrific product, or what was previously thought to be a terrific product, but if nobody's buying it, you don't want its stock.

CRASH!

The popularity of the once outrageously popular Crocs—those funky foam shoes that everybody loved for a while—took a nosedive in late 2007 and 2008, causing the company's stock to lose 90 percent of its market value in 10 months. To be fair, the stock value has rebounded somewhat, but hasn't come close to where it had been. Don't assume that a popular product will remain popular indefinitely.

Determining Market Share

To determine how much product or service the company you're looking at is selling, you'll look at its sales and earnings, something you'll read more about in the next chapter. The goal is to get a handle on where the company stands in terms of *market share*. Market share is important because it indicates how competitive a company is within its industry. If demand for baked potato chips is increasing by 10 percent a year, and Frito-Lay's baked chips market share is increasing by 20 percent a year, the company is growing its revenues faster than the snack food companies it competes against, a good thing for those invested in Frito-Lay.

DEFINITION

Market share is the percentage of sales generated by one company within a particular market during a particular time. If Coca Cola sold 32 percent of all the soda purchased in the United States during a one-year period, for instance, it would have a 32 percent market share.

To get an idea of what share of the market a company commands, you need to know the size of the market. That information is usually available in industry trade magazines or newsletters. Once you know the size of the market, compare it to the company's total gross sales revenue. If the company sold $1 million of product in a $10 million market, it has a 10 percent market share.

You can often get an idea of a company's market share from sources like regulatory bodies or trade groups, or from information released by the company. Sometimes, especially with a big company like Frito-Lay, a simple Internet search turns up an article that contains information regarding its market share.

What's the Talk on the Street?

While it's always important to check a company's sales figures and know where it stands in terms of market share, sometimes you only have to look and listen in order to know what's hot and what's not. If everybody you know (or at least it seems like everybody you know) is buying or talking about buying iPods, iPads, and iPhones, and there are lines stretched around the Apple stores, you might want to learn more about Apple, Inc. If you're hearing more and more news reports about the emergence of battery-powered automobiles, or seeing a record number of TV commercials for a particular bank, or overhearing conversations about how great the Amazon Kindle is, or hearing about shoppers waiting in line to get an item manufactured by a particular company, pay attention.

Clearly, you don't want to rush out and invest in a company because there's a holiday rush for one of its products, but if you're consistently hearing great things about a particular industry or company, you might want to dig in and find out what everyone is so excited about. An Internet search will turn up all sorts of articles from newspapers, business journals, and other sources to help you better understand the popularity (or lack of popularity) of a particular product.

Sizing Up the Competition

Checking out the competitors of a company you're interested in is an important step of your research. You might really like the company that e-mails you hot travel deals every week, but if its competitors are pulling in twice as much income from advertisers and have double the number of subscribers, you'll want to reconsider buying its stock.

Before you decide to jump in and buy the stock of your favorite fast-food restaurant, check out how the competition is doing. That's not to say you shouldn't buy your burgers from your favorite place, you just might want to buy another place's stock.

> **TAKING STOCK**
>
> Online sites such as www.hoovers.com and www.dailyfinance.com contain lots of free information about a company's competitors, along with financial information, names of executives, and more.

It's not difficult to identify competitors of a company you're interested in. Sometimes, as in the case of Coca Cola, it's obvious. If you're looking to invest in Coke, you'd do well to see what Pepsi is up to. Publicly owned companies are required to file annual reports with the U.S. Securities and Exchange Commission (SEC). Called a Form 10-K, it contains information about a variety of topics, including the company's competitors. You can access these forms from the EDGAR section of the SEC's website (www.sec.gov).

The Life Cycle of a Company

Another part of your research should be to find out how long the company you're interested in has been around. Every company has a life cycle, and you'll need to understand where the one you're thinking about investing in falls on the life cycle spectrum.

There are many theories regarding and variations on the business life cycle, but it's often broken into four stages: establishment, growth and expansion, maturity, and decline. These stages aren't measured in months and years, but by the strength and health of a company. Every company develops at its own pace, making it impossible to prescribe time periods for business stages. You can't say that a growth period will last for eight years, for instance, because the duration of growth depends on many factors.

A company that produces a toy that happens to be the one that everyone wants for Christmas one year may experience a phenomenal growth period. It might, however, last for only a very short time, until the novelty of the toy has worn off and nobody wants it anymore.

It's also difficult to predict how long any particular stage of a company's life cycle will last because companies sometimes morph in and out of a particular stage. Radio Shack, for example, was considered to be a mature company, or perhaps even one in decline, when it announced in 2010 that it was going to focus on smartphones and wireless plans, for which it would install kiosks in Target stores. Radio Shack was identified by Goldman Sachs as a potential turnaround stock, and its stock prices jumped dramatically. While the chain's last quarter of 2010 was disappointing and its CEO stepped down, its stock still enjoys much higher value than it did several years ago. The future of Radio Shack remains unclear, but it's an example of a company that morphed from a declining company to an expanding one.

Establishment

A company in the establishment stage, of course, is one that's just getting started. And while it's easy to dream that investing in a startup will result in great financial success, keep in mind that it's risky business, as more than half of all new businesses fail.

Investing in startups can be profitable, as evidenced in the 1990s when investors gladly threw money at startup dot-com companies, which were trading at record prices, but the risk, as many investors and dot-coms learned when the bubble burst in 2000, is high.

CRASH!

If you ever get an e-mail or other message announcing a Pre-IPO investment opportunity, just hit the delete button. A company will sometimes try to attract investors while it's still privately owned by promising big returns to those who buy in before the company goes public. These offers often turn out to be shams, and sometimes even illegal.

Some investors seek out companies in the establishment stage, particularly those that are private and planning to go public. Companies just starting out can be great investments, as evidenced by Microsoft, Home Depot, Dell, and others, but again, there's a lot of risk involved. A company remains in the establishment stage until it becomes profitable and more stable, accomplishments which may occur over a period of several years or longer.

Growth and Expansion

A growth company is one with earnings that are increasing significantly faster than the general economic growth, and is growing much faster than comparable businesses in the same field. These companies are more stable than startups, but still generally on shaky ground financially. Growth companies usually don't pay dividends in the form of cash, so the only way you make money is by the appreciation of the price of the shares.

Once a company has reached economic stability it can begin to look outward and think about expanding. It might add a product line, expand its facilities, or hire more employees. Companies also grow by merging with other companies. An Internet search of the company in which you're thinking of investing should turn up any rumors or news of a possible merger with, or acquisition of, another company. Industry news publications also would include this sort of information. A merger or acquisition that grows a company can increase the value of the company and increase the price of its stock.

Companies that are expanding make exciting investment prospects, but consider a word of caution. Companies that expand too quickly can be headed for financial disaster, so make sure to check all the financial information if you're interested in buying stock of a company that's on the move. Pay particular attention to the company's debt, and how it's paying for the expansion. If it's borrowing millions of dollars, what's the plan to pay off the debt? You'll learn more about financials in the next chapter.

SHARE THIS

Globalization is blamed for the decline of some production sectors in the United States, including the furniture industry, many auto part suppliers, computer manufacturers, and consumer electronics. Manufacture of nearly all of these products has left the United States, leaving businesses and industries in decline.

Maturity

Once a company is established, profitable, and stable, it's considered to be a mature company. Businesses in industries such as tobacco, oil, or automotive generally are considered to be mature. They've stood the test of time and are tried and true. It sounds like they would make great investments, and often they are valuable additions to a portfolio because they're not focused on expansion and therefore are able to pay cash dividends to investors.

Keep in mind, however, that once a company has reached maturity, its growth potential can become limited, along with the potential for its stock to continue to appreciate.

If you're looking to invest in a mature company, look for those that are diversifying by adding new products or services, or are growing by taking sales away from competitors.

Decline

Once successful businesses decline for various reasons. Mature businesses sometimes get so focused on profits and the bottom line that they forget how to be innovative, making them vulnerable as newer, more entrepreneurial companies emerge. Some lose sight of the values and goals that enabled them to be successful in the first place. Others fail due to bad investments, or because they don't have a sound succession plan. Some companies in the decline stage have simply outlived their usefulness.

An example of an industry in decline, and many of the companies within it, is the newspaper industry. Companies that publish newspapers are generally in the decline stage as consumers find other avenues for receiving information and advertising revenues fall. This type of decline is known as secular decline, as opposed to a cyclical decline, which would indicate that the decline was temporary. Most business analysts agree that newspapers are not a growth industry and, generally, companies that fall into this category don't make for wise investments.

On the other hand, some companies and businesses do return from secular decline. The retail chain Kmart, for example, filed for bankruptcy protection in 2002, with many analysts predicting it would not recover. In 2004, however, Kmart merged with Sears, another struggling entity at the time, creating a chain of 3,500 stores. When the announcement of the merger was made, Kmart stock prices jumped by 8 percent, while Sears stock prices soared more than 17 percent.

Generally, you'll want to invest in businesses that have a proven track record, and that usually means those which have been around for a period of time. Understanding the business life cycle is just one more step in helping you make smart stock picks.

Using Market Cap as a Measure

Another aspect to consider is the size of the company you're researching. The size of a company, for our purposes, isn't about how many locations there are or how many people it employs. It's about the company's *market capitalization*, often referred to as market cap.

> **DEFINITION**
>
> **Market capitalization** or market cap is the total value of all of the outstanding shares of a company. It's used to determine the size of the company.

Market capitalization is considered the standard measure of a company's size. You figure out a company's market cap by multiplying the number of outstanding shares it has by the current stock price. So if Paula's Pound Cakes has 10 million shares of stock outstanding, and each stock is valued at $10, Paula's Pound Cakes has a market cap of $100 million.

Using market cap as a measure levels the playing field and assures a uniform means of determining a company's size in comparison with that of another company. Companies are put into stock categories depending on their market capitalization. There's some disagreement about the limit amounts, but there are five basic categories: micro cap, small cap, mid cap, large cap, and mega cap. Let's take a closer look at each stock category, along with a few examples of companies with varying market capitalization. Please note that the businesses mentioned are used only as examples of companies of a particular capitalization and are not being recommended for your portfolio. Some are excellent companies, but you still need to do your homework.

Micro Cap

Micro caps are the smallest type of stock, and they're risky business. They are issued by companies with market caps of less than $300 million, which tend to be new and unproven. Micro cap stocks are sometimes referred to as penny stocks, but they're not necessarily the same. Penny stocks are those that trade for less than $1 a share. Micro stocks usually aren't making any money yet, but they aren't confined to trading for less than $1.

Public companies under a certain size aren't required to file reports with the SEC, meaning that there's often a lack of information available to potential investors, and a lack of SEC regulation of the stock. Micro cap stock is often traded in the over the counter (OTC) market instead of on one of the stock exchanges, and it's more subject to fraud than larger stock. Analysts don't research micro cap stocks and most of them aren't rated, so you'll need to do your own research if you're interested.

You should look at the company's financial information, but more importantly, because the company is likely to not yet be turning over a profit, you'll need to rely on the type of information you read about earlier in this chapter—whether the industry it falls within has the capacity for growth, how much competition it faces, and so forth—to judge whether you feel it's a viable investment.

Examples of companies with market caps of less than $300 million include the following:

- **Pioneer Southwest Energy Partners.** This Delaware-based limited partnership formed with the intention of buying oil and gas properties in Texas and New Mexico. It's listed on the New York Stock Exchange as PSE.

- **Peet's Coffee & Tea.** Peet's sells coffee, tea, and specialty foods in 75 of its own stores, by mail order, and online. More than 2,700 grocery stores offer its coffee. Based in Berkeley, California, the company is listed on NASDAQ as PEET.

- **B&G Foods.** This producer of shelf-stable foods distributed in the United States, Canada, and Puerto Rico is based in New Jersey. It's listed on the New York Stock Exchange as BGS.

- **Exponent.** This California-based company provides scientists, engineers, doctors, and consultants who analyze and offer solutions to complex issues, as well as study accidents, engineering failures, and other events. It's listed on NASDAQ as EXPO.

Small Cap

Small cap stock is that of companies with market capitalization of between $300 million and $1 billion. It's considered to be less risky than micro cap stock, and many investors love it because it's affordable and they consider it to have great potential.

It's true there are small cap companies that are growing quickly and are possibly great investments. Remember, after all, that Microsoft, Home Depot, and Wal-Mart were each at one time small cap stock. Still, small cap stock tends to be volatile, and while some might be a good addition to a portfolio, it's a good idea to keep a close watch on it. You should be sure that the company is on its way to becoming established, which usually means that it's been around for at least three years, and that it is profitable.

Examples of companies with market caps of between $300 million and $1 billion include the following:

- **Panera Bread.** This chain of bakery/café restaurants in the United States and Canada is headquartered outside of St. Louis, Missouri. In that location, Panera is still known as the St. Louis Bread Company. It's listed on NASDAQ as PNRA.

- **WebMD.** WebMD is an online medical information source that is staffed by doctors and reviewed frequently for accuracy. It's based in New York City and listed on NASDAQ as WBMD.

- **Dreamworks Animation.** This computer-generated animation company of such films as *Shrek* and *Kung Fu Panda* is known for its experienced and dynamic management team. Based in California, it's listed on NASDAQ as DWA.

- **La-Z Boy.** La-Z Boy is a leading residential furniture producer that also produces furniture for hotel lobbies, doctors' offices, and other locations. Based in Monroe, Michigan, it's listed on the New York Stock Exchange as LZB.

Mid Cap

Mid cap stock is issued by companies with market caps of between $1 billion and $10 billion. Mid cap is considered to be growth stock, and while it's considered less risky than micro cap or small cap stock, it's not considered as safe as large cap.

If you can find companies in which the financials meet your criteria (you'll learn how to make that determination in the next chapter), buying mid cap stock could be a great opportunity. Companies that fall into the mid cap category are still growing, but they've generally been around long enough to be considered established, with lessened chances of failure. What you're really doing when you buy mid cap stock is betting that it will eventually become large cap stock.

Examples of companies with market caps of between $1 billion and $10 billion include the following:

- **Aeropostale.** Aeropostale is a retailer of casual clothing with more than 900 stores in the United States, Canada, Puerto Rico, and the United Arab Emirates. Based in New York City, it's listed on the New York Stock Exchange as ARO.

- **Advance Auto Parts.** The second-largest retailer of automotive accessories and replacement parts in the United States, Advance is based in Roanoke, Virginia, and operates more than 3,500 stories in 40 states. It's listed on the New York Stock Exchange as AAP.

- **Standard Pacific Homes.** With a 40-plus year history, Standard Pacific is the eleventh-largest homebuilder in the country. Based in Irvine, California, it's listed on the New York Stock Exchange as SPF.

- **Centene Corporation.** This multi-line health-care company has two main segments: Medicaid managed care and specialty services. Based in St. Louis, it operates health plans in nine states. It's listed on the New York Stock Exchange as CNC.

Large Cap

Large cap companies are those with market caps of between $10 billion and $50 billion. Large cap stock is generally considered to be safer than its smaller counterparts because the companies usually remain stable, even during difficult economic times. That doesn't mean, however, that you don't need to do your homework regarding large cap companies—some are still better investments than others.

Examples of companies with market caps between $10 billion and $50 billion include the following.

- **Electronic Arts, Inc.** This well-known international developer, marketer, publisher, and distributor of video games is based in California. Electronic Arts is listed on NASDAQ as EA.

- **Molson Coors Brewing Company.** With headquarters in Colorado and Montreal, this company was created with the merger of Molson and Coors in 2005. It's listed on the Toronto Stock Exchange as TPX.B and on the New York Stock Exchange as TAP.

- **Goodyear Tire and Rubber.** A manufacturer of tires and rubber products, Goodyear also produces and markets rubber-related chemicals used in various applications. Based in Akron, Ohio, it's listed on the New York Stock Exchange as GT.

- **Colgate-Palmolive.** This multinational corporation produces and distributes household, health-care, and personal products, and also manufactures pet food and products under its "Hill's" brand. Based in New York City, it's listed on the New York Stock Exchange as CL.

Mega Cap

Nearly everybody has heard of the mega cap companies, which have market caps of over $50 billion. Mega cap stocks are generally considered to be less volatile than smaller stocks, although they can still be negatively impacted by economic conditions and other factors.

For instance, during the banking crisis of 2008, historically sound institutions saw stock prices crash. And when the bottom fell out of the housing market, big home builders, building supply companies, and many other businesses suffered. So although large and mega cap stocks are considered to be less risky, each stock and each economic cycle requires investors to consider the overall economy and conditions that could affect the company.

A problem with buying mega cap stocks is that, although there are bargains to be had at certain points throughout the market cycle, they're generally expensive investments. And once a company gets to be mega cap size, it may not have much room left for growth. Most investors in mega cap stock are looking for dividends and gradual appreciation of their stock.

Companies with market valuations of more than $50 billion include the following:

- **ExxonMobil.** ExxonMobil is a giant energy company that in 2008 was the most profitable company in the world. Oil prices plunged in 2009 and its profits fell by 57 percent, but the company continued to invest and expand, and remains one of the world's largest and most profitable entities. Based in Irving, Texas, it's listed on the New York Stock Exchange as XOM.

- **General Electric.** General Electric is a diversified technology, media, and financial services company, with products and services ranging from aircraft engines to business and consumer financing. Based in Fairfield, Connecticut, General Electric is listed on the New York Stock Exchange as GE.

- **Microsoft.** Founded in 1975 by high school friends Bill Gates and Paul Allen, this software giant remains extremely viable, despite serious competition from Apple. Based in Redmond, Washington, it's listed on NASDAQ as MSFT.

- **Pfizer.** Pfizer is the world's largest pharmaceutical company and producer of Lipitor, the world's most widely used drug. Headquartered in New York City, it's listed on the New York Stock Exchange as PFE.

To sum it up, large and mega cap stock historically carries less risk than small cap, but it also presents less growth opportunity. The type of company in which you choose to invest has a lot to do with your investing style and personality, as well as your financial circumstances. Investors who have money they can afford to lose can make more high-risk investments than those who don't.

Take a Look at the Management Team

Part of the job of researching a company before investing is to check out the management team. With all the information available on the web, it's not hard to do this, and it's a good idea because the performance of management can tell you a lot about a business.

CRASH!

A company's annual report can provide important financial and other information, but it's likely to sugarcoat any scandals or other bad news that's occurred. Don't rely solely on information released by the company you're researching. Be sure to check out news sources to see what the company has been up to. Stock quote pages contain a "Recent News" section that can provide interesting and useful information.

You can find the names of a company's management team on its website from a financial site like Yahoo! Finance or Bloomberg, or other online sources. You can also learn about management by reading the company's annual reports. There's a section of an annual report called "Management's Discussion and Analysis of the Financial Condition," which can provide a lot of information and is closely monitored by the SEC. Also, pay attention to the message of the chairman's letter to shareholders and read several years' worth to see if the message remains consistent. You can normally find several years' worth of annual reports that contain this message on a company's website. A company that adheres to its core values will have a steady message, even if its circumstances change.

Check to see if the management team has remained fairly intact. Of course, you expect to have personnel changes within a company, but if half of the team comes and goes on an annual basis, it conveys a sense of disorder and suggests there may be serious problems. Look for a stable management team. If it's not stable, do some digging to find out why. Most companies post press releases on their sites announcing important new hires. Reading those or news articles you find elsewhere could provide you with some information.

If a company has had the same management team for years and years, be aware that a major transition could be approaching. Management teams sometimes start out together and end up retiring or changing companies at about the same time. There's no magic formula for how long a management team will remain in place, but if most of the senior management seems to be about the same age, keep in mind that most people don't work forever, and try to get a sense of the company's management succession plan. Most publicly held companies have investor relations departments that should be able to provide you with more information if you're interested.

Try to dig up enough information to know the educational backgrounds and previous experience of management members. Where was the CEO before he took over the reins at the XYZ Company? Look for a logical career transition, and keep an eye out for management's qualifications. A pharmaceutical company, for instance, would ideally have a management team that's heavy on scientific and medical backgrounds.

It's also important to know what sort of investment the management team has made in the company. It's a good sign if management owns large amounts of stock, as it signifies confidence in the health of the company.

You don't have to spend hours and hours digging up information on a company's management team. However, taking a little time to check out who's running the show, how long they've been there, the turnover rate, consistency of the company message, succession plans, and qualifications of managers can save you from wishing you'd invested elsewhere down the road.

The Least You Need to Know

- Look to invest in companies and industries that you have researched and understand.
- Get a good grasp of what products and services the company offers and who buys those products and services.
- Take time to learn about the competition before investing.
- Consider the size and age of a company before buying its stock.
- Make sure the company's management team is stable.

Now Comes the Financial Stuff

In This Chapter

- Where to find financial information
- Understanding a company's balance sheet
- Looking at income and cash flow
- Making sense of financial ratios
- Putting it all together

Once you've taken a close look at a company, checking out its product or service, market share, customers, size, age, and other factors, you'll need to take some time to check out its finances.

Looking at a company's balance sheet, income statement, and cash flow statement will help you get a handle on how profitable it is, what sort of debt it's dealing with, what its assets are, and so forth. Studying a company's financial information is the most basic aspect of fundamental analysis, which we introduced in Chapter 12.

This chapter will fill you in on what sort of financial information to look for, and tell you how to use the financial reports mentioned above to assess an organization's financial health. Before you start moving into a company's annual reports or other financial information, however, you should take a few minutes to check out the financial information found on an analyst's stock report.

Getting an Initial Overview of a Company's Finances

Before you delve into a company's income and cash flow statements or its balance sheet, all of which contain a lot of important information, find yourself an analyst stock report. You can find these online from companies like Standard & Poor's (S&P) or Morningstar, and they're easy to read and loaded with interesting information.

An S&P stock report rates the strength of a stock from zero to five stars, gives it a letter grade, tells what industry and sector the stock falls into, lists the firm's major competitors, and provides a risk assessment. The report also provides an explanation for why the stock received the rating it did, along with key statistics and financial information. You can read a corporate overview, corporate strategy, find out who runs the company, where it's located, how many employees and stockholders there are, and much more.

TAKING STOCK

Always look for "As" or "Bs" for stock grades on analyst reports. Look to see how the stock is doing compared to the S&P 500 index and if the sales of the company are increasing. This information will give you a snapshot of the company and let you know if it's worth investing more of your time.

The value of looking at a stock report before knuckling down to assess financial information is that if the analyst's report tells you that the XYZ Company is a horrible investment, gives it zero out of five stars as a recommendation, and clearly spells out its rationale for that advice, you can save yourself some time and effort and move on to a different company.

To access a report, simply go to S&P or another rating service website and enter the name of the company in which you're interested. You have to register in order to get access to the reports, but it's free and easy to do so.

Getting Serious with Balance Sheets

If the report on the stock you're interested in is favorable, it's time to move on to an examination of the company's balance sheet. Companies are required by the government to provide balance sheets for shareholders on a regular basis in order to give them an overview of the company's financial health.

Prospective investors can also get access to a company's balance sheet from the Securities and Exchange Commission (SEC) and its EDGAR website at www.sec. gov/edgar.shtml. From the EDGAR site you can access a company's 10-K and 10-Q reports, which contain information from its balance sheets. The 10-K report can give you the balance sheet for an entire fiscal year, while the 10-Q provides quarterly reports of balance sheet information.

Checking out a company's balance sheets will give you a look at the direction in which the company has come, and that in which it is headed. You'll be able to compare assets and liabilities from quarter to quarter and year to year to assess its overall financial health. Let's have a look at just what a balance sheet is and what it contains.

What Is a Balance Sheet?

A balance sheet is simply a record of a company's assets and liabilities. It provides the value of what a company owns or expects to own soon, and what it owes or expects to owe soon. When you know the values of assets and liabilities, you can figure out equity, which is explained in the next section.

Balance sheets have three main parts: assets, liabilities, and equity. In Chapter 3, you learned about determining your net worth by adding up all your assets, and then subtracting the total of all your liabilities from that number. Balance sheets work the same way, and companies do them for the same reason that you might complete the Net Worth Worksheet in Chapter 3.

SHARE THIS

When you're studying a company's financials, keep in mind that all publicly held companies use accrual accounting when reporting their earnings. Accrual accounting is different from cash accounting, which is the system most individuals use, in that it records financial transactions (income and expenses) at the point at which they actually occur, rather than at the time payment is received or made. A company, for instance, subtracts charges for its electric bill throughout the month instead of simply paying off a bill at the end of the month. Accrual accounting provides a more realistic, "real time" picture of a company's financial picture than cash accounting.

Assets for a company are the same as for an individual—anything a company owns that has value. Liabilities are also the same for companies and individuals; they're anything the company owes. When assets and liabilities are listed on a balance sheet (hence the name), the total value of a company's assets must equal the combined value of its liabilities and equity. For instance, if a company has assets worth $10 million and liabilities worth $5 million, its equity must also be $5 million in order to balance the value of the assets.

Balance sheets vary in appearance from company to company, but normally contain the same general information. Generally, the first category is assets, which are broken down into several groups:

- **Current assets.** These include cash; accounts receivable or debts that are owed to the company; inventory and supplies; and prepaid expenses, such as insurance premiums that have been paid in advance.

- **Property and equipment.** These assets include land, land improvement, equipment, and buildings. Depreciation must be considered when figuring the total of these assets.

- **Intangible assets.** These are a little murky, and include things like the values of patents; trade names; and goodwill, which is value added to a company for its good reputation and a satisfied p ,ool of customers.

The second category of the balance sheet, liabilities, is also broken down into a couple categories:

- **Current liabilities.** These include expenses such as wages; interest; taxes; warranties; unearned revenues, which is money received for products or services not yet delivered; and accounts payable, which is money the company owes to suppliers or others.

- **Long-term liabilities.** These can include payments due on long-term loans, such as leases, or bonds that the company has issued.

The third category of a company's balance sheet is shareholder equity. This number tells you how much money is left over to divide among shareholders once all the assets have been added up and the liabilities subtracted from their total.

Why Is It Important?

The balance sheet is a simple concept, but an extremely important document for investors and prospective investors. Comparing the assets of a company to the liabilities provides a picture of the company's *equity*, which tells you if a company is financially sound.

> **DEFINITION**
>
> **Equity** is the value attached to a company, determined by subtracting liabilities from assets.

A company that is in good financial shape will have a good supply of liquid assets, or assets that can quickly be turned into cash. That's important to investors because a company that has more cash than it needs to fund future growth can use the extra cash to pay dividends to investors or to buy back stock.

By examining a company's balance sheet, you can see if the company will be able to keep expanding without borrowing huge sums of money or issuing more stock in order to do so. You can view how much it owes, what kind of income it generates, what it owns, and much more. A balance sheet is essentially the financial overview of a company, and an important tool to use when deciding whether or not to buy its stock.

Earnings, Earnings, Earnings

Another of a company's trio of major financial statements is its income statement, which measures how well a company did financially over a specific period of time, normally a quarter or a fiscal year.

Income statements are broken down into two sections: operating and nonoperating. The operating section reveals financial information related directly to the day-to-day operations of the business. If you're looking at an auto manufacturing company, for instance, the operating section of the income statement would report on all revenues and expenses that result directly from the manufacture of cars.

> **SHARE THIS**
>
> An income statement is also known as a profit and loss statement, statement of operations, statement of earnings, or statement of income. Some financial types refer to it as "the P&L," referring to profit and loss statement. However, an income statement by any other name still reports on income.

The nonoperating section reports on revenues and expenses that result from non-operating activities, such as the sale of a factory or equipment. Again, the amount of detail contained in an income statement depends on the complexity of the company and other factors. Some of the information often found on income statements includes the following.

- **Net sales.** These are the revenues a company realizes from the sales of goods or services, and they're an important factor in its ability to grow. Sales should be on the increase if you're considering buying shares of the company.

- **Cost of goods and services (COGS).** These are expenses a company incurs for materials, manufacturing overhead, and labor. COGS also includes depreciation, although that's listed separately.

- **Gross profit.** This is the amount you get when you subtract the COGS from the net sales. The greater the gross profit of a company, the better its bottom line will be. Compare the current year to the last several, because you should look to invest in companies that have increased profits.

- **Selling, general, and administrative expenses (SG&A).** These are costs incurred to sell the product or service such as rent, insurance, payroll taxes, utilities, advertising, delivery expenses, salaries and benefits, and credit card fees. Many of these expenses are considered to be controllable and an indicator of the effectiveness of management.

- **Operating income.** This is the amount you get when you subtract SG&A from a company's gross profit, and it reflects the earnings realized from day-to-day operations.

- **Pretax income.** What a company pays in taxes affects its bottom line. If a company is able to reduce or avoid taxes, it will report more income than a company that isn't able to shave off some taxes. Some investors prefer to look at pretax income as a more reliable indicator of earnings.

- **Net income.** This is where most investors look first when reading an income statement, and the figure most often used to determine a company's profitability (or lack of profitability).

For an income statement to be of real value, you need to be able to compare a current statement with past statements. You can look at an income statement and think a company is great because its net income is $6 million. If its net income from the previous year was $8 million, however, you probably want to rethink investing in the company.

SHARE THIS

Income statements that show earnings for more than one year are called comparative income statements. They allow investors and potential investors to gain perspective on a company's earnings over time, and are normally considered to be more useful than those that show earnings from just one year.

In addition to comparing earnings of previous years when looking at a company's income statement, you'll want to look for reductions in COGS. If earnings increase while COGS decrease, the company will have more gross income, which is an indicator of financial health.

Also, check to make sure that operating expenses appear to be under control by comparing them to those of previous years. If sales have increased while expenses have stayed the same or decreased, it's a good sign that the company is well managed and financially on the right track.

Cash Flow

A company's cash flow statement is the third of the major financial statements you'll want to look at when analyzing a company. It's important to investors because it indicates how much cash on hand a company has, and how much it will be able to invest back into the business to further increase productivity and profit.

Some investors don't consider cash flow as an aspect of fundamental analysis, but you should always check a company's cash flow statement when deciding whether or not to buy its stock. A company can be generating a profit, but if it doesn't have enough money on hand to pay its bills, you don't want to invest in it.

A cash flow statement is divided into three sections, each of which applies to one area of a company's business:

- **Operations.** Its operations are the primary way in which a company generates cash. This is cash that's generated from within the company, as opposed to outside of the company, as with investing and financing activities. This part of the cash flow statement takes into account net income and operating assets and liabilities.

- **Investing.** Cash flow from investing includes payouts the company makes when it buys property or equipment, investment securities, expansion from acquiring other businesses, and income obtained from selling its assets, such as investment securities, property, equipment, or even parts of the business. Investors are interested in a company's investment cash flow because it indicates whether the company is using its cash to maintain facilities and equipment so that it can continue operations.

- **Financing.** Stockholders want to make sure a company they're invested in has money with which to pay out dividends. If a company has to pay out too much cash to repay debt and interest, and isn't realizing income from selling more stock, its investors begin to fear that dividends will be cut or discontinued, which isn't a good thing.

Analyzing cash flow is a little trickier than looking at other financial statements because it's more open to interpretation. Still, it's an important part of a company's overall financial situation and helps to indicate stability and prospects for its future.

Understanding Ratios

Ratios are important tools when analyzing a company's financial situation. Getting a handle on some basic ratios allows you to compare one company against another in the same industry or sector, or contrast a company's current performance with past performance.

TAKING STOCK

Don't be tempted to compare ratios of companies that are in different industries. Comparing ratios of a soft drink company with those of a software company is like comparing apples and oranges.

Many people are intimidated by the thought of ratios and shy away from using them as analytical tools, but they're really not that difficult to understand. There are five categories of ratios, each of which applies to one financial area. Within each category of ratios there are subratios. You can buy entire books dealing with ratios, but for our purposes, we'll be considering the five broad categories of:

- Operating ratios
- Profitability ratios
- Liquidity ratios
- Valuation ratios
- Solvency ratios

Let's take a look at what each category entails and what it means to the financial health of a company.

Operating Ratios

Operating ratios, which sometimes are called asset management ratios, indicate how well a company manages its capital and other assets in order to realize a profit. They're based on factors such as the amount of inventory the company has or the amount of accounts receivable it takes to support a specified portion of the business.

Operating ratios are calculated by comparing operating expenses to net sales. They are a company's operating expenses divided by its operating revenues. In other words, operating ratios help you to know how much the company you're analyzing spends in order to produce its products or services, and how much revenue it generates from the sale of those products or services.

Common operating ratios include sales to receivables, net profits to gross income, operating expenses to operating income, net profit to net worth, return on equity, and return on assets.

Profitability Ratios

As the name indicates, profitability ratios help you to look at how profitable a company is. Remember that profit is different from income. A company might have a lot of income, but not be making much profit.

Common profitability ratios include profit margin, return on assets, and return on equity. Remember that a company's profits can vary from season to season, so be careful how you compare them. It makes more sense to compare its profitability with that of another company in the same industry and year to year, or with a previous time period that is comparable within the company you're analyzing.

If the company's profits are decreasing from year to year, that should raise a red flag that it may be facing stronger competition or that its market is falling. If its profit is much lower than that of its competitors, that's another reason for concern, as is a much higher profit, which could indicate conditions or operating circumstances that won't last.

SHARE THIS

An analysis tool popularly used in some industries is Earnings Before Interest, Taxes, Depreciation, and Amortization (EBITDA). EBITDA isn't a ratio but a process of converting net income to a number that's computed by starting with net income and subtracting interest, taxes, depreciation, and amortization. The theory behind EBITDA is that interest, taxes, depreciation, and amortization don't reflect the philosophies or business practices of current management, but are functions of laws, such as tax codes, or decisions made by prior managers. Generally, the use of EBITDA makes a company's financial ratios more attractive, so if you encounter this tool, consider it with a grain of salt.

Liquidity Ratios

Liquidity ratios indicate how easily and quickly a company can convert its assets into cash. A company could need to raise cash for various purposes, such as buying additional assets or expanding, repaying creditors, or for some type of emergency situation.

Examples of liquidity ratios include the current ratio, quick ratio, working capital turnover, inventory turnover, and receivables turnover ratio.

These ratios indicate whether a company has enough cash to pay its bills, both under normal and difficult circumstances; whether the company is able to collect money that is owed to it; how much of its working capital the company is spending; and how susceptible the company might be to high interest rates.

Valuation Ratios

Valuation ratios refer to how the price of a company's stock relates to the performance of the company. They are important to investors who are thinking about buying the stock, because they indicate whether or not the stock is a good value.

The most widely used valuation ratio is the price-to-earnings ratio, also known as the P/E ratio, which compares the price of a company's stock to the amount of earnings generated on a per-share basis. The P/E ratio gives investors an idea of how much income a company will generate in the future, and whether the current stock price is overly expensive or a good value.

The P/E ratio is calculated by dividing the current price of the stock by the earnings. It's important to compare the firm's P/E with others in the same industry, as well as with the overall P/E of the S&P 500. The P/E ratio is high for tech stocks and low for consumer staple stocks, making it irrelevant to compare the ratios of companies within those industries.

Investors who look for stock that is priced low are called value investors, as you read about in Chapter 7. Other valuation ratios include price to sales, price to book, and price to cash flow.

Solvency Ratios

Solvency is simply a matter of whether or not a company is able to stay afloat financially. Solvency ratios help to determine that by comparing what a company owns to what it owes. They indicate the long-term health of a company by looking at its financial obligations and how it might generate assets in the future.

Investors, of course, favor companies that aren't drowning in debt, either short or long term. The total debt to total assets ratio is an important solvency ratio because it indicates the percentage of a company's assets for which the company has debt.

> **TAKING STOCK**
>
> When analyzed and put together, ratios provide a wide range of information about a company, including how well it's doing compared to competitors and industry averages, overall financial health, strength of operations, liquidity, its ability to borrow money and pay off debt, profitability, and other factors. All of these are important in deciding whether or not to invest.

The closer to "0" this solvency ratio comes, the better, because that indicates low debt. If a company has two or three times more debt than assets, investors should look elsewhere. A total debt to total assets ratio of one is sometimes acceptable for young companies that haven't yet had time to pay off debt. Other solvency ratios include working capital, times interest earned, and free cash flow.

Coming to Terms with Ratios and Other Financials

You can find all the information you need with which to calculate ratios in a company's financial statements. Check the company's website, a stock report site like S&P, or the company's financial information on the SEC's EDGAR site (www.sec. gov/edgar.shtml).

Once you've located the information you need, consider using a financial analysis form to record it and provide you with an overview of a company's financial information. You can make your own form as a spreadsheet or chart. The form doesn't need to be anything fancy; just come up with a format that works for you. It should include all of the information contained on a stock report, and any other information you might find to be helpful, including the following:

- Earnings per share
- P/E ratio
- Total debt
- Company name

- Products or services

- Company risk (such as legal problems)

- Management team

- Ticker symbol and stock exchange

- Investor relations contact person and number

You should also include your impressions of a company and its financial health on your financial analysis form. Collecting all of this type of information on one form will be extremely helpful when you want to review it later.

Predicting the Success of a Company

Once you've studied a company's financial information, you can put that together with information you've already gathered about what the company does, its products or services, its market share and competition, its size, and the other factors described in the previous chapter. All of this information, when combined and viewed as a package, provides the fundamental analysis you need in order to decide whether or not to invest in a company.

Take a little time to review all the information you've acquired, putting it together so that you're relating a company's financials to the state of the overall economy, the financial health of the company's industry or sector group, the strength of its management team, how well its competition is doing, and other factors.

While financial information is vital to your analysis of a company, it cannot on its own provide the whole picture of how well a company is doing or what success it will experience in the future, since all public information available is historical. If the financial information is favorable, however, and your research regarding other aspects of the company had favorable results, you probably could feel good about buying its stock.

A big-picture approach is necessary when determining what stock to buy, along with ongoing vigilance concerning events that might affect its performance. You'll need to continue to watch for conditions and events, both within the company and outside of it, that could affect its financial well-being.

The Least You Need to Know

- Analyst stock reports are easy to obtain and provide valuable information about a company.
- Financial information can be obtained from a company's balance sheet, income statement, and cash flow statement.
- Financial ratios provide insight into many areas of a company's finances.
- Carefully researching financial and other information regarding a company will allow you to predict its success.

The Mechanics of Investing

Once you've gotten a handle on picking a company in which you want to invest, Part 4 teaches you the basics of how to buy the stock you've selected. This part walks you through the mechanics of finding and hiring a broker who can provide advice and direction as you enter the stock market, as well as advise you on buying stock on your own. You learn about different ways that companies sell their stock, different types of stock, and how not all stock behaves in the same way.

You also get some tips on how to maximize your investments using techniques like buying on margin and shorting, including the benefits and risks associated with them. We share strategies for investing during good and not-so-good economic times, and tell you how to adjust your investments in order to keep making money when the market isn't cooperating.

Investing with a Broker

In This Chapter

- What a broker does
- Different breeds of brokers
- Advantage of working with a broker
- Understanding brokerage fees
- Signing up with the best broker for you

So you've done your research, identified some companies you like, and you're ready to get started in the stock market. Now what? How does one actually go about the process of procuring stock?

Once you're confident about your decision to buy, your next step will be to locate a person or company to buy the stock you've selected. That individual or company is called a broker or a brokerage firm. Brokers sometimes are referred to as stockbrokers, account executives, registered representatives, or just "reps," and the terms can be used interchangeably.

In this chapter, you'll learn about different types of brokers, the services they provide, the advantages of having a broker, and what to look for when selecting one.

What Is a Broker?

A *broker* (or *brokerage firm*) is simply a go-between for a buyer and seller. There are real estate brokers, aircraft brokers, commodity brokers, insurance brokers, mortgage brokers, ship brokers, and other kinds of brokers, but for our purposes, a broker is someone who buys and sells stock for someone like you. Brokers don't own the stock you want to buy; they serve as agents who buy and sell for clients. For their trouble, they receive a *commission* or another form of payment.

> **DEFINITION**
>
> A **broker** is a person or firm that buys and sells stock for clients, usually for a fee. A **brokerage firm** is a company that buys and sells stock on its clients' behalf. A **commission** is a fee charged by a brokerage firm for the service of buying or selling stock.

It used to be that only wealthy people could afford the services of brokers, which meant that common folk didn't have a lot of dealing with the stock market. Then the investment world changed dramatically when brokerage firm deregulation in the form of an SEC ruling went into effect on May 1, 1975, prohibiting securities exchanges from fixing brokerage commission rates and forcing competitive prices and more opportunity for "ordinary" investors. With the advent of the Internet and online brokers, with even lower fees, just about anyone with some money to invest can now find a broker to conduct trades. Brokers provide a range of services for a range of fees.

Not just anyone can hang out a shingle and call himself a broker. Brokers are required to pass an exam and be registered with the Financial Industry Regulatory Authority (FINRA) and the Securities and Exchange Commission (SEC). Brokers need a broker/dealer to hold their licenses. It's important that you check out a broker's qualifications before allowing him to buy and sell stock for you. We'll talk more about this later in the chapter.

Different Types of Brokers

Brokers provide a range of services, with a range of fees. While one client might want a broker who simply follows her instructions to buy and sell particular stocks, another client may prefer to have a broker who makes transaction decisions on her behalf.

Hands-on investors, particularly those who buy and sell often, usually prefer to make their own decisions, relying on a broker only to conduct transactions as instructed. Investors who are unsure of what to buy, or don't have time to do the research necessary with stock market trading, are probably more comfortable with a broker who will offer advice and walk them through transactions.

There are two primary types of brokers: full service and discount. A third category is online brokers, which is your option if you trade online. You don't have a person to talk with; you make your trades yourself on the Internet. There are advantages and disadvantages to each of these types of brokers.

Full-Service Broker

Full-service brokers were once the only game in town, and there still is certainly a place for them. With the Internet so widely available, however, and investors increasingly able to research and trade on their own, the demand for full service has dropped considerably. However, they do offer valuable services.

What is referred to as a full-service broker is usually a large national firm, such as Morgan Stanley Smith Barney, Merrill Lynch, UBS, Wells Fargo Advisors, and Raymond James. Companywide, these big firms can employ 10,000, 15,000, or more individual brokers, who usually are called financial consultants, account executives, or something similar. If you hire a full-service broker, you'll be assigned a financial consultant who will handle your account. It's important to check the credentials of such a person, and you'll learn more about that later in this chapter.

> **CRASH!**
>
> A full-service broker is only as valuable as a client allows it to be. Many people sign on with full-service brokers because they are recommended by a friend or relative, or simply because they like a TV ad, and neglect to take advantage of the services available. If you choose to go with a full-service broker, be sure to find out exactly what services are available and use all of the ones that are advantageous to you. Otherwise, you'll be wasting your money.

In addition to advising on and buying and selling stock, full-service brokers offer research services, financial planning, retirement planning, and more. Your financial advisor should meet with you on a regular basis to discuss your financial goals and assess where you are in terms of meeting those goals.

A full-service broker will discuss your ideas regarding your portfolio, provide his or her thoughts, and suggest possible alternatives. These brokers are backed by research departments that provide fabulous information to supplement research you may have located yourself.

A huge advantage of employing a full-service broker is the availability of all of those services we just mentioned, but there are some disadvantages, too. These include expense—it costs more to use a full-service broker than a discount or online broker—and the fact that some of the big brokerage firms require very high minimum investments. You'll need $100,000 or more just to be considered as a client with some of the big full-service firms.

If, as a beginning investor, you feel that you require the services of a full-service broker and you have the means to meet the minimum investment requirements and pay the heftier fees and commissions you can expect to encounter, it might make sense to go the full-service route. Most investors who are just starting out, however, do fine with a discount or online broker. Some people start out with a discount or online broker and then shift to a full-service firm as their financial situation becomes more complex and requires additional advice.

Discount Broker

A discount broker buys and sells stock for you, but does not offer advice, conduct research for you, or provide the other services offered by full-service brokers. As a result, the cost of using a discount broker can be significantly less than with a full-service broker, which is a real advantage for many investors. The line between discount and full-service brokers has blurred over the past decade, as major discount firms today are more sophisticated and offer more services to clients than they did in the past.

While discount brokers don't advise you on what stocks to buy and sell, they will provide information, stock news, and more. The offices of major discount firms, such as Charles Schwab, Fidelity Brokerage Services, or TD Ameritrade, rival those of their full-service counterparts, and offer some of the same account services.

A subcategory of discount brokers is deep discount brokers, which offer even lower commission rates. They also provide fewer services, so be sure to find out exactly what is available if you choose to go with this type of broker. Some brokerage firms offer both discount and deep discount services.

Many investors of all levels are highly satisfied with using discount brokers instead of full-service brokers, because they are willing to explore stocks and the companies offering them on their own. This eliminates the need for extensive advice and counseling that one might receive from a full-service broker. Someone whose financial situation is very complex, however, or who is not interested in or willing to take the time to research stocks, may benefit from those additional services.

Online Broker

With the rise in popularity of online trading, an increasing number of brokers are offering online brokerage services. This allows clients to avoid conventional offices altogether and conduct trading entirely online. Some firms, such as TD Ameritrade and E*Trade Financial, were created expressly for Internet business, while others, such as Charles Schwab, have added online brokerage services.

SHARE THIS

Smart Money magazine rates online brokers each year, considering factors such as fees, services offered, and customer service. The top 10, in order, for 2010 are: Fidelity, E*Trade, TD Ameritrade, Charles Schwab, TradeKing, Scottrade, WallStreet-E, Firstrade, Just2Trade, and Muriel Seibert. The cost of a trade among these firms ranged from $2.50 (Just2Trade) to $14.95 (Muriel Siebert).

The big advantages to online trading are that it's convenient and less expensive than using a full-service broker, and in some cases, a discount broker. Customer service and rates among online brokers vary, however, so it pays to do your homework before signing on with one.

You'll need to check out the brokerage rate, which is what you'll be charged for buying or selling stock. Usually, the more stock you buy in one transaction, the less you'll pay "per unit." This is known as a sliding scale, and is a common practice among online brokers. You should read the contracts of the firms you're considering and compare these rates.

Also, look for account fees that are sometimes hidden within contracts, rules pertaining to how you can access the money within your account, and how long it takes for a transaction to actually occur once you place an order. Some brokers offer incentives, such as a period of waived brokerage fees or free information about companies and industries you're interested in; be sure to take those into consideration as you decide on a broker.

CRASH!

If you're considering an online broker, make certain that you can reach a representative by phone in the event of a computer problem or service interruption.

Why Having a Broker Is a Good Thing

There are many reasons why having a broker—either full-service or discount—is a good thing. Having a broker provides a vehicle for buying and selling stock quickly and efficiently, and a sense of security from having someone perform the task on your behalf.

A good broker will have extensive knowledge about the stock market and be well versed on factors that affect the market. She also has access to information, data, and tools that you may not, and can offer insights that you lack.

A full-service broker effectively serves as your financial advisor, and can assist with your investment goals and time lines. Many people like the idea of being able to pick up a phone and call someone with questions or concerns, and participating in regular portfolio reviews. If you have a full-service broker, you should work to establish a good relationship and take advantage of services offered.

Fees, Fees, and More Fees

While there are many things to like about having a broker, one thing most people dislike are fees, which, depending on the broker you choose and services offered, can be sizeable. Brokers earn their money through commissions, salaries, or a combination of the two.

Full-service brokers have historically been paid primarily through commissions, and this is a source of contention among some investors, commentators, and discount brokers. Every time a broker buys or sells stock, he gets a piece of the action in the form of a commission. Critics say this sometimes results in a practice known as *churning*, which basically means making frequent trades solely to generate commissions.

DEFINITION

Churning is the practice of actively trading stock within a brokerage account in order to increase brokerage commissions rather than customer profits. Churning is illegal and unethical.

Brokers' fees can range from annoying to distressing, but remember that commissions can be included in your purchase cost and sale price when you're figuring capital gains. If you buy 100 shares of stock for $20 a share, for example, and later sell the shares for $30, you'll have realized capital gains of $1,000. If your broker charged you $20 for each transaction, however, you get to deduct $40 from your capital gains, lowering both the gains and the tax you'll have to pay on them.

Brokers charge either on a per-transaction basis or a percentage fee, often known as a wrap account. For a stated percentage, a wrap account fee covers all administrative expenses, commissions, and management expenses either to a certain maximum number of trades, or for an unlimited number of trades per year. The wrap fee is to protect you from overtrading or churning on the part of the broker.

Brokers at discount brokerages usually receive salaries, and thereby don't have the incentive to encourage frequent purchasing and selling. Discount brokerages charge a flat fee for a trade, and make their money by having many clients and a high volume of trading.

Knowing What You're Paying For

Regardless of whether you use a full-service or discount broker, you need to know what fees are being charged and what they're for. In addition to robust fees and commissions, brokers, especially full-service brokers, may charge other fees, including …

- An annual maintenance fee on your account, which can be as high as $150 or more.
- A service fee for administrative chores such as mailing stock certificates.
- Some full-service brokers offer free trading but charge an annual fee of between 1 and 2 percent of a client's total assets in exchange. Even 1 percent of a $100,000 portfolio is $1,000 a year.
- A wrap fee, which is the cost for providing a basketful of services, such as research, advice, and trading. While this simplifies the fee process, you could end up paying as much as 3 percent of the value of your portfolio.
- Fees for a financial plan, up to $2,500 per plan.

Before you begin a relationship with any type of broker, you should get all the facts about fees and costs. Do this by carefully reading the information found on the broker's website or obtained from the company, and then following up with questions. Ask how the broker is paid, and request a copy of the company's commission schedule. Inquire whether a broker gets a higher commission on a firm's own investment products. Verify if the firm requires a minimum account balance so you can prevent minimum account fees. If there's anything you don't understand, keep asking questions until you do.

TAKING STOCK

Don't be afraid to ask a broker if he or she is willing to negotiate, especially if you have a significant amount of money to invest. A broker may be willing to lower or even drop some fees in order to get your business. It doesn't hurt to ask.

Minding the Store

Regardless of the type of broker you choose, it's your responsibility to keep an eye on your account and make sure that everything is in order. If you can access your account online, you can check it frequently. If you only receive monthly statements, be sure to review them carefully and report anything that doesn't seem right.

While you depend on a broker to buy and sell stock and perhaps provide other services, your account is first and foremost your responsibility. Don't hesitate to contact your broker immediately if you suspect there is a problem. If there is an error in your account, ask for a written explanation from a manager or compliance officer, and verify that the problem has been corrected by checking your account online or on your next statement.

If you suspect that your broker is not handling your account properly, talk to his or her manager, providing detailed, written explanations of any problems and requesting written replies. If the problem isn't taken care of or resolved to your satisfaction, you can fill out an online complaint form with the SEC. The form can be accessed at www.sec.gov/complaint.shtml.

Finding the Broker You Need

Only you can decide what type of broker is right for you. Choosing a broker should be based on your experience level, the amount of help you anticipate that you'll need, the amount of time you're willing and able to spend on your investments, and the services that you desire.

A good first step when choosing a broker is to talk to friends and family members. Ask about the types and levels of services they receive, how often they're in contact with their brokers, if their phone calls are returned promptly, what fees they pay, how easy or difficult it is to understand statements, what kind of information the broker provides, and their general level of satisfaction with the broker. Also check out Appendix D for information on choosing a broker. Once you've got some names, you can start trying to match them with the type of broker you think you'd be most comfortable with.

CRASH!

It's fine to compare notes with friends and family members when looking for a broker. Remember, though, that it doesn't make sense to choose a broker because your brother thinks she's great if your brother's investing goals and circumstances are far different from your own.

What's Your Time Factor?

If you're anxious to begin investing in the stock market but have no time or interest in researching stocks yourself, consider paying a broker to do that work for you. Trying to save money by going with a discount broker under those circumstances is short sighted, at best.

A full-service broker can make decisions for you—with your approval, of course—eliminating the need for you to spend time researching companies and deciding whether to buy or sell. You still, however, will need to pay close attention to what the broker is doing, and ask for explanations for his actions.

If, on the other hand, you're willing to put in the time to research and learn more about investing, a discount broker might be just fine for your needs.

What's Your Confidence Factor?

Some investors are interested in researching companies and choosing stocks, but don't feel that they're capable of doing so effectively. If you're a new investor and uncertain about your abilities to make sound, informed decisions, you might want to consider a full-service broker.

As with most things you do, your confidence level will increase along with your knowledge as you learn more about investing and how the stock market works. As we mentioned earlier, you could always start out with a full-service broker and then switch to a discount option when you feel that you're ready to do so.

What to Look for in a Broker

Once you've got some leads on brokers, either from friends and family members or other sources, you should check out their regulatory histories and procure some references. This sounds like it might be daunting, but it's actually pretty easy to do. There is a lot of public information about brokers available, and any reputable broker should be able and willing to provide references.

FINRA provides free information about brokerage firms and individual brokers on its BrokerCheck program, which is available online at www.finra.org/Investors/ ToolsCalculators/BrokerCheck/index.htm. The information on BrokerCheck comes from the Central Registration Depository (CRD), which is the securities industry online registration and licensing database. The site contains professional background information on about 850,000 brokers who are or were formerly registered with FINRA, and 17,000 brokerage firms.

You'll be able to find out if a broker you're interested in has the correct licenses for your state, if there have been complaints filed against him, or if he's had problems with regulators. You can also access the BrokerCheck hotline by calling 1-800-289-9999.

Once you're satisfied that the broker you're checking out isn't carrying around any serious baggage, you should call to set up an interview. When you meet with the broker, be prepared to discuss your investment goals, your timetable, and your risk tolerance. Also, have some questions prepared to ask of the broker. Here are some suggestions for what questions to ask:

- What's your experience and educational background?
- Are you involved in continuing education?
- Do you belong to any professional organizations?
- Have you received any recognition or awards?
- Can you provide me with references from current and former clients?
- Can you provide me with a full disclosure of fees and costs?

TAKING STOCK

When hiring a broker, it's important to consider what types of clients the broker represents. Different investors have different needs, and brokers tend to "specialize" in different types of clients. A broker whose specialty is retirees with $10 million or more in assets may not be able to give you, a beginning investor, the expertise or attention you deserve. Make sure the fit is right before signing on with a broker.

Get a feel for the broker's approach to investing and whether he or she specializes in any particular area of investing. Take note of the broker's interest in your goals and investing style, paying attention to whether it feels like the two of you are a good fit. If you have little risk tolerance and she's pushing a portfolio of risky stock, you probably will need to find a different broker.

Setting Up an Account

Once you've found a broker with whom you're comfortable and feel confident you can work with effectively, the next step is to set up a new account. It seems as daunting as purchasing a new car, but the paperwork is required by the brokerage firm, FINRA, the SEC, or perhaps all of these entities.

Part of the initial paperwork is a disclosure of your current annual income, your assets and liabilities, and your time frame for investing. There is usually a request for you to declare your risk tolerance. There are several questions concerning your investment experience. Some large firms require your completion of a series of questions of your understanding of the stock market and your fear of asset decline.

The brokerage firm will provide you with a contract, which includes the statement of the fees and an arbitration clause requiring the parties to resolve their disputes rather than taking them to court. You don't need to sign paperwork a prospective broker gives you at your initial meeting. You can and should take it home and read it, returning with any questions you might have. It's very important that you read and understand what you are signing.

All your personal information is gathered on the new account form, which is then reviewed by the U.S. Department of Homeland Security. The federal government wants to prohibit laundering of funds for terrorists, so your information is run through an Internet search to make sure you don't show up on a government watch list.

Finally, the broker should provide you with the firm's ADV Part II, a statement about the firm, the brokers it employs, the brokers' education and experience, and, most importantly, whether there have ever been any complaints against individual brokers, what the complaints were, how they were settled, and whether a broker has been censured or had his or her license revoked for a period of time. Don't necessarily rule out a broker or brokerage firm because of a minor complaint or proceeding noted. Most firms have run into procedural glitches that end up as notes or complaints on forms. Do, however, be sure to ask for an explanation of the note or complaint.

If you've done your homework and conducted your own research, you would have already learned of any past problems with a particular broker. Consider the information from the brokerage firm a confirmation of what you've already learned.

The Least You Need to Know

- A broker or a brokerage firm acts as a go-between for a buyer and seller.
- Primary categories of brokers are full-service, discount, and online.
- There are many advantages to working with a broker, most notable that you benefit from his or her expertise and knowledge and gain a reliable source of information and advice.
- Be sure you understand all the fees your broker charges.
- Decide what kind of broker you need based on your investing style and goals.
- Check out a broker's credentials, which are available to the public, and ask questions regarding experience and background before signing on.

How to Buy and Sell Stocks Yourself

In This Chapter

- Setting up an online account
- Understanding different types of orders
- Avoiding the middleman
- Using direct stock purchase plans
- Understanding dollar cost averaging

While many investors are more comfortable using either a full-service or discount broker, others prefer to go it alone. This doesn't mean that you would not seek advice if you needed to, but you'd rather decide what you want to trade and place the orders yourself, rather than getting in touch with a broker to complete the process for you. If that description applies to you, that's fine. Millions of people successfully buy and sell stocks on their own with few problems. It's not difficult, and as long as you know where to find help if you need it, you shouldn't experience any difficulty.

While it used to be that buying stock through a broker was the only way you could do so, today there are many online trading companies designed to allow you to trade on your own. You read a little bit about these in the last chapter, so you know that some online companies were created expressly for Internet business, while other previously established firms have added online brokerage services. The big advantage of trading on your own is lower fees than a full-service or even a discount broker. And for those who shop, conduct business, and run their social lives online, investing online on their own seems more intuitive and comfortable than ordering stock through a broker.

In this chapter, you'll learn the basics of buying and selling stock on your own. To do so, you'll need to understand a bit about different types of orders and how to decide which are the best ones to use. You'll learn about buying stock directly from a company, and taking advantage of a direct reinvestment plan, which makes investing easy and builds up your portfolio painlessly.

Establishing an Online Brokerage Account

What did we do before the Internet? There's no question that it has changed everything. Stock market investing used to require visits to a broker or involved phone calls—now you can invest with a few clicks of the mouse or via your smartphone.

Getting started by opening an online brokerage account is not difficult. First of all, just as if you were choosing a full-service broker, do your homework and find an online brokerage firm that you like. As we noted in Chapter 15, you can ask friends and family members about which brokers they use, get ratings and reviews online, and call or check out websites of different companies to get an idea of the services they offer, and what you'll be charged for them.

Remember that although buying and selling stock on your own is less expensive than going through a full-service or even a discount broker, it usually involves some fees. You'll be charged a brokerage fee for your transactions and probably some account fees, so be sure to ask.

Top online brokerage companies, as listed by *Smart Money* magazine, include Fidelity, E*Trade, TD Ameritrade, Charles Schwab, TradeKing, Scottrade, WallStreet-E, Firstrade, Just2Trade, and Muriel Seibert. Once you've located a company you like, you can set up and fund your account. The brokerage company will provide instructions as to how to set up your online account.

 TAKING STOCK

The U.S. Patriot Act requires financial institutions to collect, verify, and record information identifying each person who opens an account, so you'll need to provide your Social Security number, employer name and address, your address, and your date of birth and other information to complete your online application.

You'll choose what type of account you want to open, probably selecting from an individual account, joint account, individual retirement account, or custodial account. To trade securities, you'd want to open an individual or joint account, depending on whether or not someone else will be trading on the account.

Once you've established that, you'll need to indicate if you want a cash account or one that allows you to buy on margin:

- **Cash account.** In a cash account, your stock purchases are limited to the amount of cash you have within the account.

- **Margin account.** You'll read all about margin accounts in Chapter 18, but basically these accounts allow you to borrow money from the brokerage to buy additional stock. The brokerage uses your current portfolio holdings as collateral. You normally have to maintain a minimum balance if you want to be able to buy on margin.

- **Margin account with options.** In a margin account, you may choose to buy and sell options within the account. Options may convey the right to buy a stock, which is a call option. An option that conveys the right to sell stock is called a put. These are used to increase the returns on portfolios, protect gains, and limit losses.

If you decide to open a margin account with options, you'll probably have to sign an agreement and mail or fax it back to the brokerage. Once your application has been approved, you'll need to fund your account. You can do that either by mailing a check to the brokerage or by transferring money electronically into your online account.

Be prepared to answer questions about your personal finances. When you go through the process of opening a new account online, you will be asked questions from a credit report agency in order to verify you are who you say you are. The questions can be tricky, like who owns your mortgage and how much your monthly payment is, so be prepared with your financial records when you open an account online.

An important question included on many applications inquires about your investment objectives. You'll be asked whether your primary goal is growth of capital, preservation of capital, income, and so forth. Make sure to consider carefully what your real objectives are before stating them on the form.

Placing Your First Order

Once you've done your homework and decided on which stock you're going to invest, you're ready to place your first order. Generally, you're able to purchase almost any listed stock online. Just indicate what kind of trade you're transacting (buy or sell) and the number of shares and ticker symbol of the stock.

The ticker symbol, usually called the ticker, is an abbreviation of a company's name, developed by Standard & Poor's (S&P). The ticker is used to uniquely identify publicly traded shares of a specific stock. Some examples include:

- General Electric: GE
- Hewlett Packard: HPQ
- Google: GOOG
- Pepsico: PEP
- AT&T: T
- Wal-Mart: WMT
- McDonald's: MCD
- Oracle: ORCL
- Abbot Laboratories: ABT

You'll be asked what type of order you want, such as a market or stop order (you'll read more about different kinds of orders in the next section). When you indicate your order type, a box will appear with the information you've submitted, giving you a chance to review your order. If all is correct, you place your order, or you're able to change or cancel the order if you decide you don't want to buy or sell that particular stock or you want to buy or sell a different amount. It's not possible to change or cancel every type of order, so be sure you read your broker's policy carefully. If you change or cancel an order, you should receive a notification from your broker. If you place the order, it's normally placed and executed within a very short time period—sometimes less than a minute. There are, however, a couple of things you should keep in mind.

SHARE THIS

While stock symbols generally are pretty straightforward, some companies use them to promote products or services, communicate the company's culture, or reinforce its brands. Motorcycle manufacturer Harley-Davidson changed its ticker symbol from HDI to HOG in 2006, while Southwest Airlines uses the symbol LUV, in reference to the company's culture. The ticker symbol for United Stockyards is MOO.

In some cases, an order will be held while it's reviewed by a financial professional and won't execute immediately. It's possible—and you'll read more about this in the next section—that in the time between when you place the order and when it executes, the price of the stock could change.

SHARE THIS

Brokerage customers who are identified as day traders often are subject to additional requirements with their accounts. If you were to get into day trading, which we certainly do not advise, you most likely would be required to maintain a very high minimum balance. Restrictions may be placed on your account under certain circumstances.

This could also occur if you place an order after the markets close, because in those cases the order won't be placed until the following day. You're responsible for verifying that your orders have been executed and when, and knowing the price that you paid for the stock you ordered. If you want to sell stock, you'll need to be sure that it's listed in your account at the time you place the sell order.

Remember to check out the bid/ask spread (listed online) before you buy or sell stock. This is simply the difference between the highest price that a buyer is willing to pay for a stock and the lowest price at which a seller is willing to part with it. The bid and ask prices are never the same, and the ask price is always higher than the bid price.

If you're buying a stock, you have to pay the ask price. If you're selling, you sell for the bid price. The bid/ask spread, or the difference between the asking and selling prices, goes to the broker who handles the transaction and to pay fees associated with the transaction. Generally, the bid/ask spread isn't a big deal, but you should be aware of it because it can help you compute how much you'll be paying out, or receiving, for a transaction.

Different Types of Brokerage Orders

While it's easy to place an online brokerage order, it's important to realize that not all orders are the same. You have some options as to the type of order you want to place. Although these different orders can seem confusing, understanding what they are and how to use them can help you to keep better track of your investments and maximize your profits.

Most beginning investors use market orders, which are the most common type of brokerage order. While there are advantages to market orders, there also are good reasons to employ other types.

Market Order

A market order is an order to buy or sell a stock at its current market price. It's the most common type of order, and if you don't specify otherwise, a broker would assume it's the type of order an investor would want. Investors like market orders because they're easy, and as long as there are buyers and sellers for a stock, it's pretty much a sure bet that your order will be executed. Market orders often are the least expensive type, although that varies from one investment firm to another.

A problem sometimes encountered with market orders is that although it seeks the best price available at the time of the order, the price you pay when the order is executed might not be the same as when you ordered. You could get a real-time quote from a financial site and order the stock, only to find that the price had changed by the time it was executed. This is especially possible if you're ordering a large number of shares. In that case, it's possible that you'd end up paying more for some of the shares than for others.

As you can imagine, this problem intensifies during times that the market is very volatile and you risk getting caught up in price swings. If stock prices are changing quickly, or if orders from other traders get ahead of your order, the price you thought you were getting might not be the price you actually get. So if you'd planned to buy 100 shares of XYZ stock at $20 a share, but by the time your order was executed the price had risen to $25, you'd be spending $500 more than anticipated for the same number of shares. If the market is volatile and trading very quickly, it's a good idea to consider using a brokerage order other than a market order.

Limit Order

Using a limit order to buy or sell stock can help you avoid getting a different price than you'd anticipated. A limit order is an order to buy or sell a stock at a specified price. When you buy with a limit order, the trade can only be executed at your specified price or lower. When you sell with a limit order, the trade must be at your specified price or higher. No doubt you can see the advantage to this type of trade over a market trade, particularly in volatile markets when prices can change significantly in a very short time period.

A downside to limit orders is that they can cost you more than market orders, and it's possible that you'll place one needlessly. That happens when the price of the stock goes higher than your specified price before your order is ever executed. It's frustrating if that happens, but you can think of it as having purchased a form of insurance that prevents you from paying much more for stock than you'd planned.

Another disadvantage to a limit order is that the trade may never execute. You could put in a sell order for IBM at $145, or a buy at $137, and the stock never hits that price so the order is never executed. Limit orders are usually held on the books of the brokerage firm for up to 90 days.

Also, you may only get a partial order filled with a limit order. It could happen that you wanted to buy or sell 500 shares, but your order only fills for 300 shares.

Day Order

Day orders are those that are good to be executed during the current trading day, but don't carry over to after hours or the next day. If your order is not executed during the day of the order, it's cancelled and you'll have to place a new order. Day orders generally apply to limit or stop orders for which prices were not met during the day.

SHARE THIS

Most trading in the United States occurs between 9:30 A.M. and 4 P.M. Eastern Time, because those are the regular hours of the major exchanges. Other trading, called after-hours trading, takes place outside of those times, and there are some significant differences. After-hours trading is considered to be riskier than that conducted during normal hours because of greater volatility and less liquidity in the market.

A variation on a day order is a day around order, which is something like an all-day bus pass. Let's say that you place a limit order, ordering a particular stock with a price limit of $30 a share. After placing the order, however, you realize that you need additional funds for another purchase, meaning you'll have to either buy fewer shares or set a lower limit. Instead of canceling the order and placing another day order specifying a lower price, a day around order allows you to simply submit another order with a new price.

Good-Til-Cancelled Order

A good-til-cancelled (GTC) order is a limit or stop order with an unspecified time frame. In other words, the order stands until it's either been executed or you cancel it. If you want to sell a stock that you bought for $25 a share for $50 a share, you'd place a GTC order specifying that amount. Your order won't be executed until the selling price reaches $50 a share, regardless of how long that takes. The same principle applies if you want to buy a stock at a particular price.

Investors often use a GTC order when they're shooting for the stars and want to set a limit price that's either way higher or lower than current market prices. Because of this, most brokerages impose limits, usually 30 to 90 days, on the time a GTC order is permitted to stand. And GTC orders may cost more than other types.

Fill or Kill Order

A fill or kill order is pretty much the opposite of a GTC order, in that it must be filled within a specified time period (usually immediately) or the order is cancelled. Fill or kill orders are not common, and generally are used when buying or selling large quantities of stock or shares of a smaller company. A fill or kill order is considered to be a type of day order, but the trade must occur within a much shorter time period.

All or None Order

The name is self-explanatory. With this type of order, you set the price and specify the number of shares you want to sell. The trade is either made at that price or not at all. For example, you have decided to buy or sell 1,000 shares of a local bank stock. You know the recent price has been at $25 per share; however, if you place a market order, 100 shares can be placed at $25, another 200 at $25.50, and so forth. By placing an all or none order, the seller will need to sell all the shares specified at $25, or not sell them at all. All or none orders are cancelled at the close of the market that day.

Stop Order

A stop order allows an investor to buy or sell a stock once it reaches a specified price. That price is known as the stop price. When the order reaches the price you specify, it changes from a stop order to a market order.

Buy stop orders typically are used by investors to limit losses or protect profits on short sales. You'll read more about shorting in Chapter 18. Basically, it's selling a stock that you don't own, but have borrowed from your broker. Sell stop orders, with which the amount specified is always below the current market price, usually are used to help investors limit losses or protect profits in the event that the price of a stock continues to fall.

Investors like stop orders because they free them from constantly monitoring how a stock is performing. If you place a stop order, you are planning that your specified price will be met. Because a stop order becomes a market order once your price has been met, however, you could actually receive or pay a different price than you specified for stock sold or purchased, due to fluctuating markets. Fortunately, that problem can be controlled with a stop-limit order.

CRASH!

Brokerage firms report that anxious investors often make mistakes when buying or selling stock online. One common mistake reported is placing the same order twice. This occurs when an investor tries to confirm a trade by checking his account before the trade has been registered, panics when he doesn't see evidence of the trade, and hits the order button again. There is often some lag time between the order and the confirmation, brokers say, so don't panic and trade twice by mistake. If that does happen, call rather than e-mail the brokerage firm right away.

Stop-Limit Order

A stop-limit order, as the name implies, is a combination of a stop order and a limit order. You specify the stop price and, once that price is reached, the stop-limit order becomes a limit order. That means the stock you're buying must be executed at your set price or lower, and stock you're selling must be sold at your specified price or higher.

A stop-limit order allows an investor to control the price at which the stock will be traded. Just as with limit orders, however, you run the risk that the stock price will increase to where it's higher than your specified price before your order is ever executed, thereby wasting the order. Stop-limit orders that aren't executed occur much more frequently in a volatile market. A stock can open in the morning lower or higher than the stop-limit, so the trade is never executed. If the order isn't executed, you'll need to evaluate if you want to then chase the current price and make a market order.

Deciding Which Orders to Use

Hopefully, the explanations provided for different types of brokerage orders will help you to decide which make sense for you to use in particular circumstances.

As you read, some types of orders are based on time. Day orders and GTC orders allow you to buy or sell stock within a specified period of time. That makes sense if you want to limit the period of time during which you'll buy or sell a stock, as with a day order, so that you keep control over it. And as mentioned earlier, a GTC order eliminates the need for frequent monitoring because your order will remain.

Market orders, limit orders, stop orders, and stop-limit orders allow you to call the shots and buy or sell stock once certain criteria have been met. These orders allow you to set conditions under which you'll trade your stock. Once you've been trading stock for a while, you'll have a better understanding of how these orders work and when to use them. Begin with market orders when you first begin to trade, and then branch out by using other types of orders, as they make sense for you.

The most common nonmarket orders are stop-limit orders, which provide a means of controlling the price at which you buy or sell stock when you're unable to monitor the transaction.

Auto Investing

Some investors have embraced the concept of auto investing, which is when you open an online account at an investment firm, select stock that you wish to purchase, and sit back while your money is automatically invested at regular time periods specified by you.

Automatic investment plans are marketed toward people who don't have large sums of money to invest at one time, and who don't want to spend large amounts of time researching stock and monitoring their portfolios. The plans generally are intended for long-term investing, and sometimes targeted toward young investors with the adage that little bits of money invested over a long period of time will add up to large sums of money.

ShareBuilder, an online stock brokerage firm, offers a popular automatic investment plan in which investors can choose from more than 7,000 stocks and exchange traded funds (ETFs) and schedule automatic investments into their accounts. There are different plans investors can choose from, and prices per investment are as little as $1. The low costs, which include no account minimums, maintenance fees, or inactivity fees, appeal to some investors looking for a more relaxed way to invest in the stock market.

Buying Directly from a Company

Hundreds of U.S. companies allow investors to buy their stock directly from the company without the benefit of any sort of broker. These are called direct stock purchase plans (DSPPs), and they've become increasingly popular in recent years. DSPPs used to be offered primarily by public utility companies, but a new ruling by the Securities and Exchange Commission enacted during the 1990s allowed more companies to get in the game of selling their stock directly to the public.

Both companies and investors responded favorably to the change, and more companies started selling stock on their own. Currently, we're seeing increasing numbers of small and startup companies undertaking direct public offerings (DPOs). Analysts attribute that to the power of the Internet, which allows these companies to get the word out regarding the DPO.

Direct Stock Purchase Plans

Stock purchased directly from a company often is referred to as no-load stock. Like their mutual fund cousins, this means that there is no sales load—or fee—when purchasing the stock. Investors who go to the trouble of doing their own research regarding which stock to buy often like the fact that they don't have to pay a fee to purchase the stock. If a fee is charged, it's usually very low compared to brokerage fees.

Some companies offer DSPPs for employees. In addition to getting in on the opportunity to profit in the stock market, these types of programs can offer tax advantages for employees. If you're employed by a company that offers direct stock purchase for employees, be sure to look into what the program entails.

Some investors like DSPPs simply because they like investing on their own, even if the only broker they would have otherwise is an online one. If you're interested in participating in a DSPP for any reason, it might turn out to be a good move.

How They Work

To open a DSPP account, you should call the company's shareholders' services department or direct purchase plan center. A company's website will inform you as to whether it offers a DSPP.

Once you get through to a company that has a DSPP, you'll most likely get a message telling you how to order a company prospectus, which will be mailed to you. Once you've received and reviewed the prospectus, you can decide whether or not to order the company's stock.

All DSPPs set minimum and maximum investment amounts, so check to make sure you have enough money to get started. The company will determine how often you're permitted to invest. You probably are permitted to buy outside of the regularly scheduled times, but the frequency with which you can do so varies.

There are companies such as One Share of Stock, Inc. or Share In A Frame that allow you to buy one share (yes, it comes in a frame) of a stock of a well-known company like Disney or Harley Davidson. These not only make fun gifts, but they're also valuable, because owning even one share entitles a shareholder to enroll in the company's dividend reinvestment plan (DRIP). DRIPs are great tools for building your portfolio because you get the benefit of compound interest. You'll read more about DRIPs shortly.

What to Watch Out For

Even though you'll pay no fees or very low fees with a DSPP, there are fees involved. Some companies charge a low monthly investment fee, while others charge an annual account maintenance fee. You will also probably be charged to sell your stock.

Some financial advisors discourage repeatedly buying stock of the same company, saying it increases your level of risk through a lack of diversification.

Another negative about DSPPs is the necessity of keeping track of cost basis. Every time shares are purchased monthly, quarterly, or annually, you are adding to the basis of your holding. If you buy for 5, 10, or 20 years, the homework can be cumbersome to calculate the actual cost of the stock. To alleviate this burden, each year you will receive a statement of what was invested that year. Recalculate the cost each year when you are calculating your total return on the stock.

The Power of Compounding

DRIPs, as we mentioned, are terrific tools for painlessly building your investment portfolio. With a DRIP, stock dividends are automatically reinvested and used to buy more stock. This of course has the potential to result in bigger dividends, which in turn can purchase even more stock, and so forth and so on.

Let's say the XYZ Company offers an annual dividend of 50¢ per share, and you own 100 shares of stock. If you participate in the company's DRIP, your $50 dividend payment will automatically be used to purchase 5 more shares of stock that are selling for $10 a share. Some DRIPs offer discounted share prices for plan participants.

This increase in the value of your portfolio by adding shares of stock to it is wonderful to watch, but please know that even though you didn't receive a dividend check, the dividends amount is figured in for your taxes. These dividends increase the basis to your shares. Systematic investing in good companies has historically proven to be a sound and profitable method of increasing wealth.

Dividend reinvestment is easy; however, keep in mind that you are not controlling the price you pay for the stock, so as the share price increases, you end up paying more. If the shares decrease in price, you continue to buy a stock you will end up selling. If you are investing your dividends, watch what you are paying for your shares.

You may auto invest in mutual funds, but rarely will a brokerage firm permit you to purchase shares of a stock each month without already owning the shares.

Dollar Cost Averaging

Dollar cost averaging is a long-term investment strategy that some investors enthusiastically subscribe to. With dollar cost averaging, you would invest the same amount of money in a stock at regular intervals. Investments usually are made every month, every three months, or every six months, but the frequency can vary.

> **DEFINITION**
>
> **Dollar cost averaging** is an investment of an equal amount of money at regular intervals, usually each month, resulting in the purchase of extra shares during market downturns, and fewer shares during upturns. The practice is based on the belief that a stock or the market will rise in price over the long term.

If you're going to use a dollar cost averaging strategy, it's widely recommended that you're prepared to continue in that strategy for between 7 and 10 years—an eternity to some investors. The theory is that over time the average cost per share of your investment becomes increasingly smaller. Remember that you're putting the same amount of money into your account at each investment. That means that when the price of the stock you're buying goes down, your investment buys more shares. When the price goes up, your investment dollars buy fewer shares. Over the long term, however, it will turn out that the cost of each share is lower than the average rate per share during the investment period.

This form of investing is desirable to many people because it removes emotion from investing. And it's a great way to invest small sums in a variety of companies. You can buy four or five good companies, set up dividend reinvestment, and the shares keep growing without any further cash infusion from you. Auto investing requires additional cash, but you are buying a set investment each period.

The Least You Need to Know

- Setting up your online brokerage account is easy, but be prepared to provide a lot of personal information.
- Understanding the difference in brokerage orders will help you keep control of your investments and maximize returns.

- Buying stock directly from a company can save commission fees and offers a level of autonomy.

- Direct reinvestment plans are an excellent means of boosting your portfolio.

- Dollar cost averaging assures steady investment over time.

Buying Outside of the Box

In This Chapter

- Understanding initial public offerings (IPOs)
- Common and preferred stock
- How stock splits work
- Getting a handle on company buybacks of stock

You've read about some of the different types of stock available, and that investors must consider their own investing goals and circumstances when deciding which type of stock to buy. Not all investors are the same, and not all stock is the same; that much is certain.

When you buy stock, and under what circumstances, is as important as your decision to buy value stock, or growth stock, or income stock. In this chapter, we'll look at some special circumstances in which stock is traded, and why you might or might not want to get in on some of the action.

You read a little bit about initial public offerings (IPOs) back in Chapter 1, but in this chapter, we'll take a closer look at why some investors like them and others run from them.

Getting in on an IPO

An IPO is the occasion on which a company first offers its stock for sale. A series of actions must happen before an IPO can occur, and it's usually a pretty big deal for the company. When a company sells its stock publicly, whether it's just starting up or has been around as a privately held company, it becomes a publicly traded company.

Basically, there are two types of IPOs: startups and private companies that decide to go public. Some investors look for IPOs, and are anxious to jump in and take a chance on making some serious gains.

Startup IPOs, as the name implies, are those issued by companies that are just starting up. An entrepreneur or group of entrepreneurs effectively sells a business idea to an investment banker who agrees to fund the business by selling the startup's stock to investors.

The second type of IPO occurs when an existing, privately held company decides to go public and sell stock, usually in an attempt to generate capital. Capital raised from an IPO can be used to expand the company, invest in more equipment, hire more employees, or anything the company wishes to do.

How IPOs Work

A company that decides to go public must follow a process for doing so. It's not as easy as simply issuing a press release or putting a notice on Facebook. The first step is for the company to hire investment bankers who serve as underwriters. Basically, underwriters agree to buy all the stock the company will offer at its IPO at an agreed-upon price. They also agree that they will research the company, promote it to potential buyers, and finally issue and sell the stock.

While the underwriters are busy doing what they do, the company must register with the Securities and Exchange Commission under the Securities Act of 1933. This is done by filing a Form S-1, which contains basic business and financial information that pertains to the IPO. Investors use the S-1 to research a company before agreeing to buy its stock.

Once the underwriters have finished researching the company preparing to go public, they begin what's become known as a "road show," which is when they meet with analysts and institutional investors to try to sell the company. The analysts review all the information the underwriters have compiled, and take it to the investors to see if they will agree to buy the stock. These large investors have plenty of money and can buy a lot more stock than individuals. Usually, most of the money raised through an IPO comes from these large investors, who buy through an auction process.

Institutional investors who like what they hear and want to buy the stock subscribed in the offering are in effect agreeing on a nonbinding basis to buy the stock at a price determined hours before the offering is made public. The investors can say how much stock they want to buy, but they won't know exactly how much it will cost because a price isn't set until just before the IPO. A big demand for the stock will mean the price is higher than it would be if there was little demand.

CRASH!

Beware of IPOs for companies that are just starting up—often they offer nothing more than a roll of the dice with your money at stake. Although some startups can find investment bankers who will help them sell stock to investors, they are unproven. Those who elect to buy the stock are taking a big gamble.

Finally, a date is set for the IPO, a starting price for the stocks to be sold is determined, and the shares are released. All the shares are offered for sale at once, at the price determined. Individuals wishing to get in on an IPO normally do so by contacting their brokers, who will contact the underwriters; but under most circumstances, it's a better idea to wait for a period after an IPO to buy a company's stock.

Once the shares go public, they begin to trade on a stock exchange, known as the secondary market. It's usually quite difficult for the average investor to obtain IPOs at the initial price. They normally need to wait until the shares are offered on the secondary market, where the price usually is higher than the initial share price.

After the IPO

Issuing shares of its stock through an IPO is a proven way for companies to generate capital. Once a company has done that, its stock is traded on stock exchanges such as the New York Stock Exchange or NASDAQ.

Once a company's stock is being traded on a stock exchange, it's important to realize that the company no longer generates revenue through the sale of its stock. Transactions that occur within a stock exchange are private transactions between a buyer and seller, with no benefit to the company whose stock is being traded.

SHARE THIS

A company that goes public is not obligated to remain a publicly traded company. Aramark, a Philadelphia-based foodservice company operating in 20 countries with 250,000 employees, originally went public in 1960. In 1984, in order to avoid a hostile takeover, the company returned to being privately held through a management buyout. In 2001, it returned to the New York Stock Exchange. In January 2007, Aramark announced that an investor group led by its CEO, Joseph Neubauer, had acquired the company and its shareholders would be paid in cash for their stock, meaning that the company once again is privately held.

In order to generate more capital by selling its stock, the company has to offer additional stock for sale, and it can do so through a secondary stock offering. The ability of companies to sell shares of stock to create capital is not limited to IPOs, as companies can offer more stock to the public as they grow. This is done by either creating additional shares of stock, or offering stock that's been held previously by directors of the company or in the company's treasury. While some investors seek out IPOs, beginning investors should stay away from them, as they are risky business.

Why IPOs Are Risky Investments

If there's a lot of excitement regarding an IPO, the stock price often starts out high, and then levels off. Some investors buy IPOs and then quickly flip the stock, making big money as they do. Individual investors, however, without the expertise and experience of knowing exactly when to buy and sell, shouldn't take risks with IPOs.

Notably disappointing IPOs in 2008 included Verso Paper, a company that produces coated paper used in magazines; GT Solar, a company that provides solar equipment to manufacturers; and China Mass Media, a Chinese television advertising company that trades on the New York Stock Exchange. Verso's stock sold at $12 per share at the IPO, but fell 91 percent in the months that followed. GT's stock started out at $16.50 per share, then diminished in value by 83 percent. China Mass Media started at $6.80 per share, then plummeted 79 percent. That's not to say these will never be good stocks to own, but buying at the IPO was definitely not the way to go.

Some companies that file to go public aren't even profitable; they're operating at a loss with no sound record of profitability. More than half of all IPOs actually decline in value in the year after they're issued. Sure, IPOs are exciting for the chance that they could really take off, but most of the time it just isn't happening. Most investors will do better to keep an eye on the stock for a while and invest once the dust settles. If the company is viable and headed toward success, its stock will hold its value and be a smart buy down the road.

Common Stock

The two basic categories of stock are common stock and preferred stock, but there are variations among those two classes. You learned in Chapter 1 that common stock, the most frequently traded type of security, is popular for a variety of reasons. It's easy to buy and sell, and it entails certain rights, namely the right to receive dividends or payments made to stockholders, and to have a say in company decisions. You also read, however, that common stock is not a guarantee of dividends.

Not all companies pay dividends, even if they are profitable. A company's board of directors must declare dividends before they can be paid out, and for a variety of reasons, sometimes the board does and sometimes it doesn't.

Experienced investors know which companies are most likely to pay dividends regularly, and if they are investing for income, will buy the stock of those companies. Older, well-established companies such as General Electric, Procter & Gamble, and Exxon Mobil are examples of companies that regularly pay dividends to stockholders. Until lately, many firms have historically increased their dividends annually. However, the long and painful recession that started in late 2007 or early 2008, depending on who you ask, caused some companies to decrease or suspend dividends in 2009 and 2010.

Common Stock and Voting Rights

In addition to being eligible for dividends, holders of common stock have voting rights, which means they have a say in matters such as whether or not the company should issue new stock, merge with another company, or reorganize. These shareholders also get to help elect the company's board of directors, which is important because the board wields a lot of power, including whether or not to declare dividends. Most of these kinds of decisions are made during a company's annual meeting.

As you can imagine, most stockholders can't spend their time (or money) traveling around to vote at annual meetings. So instead, most shareholders vote by *proxy*. If you own common stock, you will receive voting materials either from the company that issued the stock, or the brokerage firm that holds the stock for you. The materials outline issues to be voted on, and provide information about nominees for the board of directors and other positions. This gives shareholders, if they choose to participate, some power in deciding how the company should operate and who should run it.

DEFINITION

Proxy is a document that allows shareholders to participate in voting without being present at an annual meeting.

Classes of Common Stock

All companies that offer common stock to investors must issue at least one class or category of stock. And while most firms do issue only one class, some companies have more than one class of stock. That can affect voting rights, dividend rates, the manner in which dividends are issued, and other factors. The primary reason a company issues more than one class of stock is that it wants to sell one class to the public (you and me), and keep another class for selected buyers, such as founders or board members.

Chapter 7 explained the characteristics of some categories of common stock, including growth stock, value stock, income stock, and penny stock. Another type of common stock is called blue chip stock, which is stock issued by the largest and most stable companies. These companies have stood the test of time, remaining profitable through bull and bear markets, and they usually pay out dividends on a regular basis.

These different categories of common stock all indicate the stage of growth of the company that issued it. In Chapter 19, you'll learn about different types of common stock that indicate reaction to a current economy. These are cyclical stock, counter-cyclical stock, defensive stock, and interest-sensitive stock.

An example of a company that offers two different classes of common stock is Berkshire Hathaway, a huge holding company based in Omaha, Nebraska, that controls a variety of businesses in many fields, including insurance, building products, apparel, and utilities. Berkshire Hathaway, of which legendary investor Warren Buffet is chairman and CEO, offers a class A stock that can sell for more than $100,000 a share. Its class B stock is still expensive, but you can buy about 30 shares of it for the price of one share of class A.

Preferred Stock

Common stock is the most widely traded type of security, but it's not the only type. Another type of stock, preferred stock, has some different characteristics than common stock, and carries some advantages to owning.

The biggest advantage of preferred stock is that preferred shareholders are required to get their dividends before common shareholders, and usually the dividends are set for the life of the stock, unless otherwise specified. If a company encounters difficult times, it tends to cut dividends paid on the common shares before the preferred shares. And at the time of issue, the dividends on preferred stock are significantly higher than on the company's common shares.

Another advantage is that if the company goes bankrupt, the claims of preferred shareholders on company assets are dealt with before the claims of those with common stock. Preferred stock, a hybrid between bonds and stocks, is often referred to as owning a bond without a maturity date. This hybrid is generally considered to be safer than common stock because it provides fixed dividends and takes precedence over common stock in the event of bankruptcy. The shares are issued at $25 per share and, when the shares mature, the owner receives $25 per share.

What's Not So Great About Preferred Stock

Preferred stock does carry some advantages, but that's not to say it is in every way better than its common counterpart. Not only do preferred shareholders usually have no voting rights, meaning they don't get the satisfaction of having a say in what goes on within the company, there's the matter of appreciation—or lack of appreciation in this case—that's distasteful to many shareholders. Preferred stock is considered a bond without a maturity date. Shares of preferred stock can be issued for as long as 40 years.

Let's say that the Green Bike Corporation comes up with a new and improved pedal-powered engine, which runs off a generator that the rider powers by pedaling. The motor, which requires no fuel and never needs to be recharged, is a huge hit and people start buying them like crazy. As a result, the stock of the Green Bike Corporation soars.

Investors who own the company's common stock are sitting pretty, but those who have preferred stock won't be nearly as happy. That's because preferred stock is less volatile than common (a trait that some people like), and not affected as much by outside influences. The value of the stock is determined by the company issuing it, and tends to remain fairly constant. That's sometimes advantageous, but in a situation like the one described previously, it's not good news for shareholders with preferred stock.

Different Kinds of Preferred Stock

Preferred stock can be broken down into many different types, with the following being the most common:

- **Callable.** With callable preferred stock, the company that issued it has the right to recall outstanding stock at its discretion, as long as the date and time are specified in the *prospectus*. Companies usually utilize this right when interest rates in the general market are much lower than the dividend rate it is paying on a preferred issue.

- **Cumulative.** Most preferred stock is cumulative. This means that if a company fails to distribute some or all of expected dividends, those dividends are considered to be in arrears and must be paid before any dividends are distributed to common shareholders. Preferred stock that is not cumulative is called noncumulative.

- **Convertible.** If you own convertible preferred stock, you have the ability to convert it to common stock if you choose to do so. The timing and conditions of the conversion are specified in the prospectus, and the company sets a *conversion ratio*. A conversion ratio of 2:1, for instance, means you could convert one share of preferred stock into two shares of common.

- **Participating.** Participating preferred stock is unusual, but it's out there. It has a fixed dividend rate and it pays shareholders part of the earnings that are distributed to investors who hold common stock.

- **Adjustable-rate.** Adjustable-rate preferred stock (ARPS) is a relatively new addition to the shopping basket. ARPS pays dividends based on factors determined by the company that issued the stock. The factors normally are tied into changes in interest rates.

DEFINITION

A **prospectus** is a legal document that contains details about stock that's being offered for sale. The Securities and Exchange Commission requires that a prospectus be prepared and filed in order to provide prospective investors with necessary information. A **conversion ratio** states the number of shares of common stock to be exchanged for one share of preferred stock when preferred stock is converted.

Companies choose to issue preferred stock because it gives them flexibility as to when they can call in the shares and the debt is not considered a bond on the firm's balance sheet. If the company is experiencing cash flow or other financial problems, it can suspend distribution of dividends. And most preferred stock is obtained by institutions, not individual investors, making it easier for a company to market at an IPO. Institutions like preferred stock because of certain tax advantages it provides.

Stock Splits

A *stock split* is a technique a company can use to affect the value of its stock. The company divides its existing shares of stock into multiple shares, increasing the number of shares outstanding. A stock split, however, doesn't increase the total dollar value of the shares. So if you own 100 shares of ABC stock with a value of $1,000 and the company decides on a 2-for-1 stock split, you would now own 200 shares of ABC stock with a value of $1,000. Companies often decide to perform stock splits when the price of a share of stock has increased to the point where the stock is perceived as being too expensive to purchase in round lots, which is 100 shares or a multiple thereof.

> **DEFINITION**
>
> A **stock split** is an action taken by a company that increases the number of its outstanding shares of stock, usually to lower the price of one share. Stockholders end up with more stock, but the total dollar value stays the same.

An easy way to understand a stock split is to think about having a $100 bill. If somebody comes along and gives you five $20 bills in exchange for your $100 bill, you have the same amount of money, you just have five bills instead of one. The same idea applies to a stock split.

What's the Big Deal?

Let's get this straight. The number of stock outstanding changes, but the value of the stock doesn't. So what's the point of a stock split? Well, in addition to altering the price of a share of stock, companies carry out stock splits for a couple of reasons.

Did you ever wonder why an item is priced at $44.98 instead of $45? It's because consumers perceive that $44 and change is a better deal than $45, even if the difference is only a couple of cents. Corporate types understand that when the price of a share of their stock gets high, some investors will think it's too expensive for them to buy and they'll look elsewhere. If the price per share is lowered, it creates the perception that the stock is a bargain, and may attract more buyers. It's all a matter of perception. Existing shareholders also perceive value as they suddenly own more stock. If the value of the stock increases, they have more shares to trade.

Splitting stock also increases its liquidity, which is the degree to which it can be traded without affecting its price. Stock and other assets that can be easily bought and sold are referred to as liquid assets, and they're usually assets that are frequently traded. Stock with greater liquidity is generally considered more desirable than those with less, because it's easier for a shareholder to get his money out of the investment.

SHARE THIS

The most common stock splits are two for one, three for two, and three for one, but splits aren't limited to those formulas. In October 2010, Facebook notified shareholders that it would execute a five for one stock split, meaning that the company would then be authorized to issue 8,851,001,400 shares of Class A common stock, Class B common stock, and preferred stock.

If a company in which you're invested is going to carry out a stock split, you'll receive a notice informing you of the action. If you own stock in certificate form, you'll receive a certificate for however many more shares you now own. Generally, you don't have to do anything, since it doesn't affect the value of your stock. Be aware, however, that stock splits often occur before the price of the stock goes up. This happens because the split generates interest, attracting more people to the stock and increasing demand. Stock splits, for that reason, sometimes are advantageous to shareholders.

Different Kinds of Splits

The type of stock split described previously is called an ordinary stock split. When you hear or read about a stock split, it's usually in reference to an ordinary split. There also, however, is an action called a *reverse stock split*, which is when a company negatively splits its stock to reduce the number of shares outstanding. A reverse stock split occurs less often than a positive split. It's usually done when the price of a share of stock has fallen significantly and the company is facing the possibility of being removed, or delisted, from the stock exchange on which it trades.

DEFINITION

A **reverse stock split** is when a company reduces the number of total shares of stock in order to boost the price of each share.

Reverse splits are also done to limit the number of shareholders. The firm reverse splits 1 share for 5 shares and then the firm buys back all shares of shareholders who own less than a set number of shares, often 100 shares. For example, if a shareholder owns 400 shares of Prudential and the company does a 5 for 1 reverse split, the shareholder then owns 80 shares and must sell his or her shares back to the firm.

Just as an ordinary stock split can positively affect the perception of a stock and boost its value by increasing demand for it, a reverse stock split can negatively affect perception and send investors running from a stock. While a reverse split doesn't change the total dollar value of the stock, just as an ordinary split doesn't, it carries negative implications that can end up affecting the stock's value.

The theory is that reverse stock splits occur because something negative has occurred or is about to occur, such as a stock is in danger of being delisted or removed from an exchange. This can occur if the price of the stock gets too low. So while a reverse split doesn't technically have a negative effect on a stock, it may have negative connotations.

Company Buybacks

In certain instances, a company will buy back shares of its own stock, thereby reducing the number of shares outstanding. These buybacks also are called share repurchases.

To buy back its own stock, a company might present shareholders with a tender offer, which is simply a notice that the company is willing to buy back some or all of their stock. The offer would include a price range that the company is willing to pay for the stock. Shareholders reply to a tender offer by stating the number of shares they wish to tender, and the price at which they're willing to sell.

Once the company has a handle on how many investors are interested in selling back shares, and how many shares it will be able to repurchase, it negotiates with investors to get the most shares possible at the lowest price possible.

Alternately, a company might buy back its stock from the open market at the going price, just like any other investor would. Companies that repurchase their stock usually spin the action in a positive manner, using the buyback to signify confidence and profitability. Stock prices often increase when a company announces a buyback because it's generally perceived as a positive action.

Why Companies Buy Back Stock

When a company buys back its stock, it reduces the number of shares in the marketplace. Because there are fewer shares outstanding, the value of remaining shares increases. Again, it's a matter of supply and demand. When supply is limited, demand increases, along with value.

Companies often buy back their stock when they feel that it's priced too low. That's a positive thing for shareholders because it signifies the company's belief in its ability to be successful, and its wish to increase the value of its stock for its shareholders.

Repurchasing its stock can also positively affect a company's balance sheet by improving its financial ratios. When a company spends a lot of money repurchasing its stock, it reduces its assets on its balance sheet, resulting in increased return on equity and return on assets. A buyback also can improve the company's price-to-earnings (P/E) ratio. All of these are viewed as positive attributes, and ones that investors look for when choosing stock. Reducing the amount of cash on hand makes companies less attractive targets for hostile takeover attempts by other companies and minimizes the effects of low interest rates.

SHARE THIS

When companies buy back stock, some of them do it in a big way. In 2010, Wal-Mart announced a $15 billion stock buyback, IBM authorized two repurchases of stock totaling $18 billion, and Hewlett-Packard Co. announced a $10 billion buyback. Not exactly small potatoes!

A company might decide to buy back stock if it's got a large employee stock option program. When a stock option program gets too large or is not managed properly, it can dilute the stock and the shareholders' equity. By repurchasing the stock, management can reduce the dilution and cause the value of stock to shareholders to increase.

Companies sometimes come under fire for repurchasing stock. Critics say that some companies repurchase stock to avoid paying dividends, to cover up weak financials, or to boost a stock price which may have fallen for good reason. If a company in which you own stock offers to repurchase it, be sure you do some digging to try to determine the reason behind it.

What It Might Mean for You

Some investors love stock buybacks, while others are skeptical regarding them. A good thing for investors is that when a company buys back a batch of its own stock, you get a bigger piece of the pie. That's because, as you read earlier, it reduces the number of outstanding shares and increases the earnings per share. This sometimes makes investors aware that the stock has the potential to increase in value, creating more demand. As a result, the price of the stock might go up, to your benefit.

A company buyback of its stock signals that the company had the necessary cash to do so, meaning it must be doing something right. You, as a shareholder, can be glad for that reassurance. Also, there can be tax advantages to having a company buy its stock from you rather than increasing dividends. Shareholders often can defer capital gains and lower their tax bills if the price of the stock increases.

CRASH!

An announcement of a stock buyback precedes the action, but don't assume that every announcement will result in a buyback. Companies sometimes announce a buyback, which results in interest in the stock and a short-lived price increase, but don't follow through to actually repurchase the stock. Some investors have gotten into trouble anticipating funds from a buyback that never happened and spending money they didn't ever get.

Company buybacks of stock are not always great news for investors, however. If a company repurchases in order to manipulate its financial ratios, achieve an artificial increase in the price of the stock, or boost the appearance of its financial health in an effort to appear to be more robust and successful than it is, there could be big trouble ahead for shareholders. Again, it's good to look at buybacks carefully and analyze why they might be occurring.

The Least You Need to Know

- An IPO can be profitable for seasoned investors, but comes with significant risk.
- Common stock is the most frequently traded type of security and is popular for a variety of reasons, including dividends and voting rights.
- There are advantages associated with preferred stock, but it also can have some drawbacks.
- Stock splits often occur when stock is perceived as having become overpriced.
- Company buybacks of their stock can signal earnings for investors, but be sure to question the motives behind repurchases.

Trading Strategies

In This Chapter

- Buying on margin to maximize investment opportunity
- Selling short to capitalize on a loss
- Timing the market to stay ahead
- Employing strategies to limit your losses

Many investors take a long-term approach to the stock market, buying stock in companies they believe will succeed and grow, and holding on to that stock for long periods of time. This "buy and hold" is a classic approach, both because of its historic rate of success, and the fact that it doesn't require constant attention on the part of the investor. Because you're not going to sell the stock the minute it dips below a certain price, you really don't have to worry too much about it. It's good, of course, to be aware of what your stock is doing, but you won't need to spend hours a day fretting about what your next move should be.

Other investors, however, delight in playing with their stock. They sell it in order to buy it back, buy it back at a lower price, and employ other tricks and techniques with hopes of generating bigger gains than they could by buying and holding the stock. In this chapter, we'll have a look at some of those tricks, and learn about their advantages and potential disadvantages.

Learning the Tricks of the Trade

This is a book written for beginning stock investors, and its content is kept intentionally simple in order to be understandable. You can buy entire books on each of the trading techniques discussed in this chapter, some of which are included in

Appendix B. Our intent is to introduce you to concepts such as buying on margin and shorting a sale so that you understand the terms and how they relate to the stock market. If you think you want to employ any of the techniques discussed, you'll need to acquire more information before doing so.

Having said that, learning your way around the stock market is fun, and pulling off a well-executed trade is an accomplishment you can be proud of. Investors do this all the time by using some techniques that allow them to maximize their money in order to acquire more stock, or to acquire stock at a more advantageous price.

Buying on Margin

Buying on margin is a strategy that enables certain investors to buy stock with borrowed money in order to increase the amount invested. It's an especially useful technique for conservative investors who, while generally risk adverse, are willing to put a portion of their money into aggressive growth investments. An investor leverages his or her current portfolio for potential greater returns.

> **DEFINITION**
>
> **Buying on margin** is the practice of borrowing money from a broker and using it to buy additional stock.

The point of buying on margin is that it allows you to buy more stock than you otherwise could. To buy on margin, you need to have a margin account established with your brokerage. When you set up an initial account with a broker, it would most likely be a cash account. Cash accounts are the most common type of brokerage account. With a cash account, when you buy stock you deposit the cost of the stock into the account. This has to be done within two days of purchase.

A margin account, on the other hand, requires that you make an initial investment of at least $2,000—and some brokerages set a higher initial investment. This investment is known as the minimum margin. After you trade, you'll also need to keep a specified amount of money in your account. That's called a maintenance margin, and the amount varies from broker to broker.

You'll need to fill out an application to set up a margin account, which may require a credit check and reviews of your investment objectives and personal circumstances. Not everyone who thinks they'd like to buy on margin is approved for an account.

Once you've applied and the margin account is approved and set up, you're permitted to borrow up to 50 percent of the cost of the stock you purchase. If you want to buy $4,000 worth of stock, you only need to come up with $2,000, and your brokerage will float you a loan to cover the other $2,000. This enables you to get twice as much stock, and doubles your returns.

It's important to understand that when using a margin account, you don't have to borrow 50 percent of the cost of the stock. You can borrow just 10 or 20 or 30 percent if you want. Some brokerages have rules stipulating that you need to borrow at least a certain percentage, however, so if you decide to set up this type of account, be sure that you understand all of the terms and requirements.

As long as you hold up your end of the deal, you can keep the money you've borrowed for as long as you wish. When you sell stock held in a margin account, the proceeds lower the margin balance until your loan is paid off. You also need to maintain a minimum account balance. You can then purchase new stock, as long as you haven't exceeded the margin limit.

Now that you know what a margin account is, let's look at how investors use them to increase their returns and capitalize on the stock market.

How It Can Make You Money

The beauty of buying stock on margin is that you can get twice as much stock as you could with a cash account, and the possibility of greater returns. Let's look at an example.

Gretchen and her friend Leah decide they want to buy the same stock. The stock is for sale for $20 per share, and they each buy 100 shares. Gretchen, using a cash account, hands over $2,000 for her 100 shares of stock. Leah buys on margin, borrowing $1,000 from her broker and coming up with the other $1,000 on her own.

Gretchen and Leah are thrilled when their stock appreciates in value to $25 a share, and they decide to sell and each collect her $500 profit. So what was the advantage of buying on margin if both Gretchen and Leah realized a $500 gain?

Gretchen realized a $500 profit on a $2,000 investment. That's a 25 percent return, and that's great. Gretchen should definitely celebrate. Her party, however, will be much shorter than Leah's, who has just realized a 50 percent return on her investment of $1,000.

By buying her stock on margin and paying only half the cost of the stock, Leah doubled her return on each dollar she invested. The $1,000 she didn't have to pay for the stock could have been put to work elsewhere, perhaps also resulting in high returns, or she could have bought twice as many shares as Gretchen did for the same price.

Of course (you knew this was coming, right?), we're talking about the stock market, and as you've read numerous times already, where there is potential for gain, there is also potential for loss.

TAKING STOCK

Rules set by the Federal Reserve Board limit stock that can be bought on margin. Generally, you can't buy penny stocks, stock sold during an initial public offering (IPO), or over the counter bulletin board stock (OTCBB)—which is considered to be a very risky investment—on margin. Brokers also may restrict margin buying on other stocks, so always check.

Of Course, There Are Risks Involved

When you receive a loan, the lender usually expects to be rewarded for his generosity. The reward is normally paid in the form of interest, which is the case with margin accounts. For as long as you keep the loan, interest is charged to your account. If you don't pay off the loan, these interest charges add up and your debt level increases. As your debt level increases, the interest does, too.

Margin interest is floating and different for every broker. Interest is usually charged bi-weekly, directly from your brokerage account. You won't see a bill; the charges just keep on happening until the loan is paid in full.

If circumstances don't allow you to pay off the loan, charges continue to grow, meaning that you'll need a big return on your investment just to break even. Generally, investors use margin accounts to buy stock they don't plan to hold for a long time for this reason. The longer it's held, the greater the return must be to pay off the loan and fees.

If the value of your stock falls below your maintenance margin (the minimum amount required that you maintain in your account), your broker issues a margin call. That means you either need to add more cash to the account or sell some stock or other investment in your brokerage account. You'll be required to meet the call within a very short specified amount of time. If you don't, your broker is entitled to sell your stock in order to increase your account equity until it's greater than your maintenance margin.

Now, think back to the story about Gretchen and Leah. Remember how Leah's return was 50 percent on her investment, while Gretchen's was half of that? That was because Gretchen had invested twice as much money as Leah, and they both earned $500.

Well, what happens if instead of realizing a $500 gain they had realized a $500 loss? Gretchen would have been upset to lose 25 percent of her investment, but not nearly as upset as Leah, who would have lost 50 percent of her investment. The big danger of buying on margin is that, in the case of a dramatic downturn of a stock, you actually lose more money than you originally invested. And you'll still owe the interest and commissions generated.

So to sum it up, while some investors swear by margin buys, particularly in up markets, they are best left to those with experience and nerves of steel. It's better to start out with a cash account until you're a more seasoned investor.

CRASH!

Regardless of how good an investment sounds, or who else has gotten in on it, or how much you think you stand to gain, never allocate more than 10 percent of your total investment funds to high-risk, high-growth stock. It's simply too speculative to risk a higher percentage of your money.

Shorting

Another strategy often employed by investors is shorting a stock, or selling short. This is when an investor sells a stock he doesn't even own, anticipating that he'll be able to sell it, then buy it back at a lower price and make a profit. Sounds weird, doesn't it? That's because shorting is counterintuitive to the tried-and-true method of buying a stock at a low price and holding it until you can sell it at a higher price. And, you may ask, how can you sell a stock that you don't even own?

When you short a stock you don't own, you actually borrow a certain number of shares from your broker, again, through a margin account. These shares are sold, and the money generated is credited to your account. Remember, though, that you still owe your broker the same number of shares that you borrowed.

Normally, there's no time limit on how long you can hold a short, though you need to settle the shares for settlement by three days. Remember, however, that you'll be paying interest because the sale of the stock occurred in a margin account.

Betting on a Loss

So you now have in your account the proceeds from the sale of stock you've borrowed from your broker. Let's say you borrowed 100 shares of stock and sold them for $30 a share. That means you're holding $3,000 in your account, less commissions and interest.

TAKING STOCK

Because a short sale loses when a stock price rises, there are no limits on how high that loss can go. There are no caps on stock prices. If you lose on a stock because the price drops, it can only drop to zero, thereby containing the loss.

Sooner or later, though, you'll need to buy back the 100 shares of stock so you can return it to your broker. Investors who short stock are betting that its value is going to decline, and that they're going to be able to buy the stock back at a lower price than for what it was sold. If that happens, and you buy back the 100 shares of stock that sold for $30 a share for $20 a share, you get to keep the $10 per share difference. So you buy back the stock, return it to your broker, and pocket your $1,000 profit, less interest. Remember, though, that the broker's fees and interest payments will be deducted.

Watch Out for the "Ouch"

While some investors have profited nicely from selling short, there are some definite risks. The first risk, of course, is that the value of the stock won't drop, but it will increase in value. If the increase is substantial enough, you could risk losing all of the money realized from the sale of the stock, and more.

And as with trading on margin, you'll be required to keep a minimum maintenance requirement in your account. If the maintenance account drops below the minimum required, your broker can issue a margin call, and you will need to come up with more cash or additional securities. If you can't, your stock can be sold. Some investors place stop-limit orders to close out their positions in the event that a stock appreciates beyond a certain point in order to minimize the chances of that occurring.

Investors should also be aware of the dangers of a "short squeeze," which happens when there is a much greater demand for a stock than there is supply. When this occurs, traders with short positions might be forced to liquidate and cover their position by buying the in-demand stock in order to cut their losses. That can cause the price of the stock to go even higher.

As with buying on margin, selling short is tricky business and best left to experienced investors. The risks we've described are not the only ones associated with shorting, and, as mentioned earlier in this chapter, you can buy entire books on selling short. If you are tempted to engage in shorting, you'll need to do much more in-depth research to educate yourself about the potential benefits and risks.

Market Timing

Some investors, usually very active traders who are willing to pull out all the stops in order to buy low and sell high, trade stock based on market timing, which is a strategy that attempts to predict the direction in which the market will move. Market timers believe that if you look long and hard enough, an investor can always find a market that's on the rise or falling, and use those movements to his advantage.

Most investors who employ market timing base their predictions on technical analysis, although others rely on daily movements, multiyear cycles, or other economic data.

TAKING STOCK

Learn everything you need to know about market timing in *The Complete Idiot's Guide to Market Timing* by Scott Barrie (see Appendix B).

Advocates of market timing claim that investors can significantly increase their returns by getting in and out of markets as they rise and fall. While it's smart to be in the market when it is rising, it's safer to get out of the market when things start to look bearish.

Critics of market timing (and there are many) will tell you that successfully timing the market is next to impossible, especially if you attempt to do so over a long period of time. Historically, the market has always recovered and achieved new highs, meaning that if you're patient you can be successful in the stock market without constantly monitoring and fretting about it.

Strategies for Limiting Loss

There are no sure bets in the stock market. Or maybe it's more accurate to say that the only sure bet is that there will be ups and downs, and periods in which you and your portfolio will fare better than others.

You read about stop orders and stop-limit orders in Chapter 16. They are orders to sell stock that has dropped to a specified price. This, of course, is done to limit the amount of loss you'll experience. It also establishes guidelines that leave you out of the decision-making process. That's a plus because it lessens the risk of you rethinking the limit or becoming emotional about a loss.

There are different types of stop orders, but all are intended to minimize your losses. A stop order can apply to just one stock, or you can have a loss limit system in place that allows you to limit losses on your total assets by stopping trading altogether, or by exiting a losing position without second-guessing yourself or being tempted to wait until things turn around. Let's look at a few other methods of limiting loss in the stock market and keeping your portfolio healthy.

Broker Triggers

Keeping up with what's happening in the stock market is the first step to limiting losses. If you can't keep an eye on your portfolio because of an extended vacation, illness, or other reason, you should definitely have stop orders in place in case values fall significantly.

Broker triggers, which are simply messages your broker shoots out when something newsworthy is happening in the stock market or within a particular business or industry, can help you be proactive with your stock. You may be able to customize your broker's trigger system to only receive alerts regarding the stock in which you're interested. You can receive alerts on your e-mail or phone.

Also, with a signup, websites like Bloomberg, The Wall Street Journal, or MarketWatch will send you market alerts that keep you up to date with breaking news and allow you to manage your portfolio in a proactive manner.

Hedging Your Bets

Another means of limiting losses is by hedging your bets. You'll hear people talk about hedging their bets in a variety of circumstances other than the stock market, but hedging applies to stock trading as well.

Generally speaking, hedging can be thought of as insurance. It doesn't stop a loss from occurring, but it reduces resulting damages. If you buy car insurance, for instance, you're hedging your bets in the event you get in an accident or your car is stolen or otherwise damaged. The damage is done, but your losses are limited because the insurance company will pay (or at least partially pay) for repairs or replacement of the vehicle.

For investors, hedging usually involves investing in two stocks that have negative correlations. By doing so, you offset the risk of unfavorable price movements by hedging one investment against the other. Hedging is usually accomplished with the use of complex financial instruments such as options and futures, both of which are derivatives. Entire books have been written about hedging, and it's a particularly complicated topic for beginning investors. Having an idea of what it entails, however, will increase your overall knowledge of investing, which is always a good thing.

Understanding Your Limitations

Employing trading strategies and attempting to limit losses are smart moves for investors, and you should learn as much about these things as you can and decide what is applicable to you and your stock portfolio.

Understand, however, that no one can be successful in the market 100 percent of the time, because the market is unpredictable and subject to unexpected twists and turns that are caused by circumstances completely out of your control.

So set your financial goals, do your homework, invest wisely, learn all you can, and employ trading strategies when it makes sense to do so, realizing that despite all your best efforts, there will be rough spots along the road of stock investing.

The Least You Need to Know

- Buying on margin can increase the amount of stock you own and the returns you realize.
- Selling short allows investors to profit when the price of a stock falls.
- Timing the market can be profitable, but it is difficult and risky.
- There are strategies you can employ to limit your losses in the market.
- Learn all you can about your investments, but understand that no one can accurately predict the stock market 100 percent of the time.

Strategies for Good and Bad Times

In This Chapter

- Investing during tough financial times
- Getting a handle on what consumers are buying (and not buying)
- Knowing which stocks make sense to buy
- Investing during up markets
- Keeping your emotions at bay

As this book was being written, the U.S. economy has been in a state of turmoil for nearly three years. Most economists agree that this has been the worst downturn in the stock markets since the Great Depression. In late 2008 and 2009, panic was everywhere, with investors pulling out of the market left and right. Slowly but surely, we are finally seeing the economy pick up steam. While unemployment still stands at around 10 percent, retail sales have rebounded to their highest point since August 2008, setting a more optimistic tone for the economy.

Economic woes have not been confined to the United States; the downturn has been termed a global recession. China, Australia, and Canada have emerged from recession earlier than the United States, raising their interest rates to slow growth during the past year. Some European countries, particularly Greece and Ireland, are weighing down the growth of Europe.

Investing internationally is good if you invest south, in Latin America, or west, in China and Indonesia.

Only lately has investor confidence improved enough for the average person to again begin thinking about entering the stock market. In this chapter, we'll look at how to invest during tenuous economic times, and we'll also share some investing strategies for when markets and economic conditions are good.

Is It Smart to Invest During a Recession?

Financial advisors and analysts have very different opinions regarding whether stock market investing during a recession is a smart move. That shouldn't be surprising, given that economic experts find it difficult to even agree on when recessions begin and end. Conflicting opinions have been the order of the day during the recession that some economists claim ended in June 2009 (others claim we were still in recession nearing the end of 2010). We now recognize that the recession began at the end of 2007, although it wasn't officially acknowledged until the end of 2008.

While some bearish financial folks have been advising that it's best to sit tight and ride out the storm, others have been urging folks to grab their surfboards and get ready for a ride. Probably, you and your investment portfolio should land somewhere in the middle of those two scenarios.

The first thing to realize is that while historically stock prices have more often fallen than risen during a recession, not every recession has been hurtful to investors.

We certainly witnessed a very dramatic drop in stock prices between late 2007 and March 2009, but the market has rallied since then. Those brave souls who invested at near bottom prices when the recession was first announced in December 2008 and held on to those stocks through the rally have done well.

Of course, it doesn't always happen that way. The markets can be volatile or stagnant, meaning that you could sit for long periods of time without seeing any return on your investment. One thing you can be sure about, however, is that sooner or later, the markets will move. It won't always be in the direction you would like, but they never remain still for too long.

Stock market activity tends to be a leading indicator, improving ahead of general economic conditions and responding positively in anticipation of the end of a recession. Economists tell us that during all the recessions since World War II, the average rate of stock market return has been 12.1 percent, only slightly below the average return of nonrecession markets.

Many investors saw the value of their portfolios drop by almost half between October 2007 and March 2009, leaving many wondering whether to sell all their investments and reinvest in money market funds or other insured investments, which return almost nothing, or to ride out the downturn. This turmoil lasted for months, but as of mid-February 2011 the market was up almost 85 percent from its low point of March 2009.

It's important to remember that every recession has ended and economic conditions improved. It's hard to keep your eye on the prize during the midst of a recession when it seems all the news you hear is bad, but it's true that recessions end and the economy gets a chance for a jump start.

Whether or not you invest during a recession is a personal decision. Some investors just don't have the stomach for it, while others are excited about the possibility of finding some bargains and coming out better in the long run. While some investors have gambled during recessions and lost significant amounts of money, others have done very well. And some investors who sit out recessions have found that they need to struggle to make up ground when they re-enter the market following the recession.

Disregarding the Market Environment

When considering buying stock during a recession, some investors lose sight of what should be their primary goal. That goal, of course, is to locate good stock at an attractive price, and buy it with the intention of holding on to it as it increases in value. It should be the stock, not the market environment, that dictates what you buy.

SHARE THIS

While some investors take a doom-and-gloom approach to recessions, economists will tell you that they are simply a piece of the overall business cycle. The four parts of the business cycle, which is spread over a period of years, are: peak, recession, trough (bottoming out), and expansion/recovery.

Those who employ fundamental analysis—which considers the big picture, including overall economic conditions before buying a stock—tend to be more hesitant about buying in a down market than those who rely on technical analysis, which focuses just on the movement and momentum of the current stock price of the company. If you combine those two strategies, however, as most financial experts advise, you should be able to get an idea of how the stock will perform, regardless of economic conditions.

Looking for Some Bargains

Seasoned investors often will find opportunities for bargains in down markets. The practice of buying stock that has decreased in value is called value investing, and it occurs when investors believe a stock is being traded for less than its real value. Investors buy the stock with the belief that better economic times will return, and, with them, the price of the stock.

Of course, you should never buy a stock just because it's cheap. If it's high-quality stock of which the price has dropped, however, and the company issuing the stock has the right fundamentals, you just might be getting yourself a bargain.

World-famous investor Warren Buffett went into the stock market in December 2008, just as we learned what many of us already knew, that our economy had already been in a recession for a year. Prices would have gone down even more had he waited for several more months to buy, but Mr. Buffett has made quite a lot of money from the holdings he purchased at that time.

Of course, if you choose to pick up bargain stocks during an economic downturn, it's extremely important that you thoroughly research the company to make sure it hasn't been affected to the point that it won't be able to recover. Analysis becomes increasingly important in unsteady economic times.

TAKING STOCK

If you're looking for some bargains at the stock store, look to a company's sales. Historically, shares with low price-to-sales (P/S) ratios have performed better than those with low price-to-earnings (P/E) ratios, especially when sales are on the increase.

Understanding Cyclical Stocks

Cyclical stocks are those that react strongly to economic conditions. Examples of cyclical stocks include steel, paper, airlines, furniture, car manufacturers, hotels, and high-end restaurants. When the economy is good, more people travel, buy new cars, redecorate their homes, build new homes—you get the picture. When the economy is in a downturn or recession, however, people tend to give up those luxuries and focus on necessities. They hang on to the cars they have, put off buying major purchases like appliances, and even cut back on clothing purchases for as long as possible.

Seasoned investors keep a close eye on the economy and trade cyclical stocks if they anticipate that bad times are around the corner. They also might buy cyclical stocks in anticipation of an economic recovery because no one can predict exactly how economic cycles will play out. However, investing in cyclical stock is risky business.

TAKING STOCK

A general rule of thumb regarding cyclical stock is to buy when interest rates are falling. That's because falling interest rates tend to stimulate the economy, meaning that cyclical stocks would be looking toward an upswing. The best time to buy is during the last year of falling interest rates, just as the rates are about to begin to rise. Because it's hard to predict how interest rates will shift, however, there is risk involved with trying to time your transactions.

While some economists in 2009 and 2010 were certain that the recession was over and the upturn had begun, others were predicting a double-dip recession with a very long recovery. If you manage to buy cyclical stock at the bottom of a down cycle, just ahead of when the economy swings upward, you can profit. If your timing is off, however, you'll feel the ouch.

A recession affects nearly all aspects of the economy, but especially cyclical stock. Growth companies, such as Apple, Panera Bread, Netflix, and Nike, continue to increase the value of their stock, even during difficult economic times, while cyclical stock suffers and sometimes doesn't survive. When the economy improves, however, cyclical stocks sometimes increase in value dramatically, leaving even growth stocks behind.

The bottom line is that cyclical stock is subject to low lows and high highs, but getting in on it at the right time is difficult and requires a good deal of knowledge, the use of stops and limit orders, and a good dose of luck. If you're interested in cyclical stock, be prepared to spend a good deal of time on research before investing.

Do Your Homework

Investment experts insist that it's possible not only to survive, but to thrive during poor economic times. Some investors use down markets to their advantage by shorting stocks and making a profit from their declining values (see Chapter 18). Most of us, however, don't have the time or stomach for such intensive and risky investing. We would not recommend at this stage of your investing career that you risk your investment nest egg on risky strategies like shorting.

What you can do, however, is your homework. Keeping up with economic news during a downturn or recession is crucial for making good decisions concerning your investments. Read the financial pages and tune in to financial news programs.

Consider what the experts have to say, but also listen and pay attention to what's going on elsewhere in your community and the world.

TAKING STOCK

While toy companies typically suffer during a recession, Lego toy company's profits increased by more than 60 percent in 2009. Its growth was attributed to expansion in Asia and increased sales in Europe, along with some help from soccer great David Beckham. Beckham revealed in an interview that he was building a Taj Mahal out of Legos, and the company's sales shot up by 663 percent. Stay attuned to what celebrities are doing, as the public responds to the things that they like.

Look for signs that the economy is starting to turn around. Are there more people in the malls? Are trucks that had been sitting idle in a distribution center parking lot starting to be put back to use? Are there more jobs advertised in your newspaper or online job board? Are your friends heading back to work, or working longer hours? Are you starting to go out to eat again, or upgrading your choice of restaurants?

Alternately, if the economy is heading for a downturn, look for those indications as well. Are young adults moving back in with Mom and Dad? Are businesses laying off workers? Did the trendy tapas restaurant shut down?

While it's important to listen to what experts have to say about global, national, state, and local economic conditions, it's also smart to be practical and make your own informed deductions based on what you see and hear.

What Are Consumers Buying?

When trying to decide which companies to invest in during a recession or lean economic times, take a look at what consumers are continuing to buy. Consider trends, such as "staycations," planting gardens, and entertaining friends at home instead of going out for dinner. Then think about what products and services will support them.

People need to eat, regardless of the economy. So while restaurant revenue and expensive wine sales decline during tough economies, consumers continue to buy macaroni and cheese, packaged cookies, meat, eggs, and milk.

Consumers continue to buy health-care products during down times, making health care–related businesses relatively recession-proof. We continue to maintain our homes and vehicles during recession, perhaps more diligently than ever to assure that they last.

Interest in gardening has blossomed (sorry for the pun!) during recent years, with consumers buying record numbers of seeds and gardening tools. People stayed at home in increasing numbers and spent money on paint and other materials for small home improvement projects. Unfortunately, tough economic times trigger feelings of insecurity, and sales of guns also have increased.

SHARE THIS

While recessionary environments are not good for stocks in general, there are many stories of companies that have flourished during hard times. A recent example is Netflix, which, with more people staying home during the recession, experienced a booming business. Redbox, with its $1 rental fees, also experienced increased business.

If you have a handle on what people continue to buy in down times, you can significantly narrow your investment search by looking to the companies that provide those goods and services.

What Are Consumers Not Buying?

You read in the section on cyclical stocks about industries that normally take a hit in a bad economy, so you probably can figure out what consumers don't typically buy during hard times. In fact, it's probable that you know what consumers don't buy during economic downturns because of personal experience.

Just for the record, consumers generally steer clear of new cars, particularly fancy new cars (Daimler, the company that makes Mercedes, realized a 20 percent drop in revenue in 2009). Fewer consumers were investing in luxury handbags, such as those made by Coach, or buying high-end furniture or jewelry. Sales at retail stores such as Saks declined, as shoppers headed to Target or even turned to second-hand shops.

Generally, consumers trim their budgets and trade down during rough economic times. Those who used to dine in upscale restaurants three times a week may cut back to once or twice. You might decide to postpone buying a new coat and wear the one you purchased last year. Stock of companies that provide nonessential or luxury products and services are likely to feel the effects of an ailing economy.

Companies That Have Kept On Earning

Look for companies that have managed to continue growing during down economic times. Journalists and economists have had great fun looking at which companies have managed to keep on earning during the tough economic environment of 2009 and 2010, including the following:

- **McDonald's.** With value meals and a dollar menu, this is not a surprise.

- **Ford.** What a difference a year makes, along with a new CEO, deep job and cost cutting, and an image boost.

- **Hershey Company.** Consumers look for small indulgences when times are tough, making chocolate the perfect recession treat.

- **Amazon.** The company constantly looks to increase its market share and introduce new products like the Kindle.

- **Kraft Foods.** It's not only college students who turn to less expensive foods in difficult economic times, and Kraft offers a variety of affordable and convenient items, such as its macaroni and cheese.

- **CVS Caremark.** Consumers always need Band-Aids and shampoo.

- **Coca-Cola.** Coke's not going anywhere anytime soon.

- **Urban Outfitters.** Analysts say that this clothing chain gets it right by investing in competent employees and offering clothing not found elsewhere, making shoppers willing to part with their money.

- **Intel.** Companies that hadn't replaced computers for employees started buying again.

Investing in Good Times

Because our economy is cyclical, downturns don't last forever. It's important to keep this in mind during the rough patches and to continue to plan for how you'll invest as conditions improve and we head toward a more bullish economy.

It's more fun to invest in a good economy than in a bad economy; however, not every stock goes up, even when the market is on a tear. It's important that you continue to do your due diligence. You should read the company reports; understand all that the company manufactures; and have a handle on operations and management.

While no one can predict exactly what the stock market will do at any particular time, history can teach us a lot if we're willing to learn from it.

Too Good to Be True?

Remember the old saying, "If it sounds too good to be true, it probably is"? As the economy strengthens, you'll no doubt be bombarded with get rich quick schemes and the names of companies with stock expected to quadruple in value.

When the market begins to expand after a period of contraction, it sometimes gets ahead of itself. It's important during an economic recovery to pay attention to the price-to-earnings (P/E) ratio of your stocks as well as the market, and to compare the two. For example, if the overall P/E of the market, based on the Standard & Poor's (S&P) 500, is 18.5, it doesn't make sense to invest in a stock with a P/E of 30.

Also, if the P/E of the market has averaged 20 for the past 30 years, and if each day the market hits new highs and the market P/E is working toward 25, it's time to think about taking some profits.

Another concept of when there are problems looming in the markets is credit spreads. That's a term that compares the difference in interest rates between investments in insured monies, i.e., bank deposits and certificates of deposit and corporate bonds. If you look at the difference between interest rates in early 2008 and late 2010, you'll see that they are the same. However, in late 2008, the spreads widened and widened until in January 2009, the spreads began to turn and the healing began. This difference warns investors of a looming downturn in the market.

In late 2007, the market hit an all-time high. That should have been a warning to investors that the rise had been too fast, and that it was time to begin taking profits and investing in more conservative investments. A steady up market is great for investors, but a market that is up day after day should warn an investor to begin to cut back holdings.

Avoid the Herd Mentality

Investors often are more influenced by events and news than they are by fundamental investment principles, and they tend to follow the movements of other investors, assuming, perhaps, that there is strength in numbers.

It's very important, especially when the market is active and people are buying and selling quickly, to resist the temptation to buy a stock just because everyone else is buying it, or you read it's going to be the next big thing. It may be a great stock, but if you're going to buy it, do so because you've researched the company and are confident in its fundamentals.

SHARE THIS

A field known as behavioral finance is emerging as experts try to better understand how psychological factors affect the way people invest. The topic is explored in *What Investors Really Want* by Meir Statman, a leading researcher in the field (see Appendix B).

Your investments should be geared toward your investing goals, and based on research and sound strategies, not public opinion. Throwing money into the stock market out of greed or fear is never a winning strategy.

Keeping Emotions Out of Your Portfolio

Many an investor has been derailed because his or her emotions took up too much portfolio space. Greed and fear are great motivators, but when applied to the stock market, they're generally not useful. When you react to news or events and either buy or sell stock based on it, you risk making poor decisions in haste. Remember that there's a big difference between reacting to and responding to an event. Investors often feel pressured to act quickly in order to capitalize on gains or avoid losses, but impulsiveness is not an asset in the stock market.

With 24-hour news and constant analysis, some of which is sound and some of which is questionable, it's easy to get pulled into the latest Wall Street frenzy or panic. And because anyone with an opinion has an opportunity to post it electronically, we're bombarded with so much information that it's hard to keep it all straight. While it's difficult to ignore commentary and news that you think could affect your portfolio, letting it dictate your decisions is not a wise plan.

Remember that when the market is volatile, it moves fast. If you make an emotional investment based on something you heard or read, chances are that the situation has already changed and the news that you were reacting to is no longer applicable.

It's always best to stick to your plan and follow your investment road map. If you trade stock, make sure you're doing so for the right reason; because you've researched it and either believe it will increase in value, or that it's going to lose value.

> **CRASH!**
>
> Do not ever get so attached to a stock that you can't get rid of it if you need to. Some investors fall in love with a particular stock for one reason or another—usually a not very rational one. Holding on to a stock because of some sort of emotional attachment is dangerous and, if it makes up a significant portion of your investment, can really derail your goals.

Resist the temptation to do anything drastic, and especially if you're tempted to do so in a hurry. If your portfolio is diversified, you have a plan to move you toward your goals, and you're invested for the long term, you need to trust that you'll be able to ride out the rough times and make up any losses you experience.

Panic Selling

Panic selling, which is the widespread selling of a particular stock, is certainly not productive behavior, and is really contrary to serious investing. Most stock market crashes are caused by panic selling, during which stock might be sold at nearly any price because investors are convinced they need to get rid of it, at whatever price they can.

Hopefully, you own the stock that you do because you've done your homework and are convinced that its fundamentals are sound. If the fundamentals change, that may be reason to sell the stock. Fear because of a rumor or speculation you've heard is not.

In our increasingly global economy, panic selling can spread across continents, as witnessed in October 2008. A huge sell-off occurred on Wall Street on Friday, October 10, resulting in a huge sell-off in Asia. European markets fell, and exchanges in Austria, Russia, and Indonesia suspended trading because so many investors were trying to unload their stock. The situation was so bad in Australia that the day was dubbed "Black Friday."

Panic can occur quickly, and it causes people to act in ways that are not reasonable or productive. Resist the temptation to unload stock quickly if the price falls. If it was a good stock when you bought it, it will continue to be a good stock.

Momentum Buying

The flip side of panic selling is momentum buying, which is when investors are buying because charts are showing the markets moving upward and everybody else is buying. Some investors watch momentum buying carefully and profit from it, but most momentum buyers are reacting based on the emotion of greed. Momentum buying occurs when investors become convinced that a certain security, commodity, or other asset is going to make them rich and they absolutely must have a piece of the action. We've seen this happen recently as investors rush to find gold, pushing it to record prices.

> **SHARE THIS**
>
> An early example of momentum buying and subsequent crash occurred in Holland during the 1600s and is referred to as Tulipmania. Many Dutch became obsessed with tulips and tulip bulbs, which had recently been introduced in the country from Turkey. As the phenomenon grew, investors were convinced that they absolutely had to buy tulips and sold their homes and spent their life savings to buy them. You got it. The tulip market crashed spectacularly, resulting in mass bankruptcy and weak economy for years.

What you can count on with momentum buying is that eventually investors will begin to get uneasy about the market they've invested in because they start to understand that it can't be as strong as they thought it was. Once that happens, you can sit back and wait for the crash.

Just as with panic selling, avoid the temptation to buy stock because someone is telling you you've just got to get it. Momentum buying drives up prices and is an unsustainable practice. In good times or bad times, you need to remain calm, assess the situation, and consider all your options before unloading or buying up stock. Remember that for every upturn there's a downturn, and down markets always come back up. Patience is essential, and it always pays off.

The Least You Need to Know

- Investing during a recession can be a good idea, but you have to assess whether it's right for you.
- Your investments should be based on stock fundamentals, not market conditions.

- Bargains can be found in down markets if you know where to look.

- Some stocks, called cyclical stocks, are more subject to market swings than others.

- Look at what consumers are or aren't buying when considering stock investments.

- Keeping emotion out of your investments will help you avoid bad decisions that could negatively affect your portfolio.

How Are You Doing?

This part looks at how you can assess how well you're progressing toward your financial goals so you can see how far you've come on that journey. You learn how to keep track of your portfolio without becoming obsessed with it, and how to minimize losses if they occur. Mistakes happen, but being aware of them and taking action to correct them before they become serious problems will minimize damage.

Because taxes are inevitable in this life, you also learn not only how they can affect your investments, but how to keep them as low as you're able to in order to maximize your earnings. We end with a chapter about starting or joining an investment club, which is simply a group of like-minded folks who pool their money to purchase stocks that everybody likes. These clubs are fun and educational, and many of them have done well over the years.

Assessing Your Performance

In This Chapter

- Keeping a close watch on your investments
- Calculating the total return for your investments
- Tracking your progress
- Knowing what you own
- Maintaining sight of your goals
- Staying on course

Once you've gotten some investments under your belt and established a portfolio, it's important that you come up with a system and a plan for staying on track toward reaching your financial goals. It can be tempting, especially if your stock investment strategy is long term, to let your portfolio take care of itself.

While that's understandable—after all, we all are busy—it's not acceptable. We don't advise that you spend hours every day poring over your stock portfolio or pestering your broker, but it's your responsibility to keep up with your statements and maintain a perspective on how you're doing.

In this chapter, we'll look at some practical methods of assessing your investment performance. Taking time periodically to review your investment goals will help you to understand where you are on the road leading to them, and whether you should consider altering your course. You'll learn how to calculate your total return and use indexes to track your performance, and why it's important to keep an open mind regarding your investments.

Understanding Your Investment Portfolio

Once you've gotten started in stock market investing and have an investment portfolio established, you should get comfortable with reading and understanding your account information and statements.

There seems to be different schools of thought regarding the monitoring of investments. While some people obsess over their stocks, others transact the investments and then pretty much ignore them. Neither of these, of course, is a healthy course, and the goal is to fall somewhere in the middle of those extremes.

Understanding your investment portfolio is simply a matter of keeping track of what you have and the activity that occurs within your account. This is easily accomplished by paying close attention to monthly statements from your brokerage, or from the company from which you've purchased stock if you bought it direct. We can't stress enough how important it is to stay on top of your investments by closely monitoring your statements. Regardless if you work with a broker or trade on your own, mistakes happen. It's a lot easier to take care of a mistake when it's discovered promptly than to deal with it months later. Little mistakes have been known to become major problems and can cost investors dearly.

 TAKING STOCK

This seems obvious, but in order to review account statements to make sure they're correct, you need to have a handle on your account activity. Make sure you keep records of your trades so you can square them with the information about your account that you get from the broker.

Many investors have gone paperless and receive their account statements electronically. If you still receive monthly statements in the mail, make sure you save them in a file—you'll need them at tax time. When you receive trade confirmations and holding statements, look them over to be sure everything is correct, and contact your broker immediately if there are mistakes or problems. Starting in 2011, brokerage houses that don't already do so will be required to include the costs of your investment on your monthly statements, as well as on the statement your broker provides for preparation of your tax return.

If there is something about your account information that you don't understand, or that doesn't seem right to you, by all means ask. Even if you trade online or use a discount broker, the brokerage firm should have someone available to answer questions.

Never be embarrassed by something you don't know or understand, and don't hesitate to question any sort of activity that you don't recognize. Identity theft is a real possibility, unfortunately, making it imperative that you keep a close eye on your accounts. You're not expected to be a financial expert, just a diligent monitor of your portfolio.

Your account report will provide an overview of all activity for the month, including deposits, trades, and fees. It will tell you if the value of your account has increased or decreased, and by how much. You should be able to view your asset allocations and see how much cash you have. The statement will list each holding individually and inform you of any transactions that have occurred during the month, whether you have margin capabilities, and if so, which funds are available for use on margin.

TAKING STOCK

A mistake that many investors make is to focus on the change in value of the account from month to month. Remember that your money is invested in the stock market and subject to gains and losses. Most brokerage statements include the account value change for the month, as well as year to date. While it's fine to note whether your monthly values have increased or decreased, keep in mind that the year-to-date numbers offer a look at the bigger picture. Don't get hung up on losses or gains from month to month.

Many brokerage statements will include estimated income from your holdings. You should already know which of your stocks pay dividends, but it's nice to see the totals spelled out from month to month. Your statement should also tell you the amount of dividends and interest you have received for the month and year to date.

Some online tracking services include a feature that allows investors to enter the usernames and passwords for other accounts, even if they're invested with another institution. The information is gathered and displayed on one screen, allowing you a snapshot of all of your investments. Others provide years of records, allowing you to review—and to download and print if you wish—the account performance and activity.

If you haven't taken some time with your account statement lately, set aside an hour or so and really delve into the features available, particularly if you use an online version. You might be surprised at how much information you're able to access in addition to your monthly account activity. It's particularly important for investors who engage in strategies that have increased potential for risk, such as buying on margin or short selling, to pay close attention to their portfolios.

You should review your statement each month; however, at least twice a year and preferably quarterly, you should conduct a thorough review of your overall portfolio. Assess your risks, take a close look at your allocations, and consider if you need to make any changes. If you have a broker or work with a financial advisor, schedule meetings at least once a year and maintain a good working relationship. If you ever encounter problems, it's helpful to have your broker know who you are and be able to put a face to the portfolio. Take notes during those meetings to review, and follow up if you have any questions or discover there's something you don't understand.

The first thing most investors look at when the statement rolls in is the total return. Let's take a look at exactly what that means and how you calculate it.

Calculating Total Return

Reviewing the *total return* for each investment in your portfolio is a good place to begin in order to see how the securities are performing. The total return reflects the change, plus income received, in the overall value of your portfolio over a given period of time.

DEFINITION

Total return is the actual rate of return of an individual investment or pool of investments over a prescribed time period. Total return includes interest, dividends, distribution, and capital gains.

When you receive a statement from your broker, it normally lists two types of total return: cumulative and average. Cumulative total return reflects actual performance of a particular stock over the time you have held the stock, while average annual total return uses an investment's cumulative return to indicate what would have happened if the investment had performed at a constant rate over the entire period, usually for the quarter, year to date, or annually. Calculating your total return allows you to assess the performance of your entire portfolio, as well as compare how well one stock performed against another.

To figure out your total return, first figure out the cost of your total investment including expenses. If you bought $1,800 worth of stock and paid $200 in fees, for example, your total investment was $2,000.

If, over a prescribed period of time, the value of your stock has increased to $2,500, you subtract the cost of the investment from the new amount, getting a total of $500. If you've received dividends on your investment, you'd have to add that amount to the new value of your stock.

Calculate your total return by dividing the profit by the cost of the investment. In this case, it's $500 ÷ $2,000 = 0.25, or a 25 percent return on investment. Congratulations!

Unfortunately, your total returns may not always be on the positive side. If you have a loss, that must factor in when you put the returns of each security together to determine total returns on your portfolio.

Once you've calculated the returns of each investment, it's time to calculate the total return for the portfolio for the time period you are interested in. Let's say you want to determine total return for the quarterly period between January 1 and March 31. You'd start by noting the value of the portfolio as of January 1. Compare that value to the current value (March 31). If you have deposited or withdrawn money from the account during the time period, it becomes a little more complicated, but the calculation is very similar to the total return for one holding.

Using your current statement (March 31), look for the market or current value of the portfolio, then subtract this value from the market value of the portfolio (less additions or withdrawals) at the beginning of the time period (January 1), divided by the beginning value. This will give you your return for the time period.

Let's say that on January 1 your investments totaled $25,000. On March 31, the portfolio was worth $30,000. To calculate return, you subtract $25,000 from $30,000, for a total of $5,000. Divide the $5,000 by the original market value of $25,000 for a return of .20, or 20 percent—a very nice return. If you use the value from the brokerage statement, dividends and interest are included. If you calculate return on an individual holding, you'll need to include any dividends during the period.

Calculating total return sounds complicated, and it can be, but it's important to understand how well each of your holdings is doing because you could have one stock that's on fire, while others are dragging your performance down. Knowing how each stock is performing in comparison to others in its sector and others in your portfolio will help you understand the bigger picture of your total investments.

Once you've figured out your total return, you'll have a handle on how each stock has performed, as well as your overall portfolio. Then you can assess how well your stocks are working together to increase the overall value of your investments, and if you may need to add or get rid of some.

Using Indexes to Track Your Progress

If you've calculated your total return and found that you're up 8 percent year to date, you're probably, and understandably, pleased. The question to ask, however, is how well should you have done? How do you know if 8 percent is a great return, just so-so, or maybe even not a good return at all?

To know how your investments are doing, you can compare them to one of the indexes that you read about in Chapter 1. Doing so will give you an idea of how well your stock is performing, as compared to the index stocks.

A guide for which index to use is that, if you're invested in only U.S. stocks, you should compare your portfolio's return with the Standard & Poor's (S&P) 500 for the same time period. Looking at the same time period will provide a comparable return for the indexes.

The Dow Jones Industrial Average gets a lot of publicity, but most investors holding U.S. stocks actually look to the S&P 500 as the benchmark. The NASDAQ is the index to use if you are invested in tech growth stocks.

If you are invested in only small U.S. companies, compare your holdings to those on the Russell 2000. International holdings generally are compared to the stocks on MSCI EAFE, which, as you read in Chapter 1, is an index designed to measure the stocks of developed markets outside of the United States and Canada.

Know What You Own

If you pay attention to such things, you might remember a 2004 presidential debate between John Kerry and George W. Bush, during which Kerry cited proceeds Bush had received from his partial ownership of a timber company. Appearing incredulous, Bush responded, "I own a timber company? That's news to me. Need some wood?"

Fact checkers revealed that Bush did, indeed, have an interest in a timber company, but the point of that story is to illustrate that investors can sometimes lose sight of what they own. A periodic overview of your investment portfolio will remind you of exactly what you own and how much you own, and allow you to assess your asset mix.

TAKING STOCK

If you have accounts in your name only, consider assigning someone to serve as your proxy in the event that you are injured or sick or unable to attend to them for another reason. Make sure that person is knowledgeable about the accounts and has access to logins and passwords.

If you've got exchange traded funds (ETFs) in addition to stock or mutual funds, it's very possible that you're not aware of what they contain. Take some time to research exactly what those accounts hold, and compare them to your stock allocation. Are the assets in the funds allocated in a similar fashion to your individual stocks? Does the allocation make sense to you? Check out the percentage of foreign, global, and international funds; large cap versus small cap holdings; and so forth. Knowing what you own helps you to make good decisions when buying additional stock.

Don't Rule Out Other Possibilities

There are many thousands of stocks available for sale. If you've got one that's not performing up to your expectations, don't feel obligated for any reason to hang on to it (except possibly if the fees associated with trading it are too high).

It's difficult for many investors to accept a loss and move on, but sometimes that's exactly what needs to be done. If you have a stock that's declining in value, ask yourself if the reasons that convinced you to buy the stock in the first place still exist. Changes occur among companies and industries, and a good stock can turn into a bad stock. Sometimes the best move is to get rid of it and find something with better value. If the value of a stock you own begins to drop, do a little sleuthing to find out why. Has the company suffered bad earnings, or has there been news that could have negatively affected it? Is the news something that the company can overcome, or is it time to accept your losses and find a better choice? Many investment publications allow you set up investment alerts for stock you own, which can help you keep up with and assess what's occurring within a particular company or industry.

Investors shouldn't stop researching companies and stock just because they have a portfolio in place. Don't be reluctant to consider stock other than what you already own. You're likely to come across good opportunities as you talk to other investors and read and listen to financial news. Don't be afraid to take advantage of them.

Keeping Your Goals in Clear View

In Chapter 4, you read about establishing investing goals and timetables based on your age, circumstances, and aspirations. Goals are set by looking into the future and identifying what you anticipate needing money for and how much you think you'll need. Once those things are determined, you can start figuring out how to fund things like your retirement, your or a child's college education, and so forth.

As you read, different investment vehicles are recommended for various types of investing. Someone who has years before she'll need her investment funds should choose different assets than someone who will need his funds in five years.

When evaluating your investments' progress, take some time to review your goals and timetables. A great time to do this is when you are gathering information for your tax returns. Review your performance for the previous year, and consider if your allocation is in line with your goals. If you established benchmarks for where you wanted to be at certain time intervals, review those to see how you're coming along. If your goals or circumstances have changed, be realistic about the fact that you may need to make some adjustments or changes to your portfolio. Revisit your goals and be willing to adjust them. We can't always anticipate the changes that life hands us, but we can remain agile and ready to alter course when necessary.

You Ready to Retire Yet?

If you're saving for retirement, you should be adjusting your stock portfolio as you move closer to the big event. The retirement portfolio of a 30-year-old, in which some aggressive growth stocks are fine, should look much different from that of a 55-year-old, whose collection of stocks should be moving toward income investing.

TAKING STOCK

Remember the old rule of thumb for retirement investing. If you subtract your age from 100, you get the percentage of stocks that should represent the total assets of your portfolio. So if you're 30, 70 percent of your portfolio should be stocks and the other 30 percent bonds. This isn't a sure bet as investors' risk tolerance, goals, and other factors differ, but it's an easy guide.

While you're reviewing your stocks, also take a good look at other retirement savings vehicles you might have, such as IRAs or a 401(k). If you're heavily invested in stock and you're more than halfway to retirement, consider adding bonds or moving assets into cash or money market funds. The stock market can offer significant gains, but if you're soon going to begin depending on your savings, you need to look at preserving wealth.

How's the College Fund Coming?

Just as with your retirement savings, your college fund portfolio should start looking more conservative as your child gets nearer to needing the money. Hopefully, you invested in a mix of stocks and bonds, beginning when your child was young. As she ages (and it happens quickly), you'll want to consider the allocation mix and move more toward bonds as the college years get closer.

When you know that you're going to need the money shortly, move at least part of it into a savings account or money market funds so its value is protected and you have access to funds as you need them. Tuition payments roll around quickly and you'll want to have money available.

Is Your Nest Egg Secure?

If you've accumulated money over the years, your focus should shift toward preserving wealth. That doesn't mean that you need to move out of the stock market altogether or cash in your investments and hide the money in your freezer, but you definitely should look to investments that incur less risk than those designed for building wealth.

CRASH!

While bonds are considered to be a more conservative investment than stock, that doesn't mean they're risk free. If you invest in bonds, be sure you understand what category of bonds you're buying, who the issuer is, tax considerations, and terms. It doesn't happen too often, but some investors have taken major hits from bond investments.

Remember that large cap stocks are considered safer than small cap. Stocks that pay you dividends are desirable, particularly if you can continue to build your nest egg by reinvesting the dividends. Look toward transferring some of the money to cash investments to assure availability.

Time to Buy a Vacation House?

When the stock market hits a bearish period, many people will begin to re-evaluate their investments and some will determine that real estate is a better place to park their money. If you fall into that category and are considering using some of your investment funds to buy a vacation home or other major purchase, there are some important considerations to keep in mind.

Owning a second home offers the advantages of having a place to visit in an area that you like, and lets you offer the home to family and friends. It can also provide a revenue stream if you're willing to rent it. Some investors insist that vacation homes can pay for themselves through rentals, but a lot depends on your expenses (the purchase price of the home, taxes, fees, and upkeep), the area in which the home is located, the availability of rental properties, and so forth.

TAKING STOCK

If you're thinking that a second home might be the way to go, invest first in *Buying a Second Home* by Craig Venezia (NOLO Press, 2009) for advice on buying a second home for investment purposes or personal use.

If you've accumulated wealth and are considering a vacation home, be sure to take sufficient time and effort to research the subject carefully and decide whether it's a smart financial move. Never buy a vacation home simply because you like the area in which it's located, for emotional reasons, or because "everyone else" is buying property there.

Staying on Course with Your Investment Approach

From time to time as you evaluate and assess the performance of your investment portfolio, you may notice that your asset allocation mix has become unbalanced. Remember the discussion in Chapter 10 about the need to periodically rebalance your portfolio to bring it back to your original asset allocation mix? Let's have a look at how you do that.

Your allocation mix gets out of balance because some investments grow faster than others. It could be that you find that stock from one industry or sector becomes overrepresented or weighted too heavily with one type of stock, such as large cap or growth stock.

This increases your risk, and you should look to making some changes. You can rebalance your portfolio in several different ways:

- Sell investments. If you're over-weighted with a particular type or category of stock, sell some of it and use the money to buy stock in under-weighted categories. If your portfolio has shifted too far toward growth stock, for instance, sell some and buy some income stock. This is known as active allocation. You sell what has grown to be too large a percentage in your portfolio, then reinvest those funds within another sector.

- Come up with some additional funds and buy stock in the under-weighted categories. This is known as passive allocation.

- Adjust any regular payments you might be making so the contributions go toward buying stock in the under-weighted categories. Keep an eye on this, however, so you'll be able to readjust the contributions once your portfolio has been rebalanced.

Before you decide how you wish to rebalance your portfolio, consider what fees you might encounter and potential tax consequences, and look for ways to minimize them.

Keeping your portfolio in balance will help to keep you on course and moving toward your investment goals. Other tips for staying on course include the following:

- Stick with investment strategies you feel comfortable with. Don't be tempted to follow fads or change strategies because you're nervous about the market.

- Continue to fund your investments so they have the opportunity to grow.

- Remain detached. Your investment portfolio is a wealth-building tool, not a friend. If one stock isn't working, find another one that will.

- Resist the urge to buy stock because you think you know what the market is going to do. Market timing is best left to the pros, and even they misjudge it.

- Don't trade depending on current market movement. By the time you do, the movement will have changed.

- Remember that you're in for the long haul and don't be overly discouraged by losses, even if they're big ones. Remember that the market is cyclical.

- Pay attention to your risk tolerance. If it changes, rebalance your portfolio to reflect the change.

The Least You Need to Know

- Once your investments are in place, it's very important to stay up to date by carefully checking statements to avoid errors.
- You can track your progress by calculating total return and using indexes to gauge performance.
- Keep a close eye on stocks and other investments such as ETFs and mutual funds to know exactly what you own.
- Be willing to get rid of a stock and buy another if necessary.
- Periodically assess where you are with your investment goals.
- Stay on course by rebalancing your portfolio when necessary.

Cutting Your Losses

In This Chapter

- Mistakes are inherent to stock market investing
- Understanding why mistakes occur
- Acting to resolve mistakes
- Knowing when to sell a stock

You read in Chapter 19 about the psychology of investing. That psychology once again comes into play when you have a stock that turns out not to be what you thought it would.

You did your homework, researched the company, crunched the numbers, and read up on the news, and thought you were picking a winner. Instead, the stock has been nothing more than a big disappointment and it's dragging down your portfolio.

In this chapter, we'll have a look at minimizing your losses, and at what it takes to get rid of an underperforming stock and find one that you'll like. One thought before we get started: all investors make mistakes or suffer losses that are beyond their control. The important thing is to be able to recognize the mistakes and respond in a positive and productive manner.

Even Experts Make Mistakes

No one buys a stock that they don't expect to succeed. That would just be counter-intuitive to investing. Buying stock that drops in value, however, happens all the time. So what you need to focus on isn't picking winners 100 percent of the time, but knowing when and how to react to losers.

During an interview in October 2010, legendary investor Warren Buffett candidly spoke of the biggest mistakes he'd ever made while investing. The biggest mistake, he said, was buying Berkshire Hathaway in 1965, which at the time was a struggling textile firm, not the hugely successful business that it is today. Buffet estimated that the acquisition ended up costing him and his investment firm shareholders billions of dollars over a period of time.

Other famous investors, including Victor Niederhoffer, Bill Gross, Monish Pabrai, and Seth Klarman, have also admitted to making major investing mistakes during interviews. The point is that even experts make mistakes when it comes to investing.

However, investors who know how and are willing to cut losses before they get out of hand are far more successful than those who deny the loss or decide to ride it out. Why is it so difficult, though, for many of us to admit we've made an investment mistake and get rid of it? Let's look at some reasons why we tend to hold on to stock that's lost value:

- **False optimism.** Investors holding stock that's dropped in value tend to think that if they just hold on to it, it will regain its value and they will break even or realize a profit. The truth is, not all stock bounces back. Many stocks that have declined in value never regain past highs. Companies falter, and while some make spectacular recoveries, others go bankrupt. Some investors, despite repeated bad news and other indicators that a company is failing, hold on to stock solely on the irrational hope that it will somehow regain its value.

- **Can't admit a mistake.** Many investors have held on to stock because they were reluctant or unable to admit they'd made a mistake. They hold on to a losing stock, rationalizing that it's only a loss on paper if they don't sell it, not a real loss. By avoiding the loss, they avoid the necessity of admitting a mistake.

- **Sentimental attachment.** Granddad worked for the railroad company his entire life and passed the stock he held in the company on to you. Now, the railroad company is on its way out, but you're hanging on to the stock because Granddad gave it to you. Sentimental attachment to an investment is not productive, and Granddad would probably only be disappointed that you're being investment foolish, not that you're planning to sell his stock.

- **Lose ability to take action.** Have you ever had a disagreement with a friend, and you stop talking to each other? You fully intend to mend the rift, but things happen and time goes on, and it becomes harder and harder to address the situation and make amends. One day you realize that six months have passed, and you and your friend are still at odds. The same thing can happen with your investment portfolio. Investors often pay close attention to their portfolios when the market is good and they're making money, only to put them aside and not want to deal with them when things are going poorly. Just like with the relationship, the longer you let it go, the harder it gets to address and fix the problems. Remember that small losses are easier to deal with than big ones.

- **Tax concerns.** Some investors put off selling low-cost stock because they're reluctant to pay the taxes associated with the sale. In reality, they would be better off to get rid of the stock before it hits bottom, despite the tax consequences.

There are other reasons that investors are reluctant to cut their losses and ditch a losing stock, but these seem to be the most common. Know that it's a common phenomenon, and many people participate in the denial game.

SHARE THIS

Wall Street slang refers to funds invested in stock that isn't going anywhere as dead money. It's sitting there, taking up space in a portfolio, with little hope of it generating any income. Dead money, essentially, is useless.

Being Honest and Learning from Experience

The stock market can be compared to a huge experimental learning center, where investors learn as they go. That's not to say that you ever want to start out ignorant, for, as you know, it's vital to put in learning time before you start. No one, though, even experienced investors, fully understands every investing nuance, or can always accurately predict what the markets are going to do.

If you're struggling in the market, take some time to assess what's causing the problem. You can't solve a problem if you don't know the reason for it. Denying that there is a problem is dangerous business when dealing with your finances, as you then deny yourself the opportunity to address it and get it resolved.

Let's take a look at some common sources of problems for investors, and what can be done to improve the situation.

Do You Understand the Companies You're Invested In?

Investors often buy the stock of a company because everybody is talking about it, or they love the company's product, or their friend made some money with it last year. None of those reasons, however, are good ones for buying stock. The only good reason to buy stock of a particular company is because you've researched the company and you're convinced that it is fundamentally sound and you'll profit from owning its stock.

If you don't fully understand what the company does, how it's structured, how long it's been around, and other factors that affect its operations and finances, you can't be sure of its fundamentals and strengths. You need to understand how the company makes its money, and then address factors that could affect its income. Is it highly susceptible to economic shifts? Has there been negative news lately regarding the company? You should understand not only the company in which your money is invested, but factors and situations that could affect the company, either negatively or positively.

TAKING STOCK

Get into the habit of reading and listening with a critical ear. Consider if the information you're receiving might have an effect on a particular company, or an industry. When hearing about the massive BP oil spill, for instance, you might have instantly thought about how it would affect the fishing industry, and what the trickle-down effects might be.

If you own the stock and don't fully understand the company, get started with learning more about it. Review Chapters 13 and 14 for a refresher course on learning about companies before investing.

Are You Making Informed Decisions?

There's no shortage of information when it comes to choosing stock, but are you relying on information that helps you to make informed decisions, or getting caught up with the constant chatter present on television or the Internet?

How well informed are your decisions? They should be based on news from reputable sources, not obtained from blogs or from sources that are biased in some way, such as those promoting a particular product. Rely on company information, but make sure to balance it, as a company will present itself in a positive light as much as possible.

Review your portfolio and remember why you purchased a stock in the first place. Was the information you based your decision on sound? Are there still sound reasons for owning the stock? If not, remember that it's by no means irreplaceable.

Are You Relying Too Much on Others' Advice?

We all get busy and tend to look for shortcuts, one of which may be looking to others for advice regarding our investments. Seeking advice is not a bad thing, don't get me wrong. Relying too much on advice from others without researching an investment on your own, however, is asking for trouble. Remember that you are ultimately responsible for your stock choices and for keeping up with what your stocks are doing.

SHARE THIS

Research has shown that, consciously or unconsciously, many investors will buy popular stocks and then, if the value decreases, rationalize their loss by pointing out that many other investors also bought the stock.

You wouldn't be reading this book if you weren't interested in learning about stock investing and how to succeed in the market. Even if you work with a broker who recommends certain securities or actions, you need to have the knowledge to understand why he or she is recommending them and how they might fit into your overall portfolio. Asking for help when you need it is a great idea. Over-reliance on advice from others without doing the work you need to do on you own, however, is not.

Are You Paying Attention?

When you're invested in the stock market, it's a really good idea to pay attention not only to what's happening with your accounts and the companies you're invested in, but to what's going on in the larger world.

Starting with your own accounts, you should be reviewing monthly statements, reconciling any discrepancies, and being vigilant for problems. If the market is volatile, sign up for e-mail alerts when the stock you own experiences a significant change in value.

Also pay attention to anything going on with the companies of which you own stock, and any factors that could affect the company. You read about the importance of top-down analysis when researching stocks, but it's no less important when it comes to avoiding problems with your stock.

If you hear about a company experiencing big problems, don't assume that those problems are confined to just one organization. When Bear Stearns collapsed in 2008, seasoned investors began to fear for the rest of the banking and securities trading industry, and with good reason. What occurs within one company, industry, or stock sector almost always has a ripple effect. If you can anticipate where those ripples are going, you'll be able to be proactive in your trading decisions.

Review the fundamentals of the companies in which you own stock several times a year. If you don't like what you see, stay on top of what's going on within the company, the industry, and the larger economy, and then act accordingly.

Are You Behaving Patiently?

That patience is a virtue applies big time to investing in the stock market. To be successful, investors need to have patience when they buy a stock, while holding a stock, and when selling a stock. Snap decisions are beneficial in some situations, but rarely in stock market investing.

Some investors decide they want a particular stock and buy it, without setting an entry price or even bothering to check out its price history. They buy the stock at a too-high price, only to have the price fall a few days later. Before buying a stock, decide what your entry price will be, based on what you think the company is worth. Then you should be willing to wait patiently until the price reaches your entry point.

CRASH!

Day traders, in our opinion, cannot be considered "real" investors, partially because of their lack of patience. Nearly all very successful investors buy long-term investments, and understand that patience is critical to their success. If you think you're more suited to day trading because you don't have the patience required for investing, I'd consider you to be a speculator, which everyone knows is a very risky field.

When holding a stock, remember that its price can be affected because the company's fundamentals have changed, or because of a market upturn or downturn. If you determine that the company is no longer a good investment, that's one thing. But impatiently throwing off a stock that's lost value due to overall market declines is quite another—and not a good decision. People buy and sell stock for all kinds of reasons, some of them sound and others not. Bouncing from one stock to the next because you lack the patience to ride out a downturn or you're too anxious to wait to buy another one will not reward you in the long run.

When getting ready to trade a stock, ask if it's reached the target price you set for the sale. If not, is there a reason you can't be patient enough to wait for it to do so? If there's a problem with the company that causes you to believe the stock will decline, it might make sense to get rid of it. Doing so because you're unwilling to ride out a temporary price dip, however, is not a good idea.

Once you select a stock, based on thoroughly conducted research, plan to hold on to it unless there are obvious reasons for doing otherwise. Patience within the stock market is a rare commodity, but it really does pay off.

Going Easy on Yourself

A teacher who punishes a student for making a mistake isn't a very good teacher. Instead, the teacher should explain to the student the reason for the mistake, and point her toward more information or other resources that can help her to correct the mistake, learning as she goes.

The same is true with investment mistakes. Accept that they're going to occur, determine that you'll figure out why they've occurred, and learn from them. If you're making a lot of poor decisions regarding your investments, the most important thing is to figure out why that's occurring. Maybe you need to find some help until you've got a bit more experience under your belt. If so, contact a financial advisor or see if your brokerage firm can provide advice. Remember that there are all types of advisors and brokers. Review Chapter 15 for a refresher course.

 SHARE THIS

Some researchers assert that investors who experience big losses in the stock market actually go through a grieving process, similar to that experienced following a death or divorce. Andrew W. Lo, a finance professor at Massachusetts Institute of Technology, said many investors will follow the traditional stages of grieving—denial, anger, bargaining, depression, and acceptance—following a significant investment loss.

Don't take your mistakes too seriously or agonize about them. Look at them as learning opportunities and move on. If you can't afford to make mistakes, you shouldn't be invested in the stock market.

Getting Rid of the Dead Wood

Sometimes the only move that makes sense is to unload a stock. If you have a stock that's performing poorly and you're no longer convinced that it will be a winner in the long run, it makes no sense to hold on to it.

That's not to say you should sell stock without doing your homework first. Know the total returns for each of your holdings, compare them to earnings of comparable investments, and draw your conclusions.

Some investors have all sort of criteria and reasons for buying stock, but none for when it comes to selling. You should establish reasons for which you'll sell stock and follow through if any of those reasons occur. Here are some reasons you might want to sell stock:

- The stock becomes overvalued. If you bought a stock at $30 a share and it's now valued at $60, the temptation is to hang on and wait for it to get to $90. If analysis tells you that the stock is overvalued, however, you'd do well to sell it off before the price starts to drop.

- There are fundamental changes within the company, such as it incurs high debt, has gone through three CEOs in less than two years, or launches a string of new products that fail.

- The reasons you bought the stock have changed. There were good reasons to invest in a home construction business when the housing market was booming. Once the bust occurred, however, those reasons no longer apply. Hopefully, you'll stay on top of your portfolio and the news and circumstances that affect your investments and be able to anticipate when the reasons that you bought a stock no longer apply.

- You need to sell stock in order to buy other investments that you are convinced are better.

- You have a financial emergency and need to sell some stock to generate cash.

Because it's difficult to know when to unload a stock, many investors rely on stop losses, which you read about in Chapter 16. Having a predetermined price at which you'll sell the stock removes the burden of the decision, along with the emotion that can accompany selling a stock.

Selling stock at a loss or sometimes even at a gain can be difficult, but there are a couple of silver linings. If you've lost money on the stock, you get to realize capital losses to either help with the loss or offset overall capital gains. Make sure that you take advantage of all the tax benefits to which you're entitled.

The other silver lining is the peace of mind you'll encounter when you've finally gotten rid of the dead wood. We often spend time and energy worrying or feeling badly about something when what we really should do is act to change the situation. Holding on to a stock based solely on hope, or not wanting to admit you made a mistake, or inertia, is not a good strategy, and will not benefit your well-being—or your portfolio.

> **TAKING STOCK**
>
> Periodically review every stock you own. For each one, ask yourself, if you didn't already own the stock, would you buy it? If you answer yes, stick with it. If there's no way that, knowing what you know now, you'd buy that stock today, it's time to get rid of it.

Anyone who invests in the stock market needs a strategy and the will to stay with that strategy. If you're investing for growth, then you need to be prepared to hang in, even when it gets to be a wild ride. Succumbing to fear when conditions get tough and selling your assets takes you out of the game and eliminates your opportunity to profit when markets rebound.

You should write down your investment strategy and refer to it often, using it as your road map. Not only will this remind you of your goals and investment conditions, if you stick to your strategy, you will minimize the risk of acting based on emotion.

The Least You Need to Know

- If you've made some mistakes with your stock investments, you're in good company; even experts make mistakes.
- The most important thing is that you learn from mistakes.
- Investors make mistakes for reasons that are easily avoidable.
- Selling stock can be difficult, but it's important to know when it's time to get rid of it.

Tax Considerations

In This Chapter

- Benefiting from the stock market comes with tax consequences
- Understanding how your earnings are taxed
- How dividends are taxed
- Minimizing your tax bill
- Keeping it legal
- Finding tax breaks where you can

You read in Chapter 4 about how investments can affect your taxes, and some of that information will be reviewed in this chapter. Taxes are an important consideration when you're investing in the stock market, and you'll need to have a sound understanding of how they can affect your investments and your bottom line.

While everyone has to pay taxes, there are techniques you can use to help you hold on to as much of your money as possible. With that accomplished, you can reinvest, or use the money to fund those goals that caused you to start investing in the stock market in the first place!

In this chapter, you'll read about what gets taxed and at what rates, and how to minimize the taxes you'll need to pay. You'll also learn the importance (if you haven't learned this already) of keeping good tax records, making sure you have all the forms and paperwork you need, and making sure you comply with all tax codes and regulations.

The Downside of Winning

Whether you win the lottery, hit the jackpot in Las Vegas, or get a big bonus from your employer, you're going to have to pay taxes on your earnings. Paying taxes is a fact of life, and, as some savvy accountants say, "proof that you made some money."

If you're going to invest in the stock market, you need to realize that you'll be taxed on your earnings, just the same as if you'd won the lottery. And you should realize that those taxes could reduce those earnings significantly. Before you begin investing in the stock market, you should review the significant tax advantages associated with retirement funds, such as 401(k) plans or individual retirement accounts (IRAs). And as you've read previously, you should invest in any applicable retirement accounts before getting started in the stock market.

How Your Earnings Are Taxed

Basically, your stock market investment earnings will be taxed in one of two ways. Taxes will be at the same amount as your regular income tax rate, or at a lower rate for gains on investments you've held for more than a year. Having read that, it probably sounds obvious that the best thing to do is to hang on to your investments so you end up paying less in taxes. And in many cases, that's true.

SHARE THIS

At the time this book was written, income tax rates were set at 10, 15, 25, 28, 33, and 35 percent. Starting incomes for each of those categories for a single taxpayer were $7,825; $31,850; $77,100; $160,850; and $349,700. For those married and filing jointly, the starting incomes for each tax bracket were $15,650; $63,700; $128,500; $195,850; and $349,700 (same as a single earner).

The nature of the stock market, however, necessitates that you remain attentive, nimble, and willing to take action when necessary. Certainly taxes are one factor that affects your investment. Remember, though, at any given time there could be other factors that crop up and affect the stock you hold. And sometimes, for a variety of reasons, it could make more sense to get rid of the stock while you can, even if the tax consequences are severe.

Let's review how your stock market earnings, or capital gains, are taxed.

Capital Gains Taxes

Capital gains taxes are incurred not only on money realized in the stock market, but from the sale of bonds, real estate, precious metals, and so forth. Not every country imposes taxes on capital gains, and for those that do, the rate varies dramatically.

Just as a sampling, Canada imposes capital gains taxes at an individual's regular tax rate on only 50 percent of realized capital gains, with no need to pay on the other half of the earnings. France levies a flat 30.1 percent tax on capital gains; Ireland has a flat 25 percent capital gains tax; Jamaica imposes no tax on capital gains; South Africa's capital gains tax can be as high as 50 percent; Sweden taxes capital gains at 30 percent; and Switzerland does not tax them at all.

In the United States, capital gains are classified as either long-term gains or short-term gains, depending on how long you've owned a stock. If you hold an investment for less a year, the gain (or loss) from that investment is considered short term. If you hold an investment for more than a year, it's considered a long-term investment, and your gain (or loss) is considered a long-term gain.

It's important to understand that only *realized capital gains* are taxed, and only *realized capital losses* can be deducted or netted against gains. If you just hold the stock instead of selling it at a profit or a loss, there are no capital gains or losses. The gains and losses shown on a statement are known as unrealized gains or losses. The tax consequences aren't reported on your tax return until the stock is actually sold.

> **DEFINITION**
>
> **Realized capital gains** are profits to an investor realized through the sale of stock that has increased in value. **Realized capital losses** are losses incurred through the sale of stock that has decreased in value. Only realized gains are taxed, and only realized losses can be deducted or netted against gains.

Short-Term Capital Gains

If you end up with a short-term capital gain, meaning that you sold an investment for more than you bought it for a year or less after the stock was bought, it is taxed at the same rate as ordinary income—that is, the same rate as your regular income tax rate.

If you're in the 25 percent tax bracket, for instance, a full quarter of those short-term gains will go to the government. Instead of realizing a $1,000 gain, you'll have to settle for $750. If you're taxed at the 35 percent rate you'll have to settle for just $650 of your grand. Because holding a stock short term rather than long term can significantly affect your taxes, be sure to keep careful records regarding when you buy stock, and how much you pay for it.

Long-Term Capital Gains

Long-term capital gains are a bit more interesting, and a lot easier to take than short term. Investors who are taxed at the lowest rate of 15 percent see their capital gains taxes drop to 10 percent, provided they've held the investment for longer than a year. If you're in the 25 percent or higher tax bracket, your long-term capital gains are taxed at 15 percent.

A consideration to understand regarding the tax on long-term capital gains is that, at least currently, they can't be higher than what you would pay on ordinary income. If you are in the 25 percent tax bracket, for instance, but you realize capital gains that boost your earnings into the 28 percent bracket, the gain is still taxed at your normal tax rate of 25 percent.

The taxes you don't end up paying on long-term gains add up, making it desirable to hang on to your investments for longer than a year.

Income Tax on Dividends

Dividends, like any form of income, are nice to get, but you'll be taxed on them. Most dividends are considered income and taxed at an investor's regular income tax rate. You can assume that any dividends you receive are considered ordinary or taxable dividends, unless the corporation distributing them tells you differently.

Some dividends, known as qualified dividends, are not taxed as ordinary income, but at a rate that's typically not higher than 15 percent, your capital gains tax rate. Qualified dividends, which were established as part of the Bush administration's tax cuts, include most dividends earned through mutual funds. Requirements concerning the length of time stock has been held also factor into whether dividends qualify as qualified dividends. The idea behind qualified dividends was to prevent the double taxation of corporate earnings. Corporations would pay tax on their profits, and then distribute dividends to shareholders, who would again pay income tax on the dividends at their income tax rates.

Dividends must meet three criteria in order to be considered qualified dividends:

- They must have been paid out by an American company or a company that meets certain qualifications set by the IRS.

- They cannot be listed with the IRS as dividends that do not qualify.

- They have met the required dividend holding period.

President Obama signed a two-year extension of the Bush tax cuts at the end of 2010, so the reduced rate on dividends will remain in place at least until 2012.

Don't Pay More Than You Have To

Everyone who is successful in the stock market will have to pony up taxes to the Internal Revenue Service (IRS)—there's just no getting around it. The trick is to understand how to hang on to as much of your gains as possible.

Some investors get so hung up on taxes that they lose sight of their investments. While taxes should be a factor in your decisions concerning your investments, you should never make decisions based solely on tax considerations. Other considerations, such as brokerage fees and transaction costs, also should be kept in mind when deciding whether to buy or sell stock. Keep careful records, and when considering a sale or purchase, assess all of the factors that will affect it before making a decision.

Netting Capital Gains Against Losses

If you've realized a capital gain, give yourself a little pat on the back. The gain indicates that you did your homework and selected a sound stock that resulted in a win for you. Having said that, let's have a look at how you can minimize the tax you'll need to pay on that gain.

If, while realizing capital gains on one stock, you've realized capital losses on another, don't despair. For one thing, you usually can deduct capital losses on your tax return, up to a maximum of $3,000 per year, lowering your yearly income, and the tax you'll pay on it. Another good thing about capital losses is that they can be netted against capital gains, thereby lowering the amount of tax you pay on your earnings.

Let's say you realized a $5,000 gain on a stock you sold. Once you're done celebrating, you start thinking about the tax you'll need to pay on it. You remember, however, the $2,500 hit you took on a stock you sold earlier in the year, and wonder if you can somehow use the loss to offset your earnings. The answer is yes. The loss will reduce your capital gains earnings to $2,500, and that's the amount you'll pay taxes on. This pertains to long-term and short-term losses and gains. A long-term loss can be netted against a short-term gain, and vice versa. Always check to see if losses in your portfolio can be netted against gains, and take advantage of the tax benefits you'll get from doing so.

Holding On to Delay a Tax Payment

Another way to minimize the taxes you'll pay is to pay attention to short-term and long-term investments, making sure to hold on to an investment for more than a year before you sell it. If you sell a stock before you've held it for a year, sell it after the end of the calendar year so you can delay the realization of the gain until your taxes are due on April 15—more than a year later.

CRASH!

If you decide to put off selling a stock you want to get rid of in order to delay the tax consequences, remember that you run the risk of the value of the stock declining before you get around to making the sale. Nobody ever said the stock market is without risks!

Holding on to a stock for an extended period of time is generally a favorable investment strategy, as well as useful for tax considerations. Unless there is a compelling reason to unload a stock quickly, check to see how long you've held it. If it hasn't been a year, and the sale will result in a short-term gain, consider holding on to it until the gain will be long term and taxed at a lower rate.

Keeping It All Legal

If you're like most investors and taxpayers, you have a healthy respect for the IRS and a strong desire to not attract the attention of its agents. If you hire an accountant or tax preparer to do your income tax, the burden of the preparation is not on you, except to provide all the necessary information and documentation, and to make sure that the information on the form appears to be correct. Remember that it's always important to verify all information. If you notice something that doesn't look right, be sure to ask about it. Remember that someone else's mistake could become your problem.

If you, like an increasing number of people each year, prepare your own tax form, you're likely to feel some significant pressure to get everything correct. Using a good tax software program like Intuit's Turbo Tax or Block Financial's Kiplinger Tax Cut will provide a lot of useful information and guide you through the preparation of your return.

SHARE THIS

About 1.5 percent of all taxpayers who submit returns get audited by the IRS each year. Most of the returns that result in audits contain deductions that are too high in relation to income, blatant errors, claims that require proof, or other red flags. Generally, the higher a person's income, the more likely he or she will be audited.

Gathering all the information and materials you need before starting on your tax return will save you time and keep you focused on the task. You'll need to get some information from your broker to give to your tax preparer or use as you prepare your taxes.

Forms and Schedules You'll Need to Have

Before you can prepare, or have someone else prepare, your individual income tax return, also known as Form 1040, you'll need some information.

If you've sold stock you'll need a Form 1099-B, which reports the date of every sale of stock, proceeds, the number of shares traded, and other information. Your broker should provide you with the 1099-B form, and will submit one to the IRS as well. You'll need the information from the 1099-B form in order to complete a Schedule D, which will be attached to your return.

Be sure that the information on the 1099-B matches that on the capital gains and losses section of your individual income tax return, especially the total, or proceeds, or you could be inviting a tax audit. If you want, you can read a lot more about the 1099-B form (and lots of other forms) on the IRS's website at www.irs.gov/instructions/i1099b/ar02.html.

If you've received dividend income, you should get 1099-DIV forms from each company that paid the dividends. You'll need to add up all the dividend amounts received from these forms and then report your dividend earnings on your individual income tax return. If you've received more than $1,500 in dividend income, you'll need to detail your earnings on Schedule B and attach it to your tax return.

A form 1099-INT reports any interest income you might have received during the year. Information from this form also must be included on your tax return. You may also receive bank statements containing investment information, and some brokerage firms provide tax-related information to clients as well.

Staying on the Up and Up

According to the IRS, a high percentage of completed tax forms contain mistakes. This isn't referring to intentional misinformation, just good old-fashioned mistakes. Regardless of whether you prepare your own tax returns or have someone else do them for you, be sure to look them over carefully before submitting them.

> **CRASH!**
>
> A good way to get the IRS upset is to sell a stock at a loss, claim a loss on your tax return, and then buy the same stock back a few days later. To get around this, the IRS has a rule called the wash-sale rule, which says you can't claim a loss on a stock if you buy it back within 30 days. If you attempt to do so, you could be looking at a penalty.

It's a good idea to complete the forms and then let them sit for a day or two before going back and giving them a careful check. And be sure to give yourself enough time to complete the forms without having to rush at the last minute, increasing the likelihood of mistakes. Making sure that you have all the necessary information, staying organized, and leaving enough time will ensure that you remain on the up and up with the IRS and save yourself some potential problems.

Finding Tax Breaks Wherever You Can

While it's important to remain in strict compliance with IRS regulations, it's also important to take advantage of the tax breaks that are available to you. Some expenses related to your investments can be deducted from your income taxes. You'll need to itemize the expenses on Schedule A and attach it to your 1040.

The IRS Publication 550, Investment Income and Expenses, provides a lot of information about expenses that can be deducted, what's considered taxable income, and so forth. You can access it on the IRS website at www.irs.gov/publications/p550/indes.html. Let's take a look at some deductions to which you may be entitled.

Deductions

Nobody wants to pay more taxes than are necessary, and being aware of deductions to which you may be entitled can help keep your tax bill to a minimum. Consider the following possible deductions:

- **Brokerage transaction fees.** These fees become a part of the cost and sale of a stock. You don't have to keep track of each brokerage commission, because the fee is netted out at the brokerage house. It is important, however, to understand the fees. Brokerage fees increase the cost of the shares purchased. They also lower your profit or increase your loss when the shares are sold. This is especially significant if you use a full-service broker, as the fees can be quite extensive. Also, if you would incur any legal fees associated with stockholder issues, those also are deductible.

- **Rent on a safe deposit box or a home safe.** If you rent a safe deposit box or buy a safe in which to hold your stock certificates, you can deduct those expenses.

- **Computer.** If more than 50 percent of the use of a computer is attributed to managing investments, you can depreciate some of its value in the form of a deduction.

- **Travel.** You can deduct travel costs for trips to your financial advisor to discuss your stock investments.

- **Advisory services and publications.** If you subscribe to investment advisory services or buy an investment newsletter or *Bloomburg Business Week*, it's deductible. Keep your receipts!

- **Margin interest.** An important deduction to remember is margin interest, which you incur when you borrow money against your stock. If a stock is listed on an exchange and in a brokerage account, you can borrow up to 50 percent of its value. That money is called a *margin loan*. The interest rate on margin loans usually is less than it would be on other types of loans. That's because if you don't pay back the loan, the lender has collateral—your stock. If you incur interest on a margin loan, you deduct it from your income tax up to the amount of your annual portfolio income including dividends, interest received, and capital gains.

DEFINITION

A **margin loan** is a loan from a broker to a client. The loan, which is secured with stock owned by the client, can be used for any purpose.

- **Donated stock.** Another type of deduction can be taken if you donate stock to charity. This can be advantageous when you donate stock that has increased in value, because you get to deduct the value of the stock at the time it's donated, not the value of when you purchased it. If you want to send a year-end donation to your church, and you also want to sell your shares of IBM, gift the shares to the church. The full value of the stock is deductible, and you have gifted away the capital gains.

Remember, though, that a charity has to be approved by the IRS before you can claim a deduction if you donate stock. And the Obama administration's proposed budget for 2012 limits the value of deductions for charitable gifts for some people, so be sure to do your homework if you're thinking about donating some of your stock to charity. More information about these deductions and which charities are IRS approved can be found on IRS Publication 526, Charitable Contributions. You can find it online at www.irs.gov/publications/p526/ar01.html.

Tax-Friendly Investment Vehicles

While this book is about stock market investing, it would remiss not to remind you of the advantages of tax-sheltered retirement funds, such as 401(k)s and IRAs. With these funds, you don't have to worry about tax factors because your investments aren't taxed until you make withdrawals from the accounts. These are called tax-deferred investments, and it means that your money grows and you're not taxed on your earnings until you take them out of the fund.

There are several types of IRAs in which you can deposit up to $5,000 a year, and you can stash up to $15,500 in a 401(k). These types of investments can be extremely beneficial from a tax viewpoint and are worth investigating with a financial advisor or tax preparer.

The Least You Need to Know

- Stock market earnings are taxed as capital gains, which can be either short term or long term.
- Short-term gains are taxed at a higher rate than long-term gains.
- Dividend payments are considered taxable income.
- There are strategies you can employ to minimize the amount of taxes you'll need to pay on earnings.
- The tax world is fraught with legal regulations you'll need to be mindful of in order to stay on the right side of the IRS.
- Learning about deductions can help you decrease your tax bill.

Considering an Investment Club

In This Chapter

- How investment clubs work
- Finding a club that fits
- Starting up your own club
- Understanding the legal considerations
- Education is key
- Looking into online clubs

Interest in investment clubs has dwindled from its peak level during the 1990s, but there still are about 13,000 clubs affiliated with the National Association of Investors Corporation (NAIC), and many thousand independent clubs that meet faithfully to learn, share ideas, and of course, invest.

In this chapter, we'll discuss the purpose of investment clubs, how they're normally set up and how they operate, and what's involved in getting one started. Of course if you decide you want to start a club, you'll need a lot more information than it's possible to provide in this chapter. Once you've learned a little bit about them, you might be motivated enough to get one started in your community—either physical or online.

Investment Club Basics

Basically, members of investment clubs pool monetary resources to purchase stock, bonds, or other assets. Some groups buy only mutual funds or exchange traded funds (ETFs), while others only invest in individual stocks. Some clubs call themselves stock clubs or bond clubs, depending on their choice of investment.

The idea behind an investment club is to maximize investments by having each club member contribute a small amount of money on a regular basis, then to make sound, informed investments that should result in good returns. That amount contributed varies from club to club and is the decision of club members—there are no regulations that apply to independent investment clubs.

The money is kept in a joint savings account (never a personal account of one of the members) or other safe investment, where it can be accessed by authorized club officers as needed. When club members, who often but not always are friends or co-workers, have agreed on an investment they want to buy, the money is used to make the purchase.

What They Do

Investment clubs normally meet once a month to discuss various investment possibilities and debate the pros and cons of each one. Some clubs meet once a week, but unless all members are extremely dedicated to the concept, it's usually difficult to get people together that often on an ongoing basis.

Usually club members take turns researching companies in which the club is interested in investing, either individually or in groups. The designated researchers then report back to other members, who collectively debate the pros and cons of the particular investment, consider whether or not to invest, and decide by voting. Meetings should provide a forum for all members to express their opinions and share knowledge regarding a proposed investment. Establish ground rules (how long each member has to speak, no interruptions while someone is speaking, the meeting will start on time, and so on) and make sure these rules are understood by all members.

The best clubs focus on education, as well as the actual investing. They often will invite a member of the financial community to speak about investments during a meeting, or designate one member to review a book dealing with investing and finances. Members sometimes will research one specific aspect of investing, such as minimizing capital gains taxes, and report back to the group on his or her findings.

Investment clubs aren't much different from individual investors in that, over time, their investments will become more sophisticated and smarter, due to an increase in individual and collective knowledge.

How They Started

The first investment club in the United States is thought to have been started just before the turn of the twentieth century in Texas, and they've been a part of the financial stage ever since. Many thousands of clubs have come and gone since then, becoming increasingly sophisticated as they diversified, moved online, and took advantage of other technological advances. Basically, most clubs started for the purpose of boosting their buying power while keeping costs relatively low for each member. They're a great example of the power of investing and what teamwork can achieve.

The Mutual Investment Club of Detroit, founded in 1940 by a group of young men interested in investing but without the financial resources to do so individually, is considered a model investment club. Organized by Frederick C. Russell, who like many people at that time was out of work, the club was formed as a means of raising money with which to open a small business.

Members included a broker and several of Russell's fraternity brothers. When some of the young men went off to serve in World War II, the others kept the club afloat, and by the time the war ended there were a dozen members. The club persevered through both good and bad economic times, holding steady to its three core principles:

- Investing every month

- Reinvesting all dividends

- Buying the stock of growth companies

It was one of four clubs to form the NAIC in 1951, an organization that has become the definitive authority regarding investment clubs. The founding of the NAIC caused increased recognition of and interest in investment clubs, and Americans jumped on board.

SHARE THIS

One of the earliest documented investment clubs was an art fund established in 1904 in Paris. The group for 10 years invested in art, collecting works of greats like Picasso and Matisse, which they hung in their homes. Just before the First World War, they sold the collection, with each member receiving four times his or her investment.

By the 1990s investment clubs had become the next big thing, especially toward the end of the decade when every investor was sure he or she could get rich quick by buying some technology stock. Investment clubs were founded as quickly as dot-coms were going public, many of them with a focus on technology stock. Club membership grew by leaps and bounds during that heady, optimistic investment fest.

Many clubs, however, forgot one of the most basic rules of investing as they became overly enamored of dot-coms: diversification. And then came the burst of the dot-com bubble in 2000, and the beginning of a new era for investment clubs. Many clubs have disbanded since then, while others have soldiered on, wiser, although perhaps poorer. Clubs that have stuck around tended to look for safer, more reliable investments, and hopefully have learned the hard lesson that buying too many stocks in one industry can teach.

Why They Can Work

You read a little while ago that members of investment clubs contribute money to be invested on a regular basis. And clubs that take a lesson from the Mutual Investment Club of Detroit and understand the basic lessons of the stock market understand the power of hanging tough, making sure a portfolio is well diversified, reinvesting dividends, and choosing companies that will succeed and result in returns. Those are the primary factors that result in success for investment clubs, and if members agree to and do adhere to those rules and operate in a disciplined, structured manner, they should succeed.

Investing with others isn't so different than investing on your own, except there needs to be consensus. Clubs work when members are diligent about researching potential companies in which to invest, and when they invest regularly.

The beauty of regular investing is that your investment within the club grows as the value of the total club portfolio increases. Your share of the portfolio depends on how many members are in the club. If you are one of 20 members and everyone contributes equally, you own 5 percent of the portfolio. If 20 people invest $1,000 each, and that $20,000 grows to $40,000, your share has doubled and is now worth $2,000.

Investments work when members communicate well with one another, can agree to disagree, and understand that the most important act of the club is regular investment in solid companies.

Finding a Club to Join

If you're thinking about joining an investment club, there are some factors you should consider before committing. Remember that belonging to a club requires a regular financial contribution. And while most clubs don't require a huge amount of money, if you're already scraping the bottom of the money barrel, it could be tough to come up with extra each month.

Just as deciding whether investing in the stock is right for you as an individual, you'll need to determine whether it makes sense to invest as a club member. Take a few minutes to review Chapter 3. If you're carrying credit card or other high-interest debt, are spending more than you're earning, don't have an emergency fund, or are not contributing to a 401(k) or other type of retirement fund, you probably should rethink investing in the stock market in general. If you're in good shape in all of those areas, however, here's what to look for when considering investment club membership.

Is It the Right Fit?

As with any group or organization, some investment clubs will provide a better fit for you than others. You'll read more about matching up investment philosophies and experience levels a little later in the chapter, but a basic consideration before joining a club is your comfort level. Are you comfortable with the other club members?

Understand that some clubs are laid back and like to have a good time as they go about the business of investing, while others are serious and all business all the time. Some groups are more insistent on consistent attendance than others. If your job includes frequent travel, a club with mandatory attendance won't be for you. Some clubs have more and stricter rules than others regarding research and reporting, contributions, and other matters. You need to identify the type of club in which you think you'd be most comfortable and seek it out.

Remember, too, that some investors fare much better on their own than they would in an investment club, where compromise sometimes is necessary and they don't get to call all the shots themselves. Be honest about your temperament and how well you work with others before committing to joining an investment club.

What's the Contribution?

Another consideration, of course, is the amount of the contribution the club requires, both initially and on a monthly basis. Clubs that wish to begin investing immediately sometimes require a hefty initial investment from each member in order to get started. Others require just a small contribution to cover startup costs and then wait until they've collected enough monthly dues to start buying stock.

How much each member of your club contributes is entirely up to you and the other members; there are no rules regarding the amount to be invested. The size of the contribution normally varies depending on the number of members in the club. It's often necessary for members of a large club to contribute less than those of a smaller club. The amount contributed each month isn't set in stone. Many clubs increase their contributions as they become more experienced. The amount that members will contribute should be determined as the club is being formed, and members should vote on whether or not to change the amount as the club progresses.

It's important that each member of an investment club contribute each month, regardless of whether or not he or she attends the monthly meeting. Without regular contributions from each member, the percentage of ownership becomes uneven and can result in problems. There are methods of dealing with uneven contributions within a club, but it's easiest if everyone contributes the same amount each month.

TAKING STOCK

Be sure to get all the information you need about club contributions, and consider carefully if the fees are doable before agreeing to join. Ask if there will be future funding requirements in addition to the regular monthly contributions, and if so, find out what they are and how much. An investment club should be a financially rewarding experience, not a draining one.

Startup costs can include software programs, legal fees, office supplies, membership in the NAIC, and other expenses. Remember that the more members the club has, the greater the ability to share startup costs. Seven or eight members would have to each pony up considerably more than those in a club with 15 or 20 members.

Locating a Club

The most obvious place to start looking for an investment club is to ask people you know. Do you hear friends or family members talking about any clubs? Do you know anyone who already belongs to a club? If so, you can get more information and find out if the club is accepting additional members.

The Internet, of course, is a great place to look for almost anything, including investment clubs. Check out Facebook, LinkedIn, and other social networking sites, and use a search engine to see if there are clubs that have websites or are listed on other sites.

What to Consider Before You Join

Once you've located a club that you feel might be a good fit for you, be sure to do your homework before agreeing to become a member. Just as you'd want to check out a class before signing up for it, take some time to look into and evaluate your prospective investment club. Be sure to spend some time getting to know the members and club policies before making a decision. Here are some suggestions for what to look for in a club and what to keep in mind before you join:

- Attend a regular club meeting (some experts recommend you attend as many as three) to get a feel for its dynamics. Do you enjoy the company of the other members? Do you feel comfortable?

- Review the club's bylaws and partnership agreements.

- Pay attention to the club's process for researching and selecting stocks.

- Get a feel for the club's investing approach. Are members aggressive investors, conservative investors, or somewhere in between?

- Inquire about the club's investing track record. How do its returns stack up against the Standard & Poor's (S&P) 500 or another major index?

- Ask questions concerning the long-term goals of the club.

- Make sure you understand the fee structure and what you'll be expected to contribute up front. Some clubs require members upon joining to contribute the total of what each other member has invested up to that point.

- Find out what your club responsibilities will be. Clubs typically divide up duties such as distributing educational materials or e-mailing meeting reminders.

- Learn the terms (and possible penalties) of leaving the club.

Starting Your Own Club

Just as Frederick C. Russell did in Detroit in 1940, you can start your own investment club. This will take some time and organizational skills, so think carefully before committing to starting a club. Forming an investment club is not rocket science, but if you're already working full time and have family demands and other obligations, you may not be able to put in the necessary time.

TAKING STOCK

The ability to network will be important if you decide to start up an investment club. Use personal and online resources to locate others who might be interested in joining a club. Once you find a potential member, ask if she knows of any other potential members. Look to family, organizations of which you're a member, your workplace, and other logical groups of people. The NAIC website (www.betterinvesting.org) provides resources for connecting people interested in joining an investment club.

There are all sorts of investment clubs. Some are made up of family members, groups of friends, co-workers, and special interest investors. The type of club you want to have is up to you, assuming you don't have problems locating members.

One of the first steps is to determine how many members you'll include. Club memberships range from 3 to 50—and there are advantages and disadvantages to all sizes. Keep the following points in mind when deciding how many members makes sense for your club:

- It could be difficult for just a few members to come up with a sizeable enough monthly contribution for you to invest on a regular basis.

- Having more members allows you to spread out the work of keeping the club up and running, and allows for the club to research a greater number of companies for possible investment.

- Too many members can be difficult to keep track of and unwieldy to manage.

- Life is busy for most people. Remember that the more members you have, the greater number of schedules you'll have to work around.

- Larger groups tend to be livelier and more exciting than small groups.

- Larger groups have more potential for conflict but also for sharing ideas and collaboration.

Remember, there are practical aspects of starting an investment club. You'll need to consider things like naming the club, finding a place for the club to meet, choosing a day or evening of the week and a time to meet, what rules you'll ask club members to adhere to, and how long your meetings will last, to name a few.

Starting any kind of club (if you're an adult, anyway) requires careful planning and some common sense. Consider how much time you have to spend organizing a club, your prospects for finding members, and practical matters such as a meeting location. Once you've nailed down the basics, you can start thinking about more investment-specific topics you'll need to consider.

Evaluating Investment Philosophy and Setting Goals

The last thing you want within an investment club is members with wildly different investment philosophies. In Chapter 5, we discussed the different levels of risk investors are willing to assume, and other aspects of investment philosophy. It's really important, within an investment group, for members to have similar expectations regarding risk tolerance and the seriousness with which they approach the club.

For that reason, you'll need to get a good idea of risk tolerance of prospective members before they join the club. Ask them to take a risk tolerance assessment, such as the ones from Kiplinger or Money Central that were mentioned in Chapter 5. It's not that one level of risk tolerance is necessarily better or worse than others, but it's not a good idea to mix extremely conservative investors with big risk takers.

If some members want to be in the club primarily because it gives them a night out with friends, and others are there strictly to learn about investing, you're looking at an investment philosophy gap. Some gentle screening of potential members can go a long way in avoiding problems once the club is underway. Before agreeing to allow someone to join the club, determine the following information about the prospective member:

- Investment approach (conservative, aggressive, or moderate)
- Current knowledge of investing and finances
- Willingness to assist with club duties
- Ability to attend regular meetings
- Ability to meet the club's financial requirements
- Whether his or her personality is a good fit with other club members

It's likely that an investment club would have investors of different ages who would be investing with different goals in mind. As a club, however, it's important to establish collective goals, as the Mutual Investment Club of Detroit did.

The following are some goals worth considering for your club:

- Invest every month
- Reinvest dividends
- Buy diverse stock
- Keep all members involved
- Research all stock
- Identify group risk tolerance and invest accordingly
- Look for growth company
- Have a good time as a group
- Increase your investing knowledge
- Improve your investing skills
- Beat the S&P 500 index average annual gain

Goals should be known to all members, posted on the club's website, and reviewed occasionally. You also might consider coming up with a mission statement that would clearly state your goals and serve as a reminder to members why the club exists.

What's the Experience Level?

The experience level of club members is another factor to consider when establishing an investment club. It's a good thing, actually, to have some members with more experience than others so they can pass along their knowledge. You'll just need to watch that less-experienced members don't feel intimidated and are not looked down upon by their more savvy peers.

> **CRASH!**
>
> Beware of the concept of groupthink, a word coined by Yale research psychologist Irving Janis. Groupthink, purported Janis, is the idea that smart, informed people, when grouped together, sometimes make terribly bad decisions. This occurs, Janis said, when the need for group members to concur on a decision overrides the need for rational, thoughtful decisions. When groupthink occurs within an investment club, nobody wins.

You'll need to assess potential members regarding investment experience, just as you'll assess risk tolerance. More experienced investors should assume leadership roles in the club, with the understanding that those who are less experienced will eventually rise to the point where they can step in.

Legal Considerations

Don't be tempted to think you can start an investment club without obtaining legal advice. It's very important that you follow the necessary legal guidelines as your club gets up and running, as investment clubs must comply with regulations of the U.S. Treasury Department. At the very least, you should become a member of the NAIC and take advantage of its startup materials and advice you can access from its website.

Most investment clubs are structured as *partnerships*, but some form as *corporations*. These are two types of legal entities, each subject to different regulations. A partnership is nothing more than a group of people who get together for a common purpose. They agree as to how they'll conduct the club, and how the profits, risks, liabilities, and losses will be distributed among them.

> **DEFINITION**
>
> A **partnership** is a legal agreement between two or more people who get together to form a business or club. A **corporation** is a legal entity that is separate from the people who are its members.

Partnerships are fairly straightforward, but you need to be sure you have a sound operating agreement. You'll need to register a partnership with the county or state in which the group will operate, and regulations will vary, depending on where you are. And once you're registered, find out how to keep your registration current. You'll need to renew it periodically.

The big advantage of a corporation is that legally, it's separate from its members. It limits the liability of each stockholder or member to the amount of his or her investment. If a corporation fails, or is found liable in a lawsuit, it's the corporation that's responsible, not the people who own it.

You'll also need to choose a place to keep members' contributions until you're ready to buy stock. This can be your local bank, a credit union, or an online account; just be sure that club members are in agreement and accounts are correctly established and maintained. Never mingle club money with that of a personal account, and make sure that money is handled properly at all times.

CRASH!

Do not under any circumstances be tempted to hold on to club funds until you're ready to purchase stock. The handling of money must be beyond possible reproach in order to keep a club running smoothly.

Obviously, if you're thinking of forming an investment club, you'll need a lot more legal information than what is provided here. Again, don't be tempted to take short-cuts in this area, as it could come back to haunt you later.

Organization Within the Club

An investment club should have officers who are willing and able to put in the time necessary to keep it running smoothly. Plan to elect new officers each year to avoid burnout and give different people a chance to lead. If an officer is doing a great job and wants to stay on for another term, however, save yourself some aggravation and agree to that.

Most clubs will elect a president, vice president, secretary, and treasurer. They're all important, but the treasurer's job is crucial to the group. Ideally, he'll have investing experience and a good grasp of financial matters. The treasurer normally places orders with your club's broker to buy and sell stocks, and gathers members' monthly contributions. He also keeps track of all the club's financial records, is responsible for putting together a monthly statement of club receipts and disbursements, and keeps track of each member's investment.

If your club treasurer is a financial wizard (or a professional tax preparer), some clubs would have him prepare yearly tax information for each member. Because that entails a significant amount of work, however, most clubs hire an outside person.

SHARE THIS

The job of secretary within an investment club is very important because meeting minutes provide a history of the club's operations. Meeting minutes are important and should be well maintained and organized.

Large clubs sometimes assign certain members to serve on a nominating committee to identify people to fill the positions of officers and to contact those people to see if they're willing to serve. If so, the nominating committee would bring the names to other club members for a vote.

The club president conducts monthly meetings, organizes various committees, and maintains oversight of how the club is doing and what's going on.

The vice president takes over for the president in her absence, and sometimes takes responsibility for a certain aspect of club business.

The secretary is responsible for taking minutes of the meeting and distributing them to all members in a timely manner, and for handling all club correspondence.

Finding a Broker

Most beginning investment clubs choose to start out using the services of a broker (see Chapter 15). Remember that you'll need a broker if your club wants to invest in ETFs.

Basically, a broker buys and sells the securities within your investment club's accounts. An important distinction is that he can do this only when you tell him to. If your broker is making trades without your knowledge, find a new broker immediately. Some brokers, called full-service brokers, will advise your club on what to buy, but you'll pay more for that advice.

Some clubs, especially those that have been in place for a while and whose members possess a good deal of investing experience, feel that since members spend a considerable amount of time researching stock before they make a decision to buy, they don't need additional advice from a broker. For most clubs, however, having a broker makes sense.

The Education Piece of Investment Clubs

Along with investing in the stock market, a major goal of your club should be education for its members. The more you learn about the stock market and investing, the better qualified you will be to make investments. Clubs that are NAIC members have access to investment education webinars, conferences, and other educational opportunities. Some clubs invite members of the financial community to address members about a particular topic, such as mutual funds or economic cycles. In some clubs, members take turns reporting on a financial education topic.

Online Investment Clubs

Online investment clubs operate in much the same manner as traditional clubs, except that members interact electronically instead of face to face. This option doesn't work for every club, as many people enjoy getting out of the house and being in the company of others. In our busy society, however, online everything—from shopping to dating—has become increasingly popular.

Online clubs have the advantage of allowing people who work different schedules or don't live in the same geographical area to stay in touch with other members. Investors who belong to clubs whose members are spread out geographically say the distance allows them a broad perspective regarding economic conditions and demographic trends. Operating online also permits greater flexibility and faster decision making. When a club member recommends the purchase or sale of a stock, other members can weigh in by e-mail or on a blog instead or waiting for the next meeting.

TAKING STOCK

Members of most traditional investment clubs stay in touch electronically between meetings, which makes the actual meetings run more smoothly and quickly.

A potential problem with online clubs is that requirements vary from state to state. It's important that all members understand the need to adhere to the rules of the state with which the club is registered. If you opt for an online club, be sure that membership agreements, club rules, and goals are clearly stated and understood by members. You also should pay special attention to computer security issues to avoid the possibility that a nonmember will gain access to online material or information that's meant only for members or club officers.

Resources Your Club Can Use

In addition to the NAIC, there are a variety of resources available to investment clubs and their members. You might want to check out *The Complete Idiot's Guide to Starting an Investment Club* (see Appendix B) as well as the following resources. By all means expand your search, however, as there are thousands more resources available in libraries, bookstores, and online:

- **United States Securities and Exchange Commission.** You'll need to check out the SEC site for information about regulations pertaining to investment clubs. www.sec.gov/investor/pubs/invclub.htm

- **World Federation of Investors Corporation.** This organization has chapters around the world to support investors in many countries. The NAIC is a member of this group. www.wfic.org

- **The Mining Company: Investment Clubs.** Provides links to resources for investment clubs. www.investmentclub.miningco.com

- **Bivio: Invest with Your Friends.** This website is a wealth of information presented in a fun, down-to-earth manner. www.bivio.com/index.html

The Least You Need to Know

- Clubs maximize their resources with regular investments, and also benefit from reinvestment of dividends.

- Member contributions are pooled and then invested in stocks that have been thoroughly researched.

- All members must have input regarding, and agree on, which stock to buy and sell.

- Clubs should establish clear goals and rules and must follow strict guidelines regarding the handling and placement of club money.

- Education should be a key component of any investment club, with each member responsible for contributing to the collective knowledge of the club.

Glossary

52-week high   The highest price the stock achieved during the past 52 weeks.

52-week low   The lowest price the stock achieved during the past 52 weeks.

active allocation   The strategy of selling off stock in a category of your portfolio that has become overweighted, and using the proceeds to buy stock in underweighted categories in order to achieve a balanced allocation mix.

active mutual funds   Mutual funds that are actively managed by fund managers who try to outperform average returns of overall markets or specific market segments or sectors.

adjustable-rate preferred stock   A type of security that pays dividends based on factors determined by the company that issued the stock. As the name implies, the dividend rate changes periodically.

all or none order   A trade order in which a client instructs a broker to fill the order completely. If there is not enough stock available to meet the specifications of the order, it is canceled at the end of the market day.

American Stock Exchange (AMEX)   The third largest American stock exchange, handling about 10 percent of all funds traded in the United States. It was acquired in 2008 by NYSE Euronext and was renamed the NYSE Amex Equities in 2009.

angel investor   An individual or group that seeks out promising startup businesses, guides them, and invests in them, betting on high returns as the company grows.

ask   The price a seller is willing to take to sell a stock.

ask size   The number of shares a seller is selling at a quoted ask price.

asset allocation   The process of assigning investment funds to different families of assets with the goal of achieving diversification.

average daily trading volume   The average number of shares traded within a day.

balance sheet   A financial report listing assets, liabilities, and owner's equity as of a certain date.

balanced fund   A fund that contains both stock and bond investments.

bear market   A period of time during which stock prices remain flat or fall and investors exhibit a widespread fear of stocks and the stock market.

bid   The price that a trader names to buy a stock.

bid size   The number of shares a buyer is willing to purchase at the quoted bid price.

bid/ask spread   The difference between the highest price a buyer is willing to pay for a stock and the lowest price at which a seller is willing to sell it.

blue chip stock   A high-quality stock involving a lower than average risk. Blue chip stock generally refers to that of companies with a long history of sustained earnings and dividend payments.

bond   A debt instrument. The issuer promises to pay the investor a specified amount of interest for a period of time and to repay the principal at maturity.

bond mutual fund   A mutual fund that invests in bonds. Bond funds are considered less risky than stock funds, and are usually set up to mature periodically.

bottom-up investing   An approach to investing that emphasizes the specific financials and business of a particular company rather than its industry or sector, or the overall economy. A bottom-up investor analyzes a stock, but pays little attention to market cycles or the state of the economy.

broad-base index   An index that represents the performance of the entire market rather than a segment of the market.

broker   A person who earns a commission or fee for acting as an agent in making contracts or sales.

broker trigger   Messages a broker sends out to alert clients to price targets, or to when something newsworthy is happening in the stock market or within a particular business or industry.

brokerage firm   A company that buys and sells stock on its clients' behalf.

bull market   A period of positive movement within the stock market, during which time prices increase and investors exhibit a widespread enthusiasm for stocks and the stock market.

business life cycle   The stages a business passes through during the time between founding and demise. The stages are establishment, growth and expansion, maturity, and decline.

business risk   Risk based on the manner in which a business is managed and run.

buying on margin   The practice of borrowing money from a broker and using it to buy additional stock.

callable preferred stock   Stock for which the company that issued it has the right to recall at its discretion.

capital gain   Profit realized on an investment.

capital loss   Loss that results from losing money on an investment.

capitalization-weighted index   An index in which the stocks of companies with the most market value figure more heavily than the stocks of companies with less market value. Also known as a market value weighted index.

cash account   An account in which your stock purchases are limited to the amount of cash you have deposited in it.

churning   The practice of actively trading stock within a brokerage account in order to increase brokerage commissions.

closed-end mutual fund   A mutual fund that contains a limited number of shares.

coincident indicator   An economic indicator that moves along with the economy, such as the gross domestic product.

commission   A fee charged by a brokerage firm for the service of buying or selling stock.

common stock   A type of security that entitles you to a share in the ownership of a company.

composite index   A grouping of several indexes or averages that is considered in a specific manner to provide a statistical measure of the performance of the market or a sector of the market over time.

compounding   A mathematical formula that involves adding interest earned on an investment to the principal and any previous interest.

conservative investor   An investor who wants to see his net worth increase without risking any of his principal.

conversion ratio   A ratio that states the number of shares of common stock to be exchanged for one share of preferred stock when preferred stock is converted.

convertible preferred stock   Stock which can be converted from preferred to common.

corporation   A legal entity that is separate from the people who make up its membership.

counter-cyclical stock   Stock that tends to perform well during economic downturns, and not as well during periods of expansion.

cumulative preferred stock   Stock that assures those holding it will receive company dividends before common stockholders when the dividends are considered to be in arrears.

cyclical market trend   A shorter-term cycle within a primary, secular trend.

cyclical sectors and industries   Those sectors and industries that perform well in good economic times but drop off in down times. Examples include manufacturing, transportation, and construction.

cyclical stock   Stock for which the price is affected by general economic conditions.

day order   A trade order to be executed during the current trading day, but not to be carried over to after hours or the next day.

day traders   Traders who buy and sell securities within a single day.

day's high   The highest price a stock achieved during a particular day.

day's low   The lowest price a stock achieved during a particular day.

defensive sectors and industries   Those sectors and industries that provide food, power, gas, water, and other essentials, causing them to not be heavily affected by overall economic conditions.

defensive stock   Stock that provides dividends and earnings regardless of economic conditions.

direct stock purchase plan (DSPP)   A plan under which investors can purchase stock directly from a company without the benefit of any sort of broker.

discount broker   A broker who buys and sells stock, but does not offer advice, conduct research, or provide other financial services.

diversification   The acquisition of a group of assets in which returns on the assets are not directly related over time. Proper investment diversification, requiring a sufficient number of different assets, is intended to minimize investment risks.

dividend reinvestment program (DRIP)   A program in which stock dividends are automatically reinvested and used to buy more stock.

dividends   Payments a company makes to stockholders.

dollar cost averaging   Investment of an equal amount of money at regular intervals, usually each month, resulting in the purchase of extra shares during market downturns, and fewer shares during upturns. The practice is based on the belief that a stock or the market will rise in price over the long term.

Dow Jones Industrial Average   The oldest stock market index, founded in 1896 by Charles Dow.

economic indicator   A piece of economic information used by investors to measure the overall strength of the economy and predict opportunities for successful investments based on economic trends.

emerging growth stock   Stock of a young company operating in an industry with very good growth prospects. This type of stock is associated with well above average investment risk.

emerging market   A country or region with an expanding economy that is experiencing growth and industrialization.

equity   The value attached to a company; determined by subtracting liabilities from assets.

established growth stock   Stock of an established, strong company operating in an industry with very good growth prospects. This stock carries less risk than emerging growth stock.

exchange traded fund (ETF)   An investment fund that contains a collection of assets, similar to a mutual fund, but trades on a stock exchange.

expense ratio   The cost to an investment company to operate a fund. It's calculated by dividing the cost of a fund's operating expenses by the average dollar value of its assets.

fill or kill order   A trade order that must be filled within a specified time period or the order is cancelled.

financial risk   Investment risk based on the possibility that an investment will lose value because the company loses money or goes bankrupt.

foreign exchange risk   The price volatility of an investment caused by the movements in the exchange rate of the investor's home currency and that of the currency in which the underlying investment is priced.

full-service broker   A broker or brokerage firm that places trade orders and provides services such as advice to clients, research, and financial consultations.

fundamental analysis   The process of researching a stock by studying the financial health of the company offering it.

global investing   Investing in stock of U.S. and foreign companies.

good-til-cancelled (GTC) order   A market order or stop order with an unspecified time frame. The order stands until it has either been executed or cancelled.

growth stock   Stock with earnings that are growing at a faster rate than that of the overall market.

hedge   A strategy investors use to reduce the risk on an existing investment position. A hedge usually involves investing in two stocks with negative correlations to offset the risks of unfavorable price movements.

high-risk investor   An investor who can tolerate losing one quarter of his or her investment portfolio within a year's time.

income investing   Investing in an income stock that has a relatively high dividend yield.

income statement   A financial report that lists revenues and subtracts expenses in order to determine net income.

income stock   Stock with a relatively high dividend yield, usually from a firm that realizes stable earnings and dividends and operates within a mature industry.

index   A group of securities that, together, are used to measure changes in the market.

index fund   A mutual fund that tracks the performance of a market index, such as the Dow Jones Industrial Average or the Standard & Poor's 500, by buying and holding all or some of the securities in the index.

industry index   An index that measures only one segment of the stock market, such as oil or technology stocks.

industry risk   Investment risk based on perils that are unique to a certain industry or sector, such as product recall in the food industry or crashes in the airline industry.

initial public offering (IPO)   A process by which a company sells its stocks to the public. Under the Securities Act of 1934–1935, the company is required to follow specific steps with regard to documentation and communication with prospective investors.

institutional investors   Large investors who invest in a company through an auction process prior to the company's initial public offering.

interest rate risk   Investment risk based on the possibility that the value of an investment will change due to a shift in interest rates.

interest sensitive stock   A stock that tends to move in the opposite direction of interest rates.

international investing   The process of buying stock of foreign companies that do not have corporate headquarters within the United States.

investing   A long-term process based on the study of fundamentals such as a company's earnings, sales, debt, and industry outlook.

investment risk   The possibility that your investment will decrease in value.

lagging indicator   An economic indicator that occurs after the economy has shifted, such as unemployment.

large cap company   A business with a market capitalization of between $10 billion and $50 billion.

leading indicator   An economic indicator that occurs before the economy changes, signaling the forthcoming change.

limit order   An order to buy or sell a stock at a specified price.

liquidity ratio   A set of ratios that indicate how easily and quickly a company can convert its assets to cash in order to pay off short-term debt obligations.

load fund   A mutual fund that pays sales commissions to a broker when bought or sold.

long-term investing   An investment that is held for longer than three years.

low-risk investor   *See* conservative investor.

macroeconomics   A broad-based view of the economy, based on past and current trends and shifts.

margin account   An account that allows an investor to borrow money from a brokerage with which to buy additional stock.

margin loan   A loan from a broker to a client, which is secured by the investment purchased.

market capitalization   The total market value of all of the outstanding shares of a company; used to determine the financial size of the company.

market cycle   A pattern of stock movement over time in a specific market environment.

market order   An order to buy or sell a stock at its current market price.

market report   A compilation of news affecting either a particular market or the general stock market.

market risk   Investment risk based on the tendency for stock to move with the market.

market share   The percentage of sales generated by one company within a particular industry during a particular time.

market timing   A strategy that attempts to predict the direction in which the market will move.

mega cap company   A business with a market capitalization of over $50 billion.

micro cap stock   Stock issued by companies with market capitalizations of less than $300 million, which tend to be new and unproven.

microeconomics   A narrow-based view of the economy that focuses on specific issues which affect a particular company and/or industry.

mid cap stock   Stock issued by companies with market capitalizations of between $1 billion and $10 billion.

moderate-risk investor   An investor who can tolerate the thought of losing 15 percent of his or her portfolio during a given year.

momentum buying   The practice of widespread buying or selling of a stock because charts are showing the markets moving upward and the perception exists that everyone else is buying the stock.

money market fund   Funds in which the value of the original investment doesn't change.

moving average   A running tally of the average stock price of a specified time period to measure stock price trends.

mutual fund   A managed collection of stocks, bonds, and other assets purchased with money from many investors.

NASDAQ   A computerized market formerly known as the National Association of Securities Dealers Automated Quotation System. Although not technically a stock exchange, the NASDAQ serves as one because many companies are traded on it.

net worth   The total of financial assets minus financial liabilities.

New York Stock Exchange (NYSE)   The largest stock exchange in the world, founded in 1792. More than 3,600 companies are listed on the exchange.

niche company   A company that dominates one market segment of a larger industry, in this case, such as a spice company within the larger food and beverage industry.

no-load fund   Mutual funds sold without sales charges.

odd lot   Group of less than 100 shares of stock.

online broker   A brokerage firm that operates solely on the Internet, with no personal service available to clients.

open-end mutual fund   Mutual funds that have no size limit and no limit to the number of shares they can hold.

operating ratio   A ratio that indicates how well a company is doing, based on factors such as amount of inventory the company has, the amount of accounts receivable it takes to support a specified portion of the business, or other factors related to operations.

over the counter bulletin board (OTCBB)   An electronic quotation system providing information about over the counter stocks.

over the counter (OTC) market   A market on which the stock of companies not listed on a stock market is traded.

panic selling   The widespread selling of a particular stock, based on rumor and fear. Most stock market crashes are caused by panic selling.

participating preferred stock   Preferred stock that has a fixed dividend rate and pays shareholders part of the earnings that are distributed to investors who hold common stock.

partnership   A legal agreement between two or more people who get together to form a business or club.

passive allocation   The strategy of buying stock in underweighted categories of your portfolio in order to bring the allocation mix back into balance.

penny stock   A stock that trades at a relatively low price, usually outside of the major stock exchanges. Some investors consider penny stocks to be any that trade for less than $5 a share.

performance-based index   An index that takes into account not only the performance of stocks, but the dividends and other cash paid by companies to shareholders.

personal finances   Everything financial as it applies to an individual or family.

personal risk   Investment risk based on how a decrease in your investment would affect you and your life.

political risk   Investment risk based on the possibility of political movement within an international market that results in the market being inhospitable to foreign investors.

portfolio   A group of investments assembled to meet an investment goal.

portfolio manager   An individual or team of researchers who are responsible for investing money pooled for the purchase of mutual funds.

preferred stock   A special type of security that provides some preferential treatment to owners, but usually doesn't include voting rights.

previous close   The price at which a stock closed on the previous day of trading.

price-to-book (P/B) ratio   A ratio used to compare the stock market's value to its book value, calculated by dividing the closing price of stock by the book value per share.

price-to-earnings (P/E) ratio   The current price of the stock divided by the earnings per share, usually used by an investor to value a company's stock.

price-to-sales (P/S) ratio   A company's current stock price divided by its sales for the last 12 months, mainly used to compare the success of similar companies.

price-weighted index   An index that considers each stock in proportion to its price per share.

private placement   The sale of a relatively small amount of stock to selected investors as a means of raising capital.

profitability ratio   A type of ratio that measures how profitable a company is.

prospectus   A legal document that contains details about a stock or mutual fund being offered for sale.

proxy   A document that allows shareholders to participate in voting without being present at an annual meeting.

purchasing power risk   Investment risk based on the possibility that inflation could erode the real value, as opposed to the nominal value, of your investment.

rating service   A company that rates the strength of stock and other securities. Standard & Poor's and Moody's are examples of rating services.

ratios   Tools used when analyzing a company's financial situation.

realized capital gains   Profit to an investor realized through the sale of stock that has increased in value.

realized capital losses   Losses incurred through the sale of stock that has decreased in value.

relative strength indicators (RSI)   Indicators that measure a stock's performance relative to the overall market indexes or averages to determine if a stock has outperformed or underperformed the market.

reverse stock split   The act of a company reducing the number of total shares of stock in order to boost the price of each share.

risk tolerance   The level of risk an investor is willing to take as it applies to her investment portfolio.

round lot   Shares of stock sold in groups of 100.

secondary market   A market in which investors buy stock or other assets from other investors, usually large institutional investors, instead of from issuing companies.

securities   Investments that represent evidence of debt, ownership of a business, or the legal right to acquire or sell an ownership interest in a business.

Securities Act of 1933   A federal law enacted in 1933, following the Great Depression. It was intended to protect investors from financial irregularities that contributed to the collapse of the stock market which resulted in the Depression.

Securities and Exchange Commission (SEC)   A government commission charged with regulating the securities market in order to protect investors.

selling short   *See* shorting.

short-term investing   An investment in the stock market that is held for less than three years.

shorting   The act of an investor selling a stock in anticipation that he'll be able to sell it, then buy it back at a lower price and make a profit.

small cap stock   Stock of a company with a market capitalization of between $300 million and $1 billion.

socially responsible investing   The practice of investing in companies and industries that represent the social and political preferences of the investor.

solvency ratio   A ratio that helps determine the long-term health of a company through looking at its financial obligations and how it might generate assets in the future.

speculation   The act of purchasing stock or another investment with the sole expectation that its value will increase and it can be sold for more than the purchase price.

Standard & Poor's (S&P) 500   An index regarded as the best indicator of the performance of the stock of the country's largest companies.

stock   A type of security that signifies ownership in a corporation and represents a claim on part of the corporation's assets and earnings.

stock exchange   An institution that hosts a market where stocks and other securities can be bought and sold.

stock fund   A mutual fund that is invested in stocks.

stock market   The organized securities exchange for stock and bond transactions.

stock sector   A section of the stock market, such as health care, information technology, or utilities.

stock split   An action taken by a company that increases the number of its outstanding shares of stock, usually to lower the price of one share.

stocks of local interest   The stocks of companies based within a newspaper's readership area or those that otherwise have ties to the community.

stop order   A trade order that allows an investor to buy or sell a stock once it reaches a specified price.

stop-limit order   A trade order that specifies a stop price, and once that price is reached becomes a limit order. The stock you're buying must be executed at your set price or lower, and stock you're selling must be sold at your specified price or higher.

story stock   A stock with a value based on something that's expected to happen or that has happened, rather than a company's financials.

technical analysis   A method of evaluating stocks by looking at statistics based on market activity, such as volume or pricing. Technical analysis involves the use of charts and other tools to spot patterns, which are considered as predictors of future activity.

time willingness   The amount of time an investor is willing and able to put into managing and monitoring investments.

top-down investing   An approach to investing that focuses on general economic conditions, attempting to predict how certain companies will perform within those conditions. Top-down investing is considered to be the opposite of bottom-up investing.

total return   The actual rate of return of an individual investment or pool of investments over a prescribed time period, based on price movement plus reinvestment of income and other distributions.

trading   A quick succession of buying and selling of stock, based not so much on fundamentals as on what the market is doing at any given time.

valuation ratio   A ratio that compares the price of a stock to the financial results of the company offering it.

value investing   The practice of buying stock that has decreased in value, which an investor believes is being traded for less than its real value.

value stock   Stock that sells at a price considered to be less than normal valuation.

volume   The total number of stocks traded within a specified time period.

wash-sale rule   A ruling from the Internal Revenue Service which states you can't claim a loss on a stock if you buy it back within 30 days.

yield   The income return on an investment; also known as a return.

While you've learned a lot about stock market investing from this book, there's always more to know. The books and online resources listed here will help you to become even better informed about your finances and stock market investing.

Books

Anderson, Seth, and Parvez Ahmed. *Mutual Funds: Fifty Years of Research Findings.* Spring-Verlag, LLC, 2010.

Barrie, Scott. *The Complete Idiot's Guide to Market Timing.* Alpha Books, 2003.

Bernstein, Jacob, and Elliott Bernstein. *Stock Market Strategies That Work.* McGraw Hill, 2002.

Bogle, John C. *The Little Book of Common Sense Investing: The Only Way to Guarantee Your Fair Share of Stock Market Returns.* Wiley Publishing, Inc., 2007.

Clark, Ken. *The Complete Idiot's Guide to Getting Out of Debt.* Alpha Books, 2008.

———. *The Complete Idiot's Guide to Boosting Your Financial IQ.* Alpha Books, 2009.

———. *The Complete Idiot's Guide to Paying for College.* Alpha Books, 2010.

Davidson, Alexander. *The Complete Guide to Online Stock Market Investing: The Definitive 20-Day Guide.* Kogan Page, Ltd., 2007.

Elder, Alexander. *The New Sell and Sell Short: How to Take Profits, Cut Losses, and Benefit from Price Declines.* Wiley Publishing, Inc., 2011.

Feldman, Jeffrey. *Three Paths to Profitable Investing: Using ETFs in Healthcare, Infrastructure, and the Environment to Grow Your Assets.* FT Press, 2010.

Fisher, Sarah Young, and Susan Shelly. *The Complete Idiot's Guide to Starting an Investment Club.* Alpha Books, 2000.

———. *The Complete Idiot's Guide to Personal Finance in Your 20s & 30s, Fourth Edition.* Alpha Books, 2009.

———. *The Complete Idiot's Guide to Personal Finance in Your 40s & 50s.* Alpha Books, 2001.

Graham, Benjamin, and Jason Zweig. *The Intelligent Investor.* Harper Collins, 2006.

Greenblatt, Joel. *The Little Book That Still Beats the Market.* Wiley Publishing, Inc., 2010.

Hirsch, Jeffrey A. *Stock Trader's Almanac 2011.* Wiley Publishing, Inc., 2011.

Jones, Chris. *Hedge Funds of Funds: A Guide for Investors.* Wiley Publishing, Inc., 2008.

Kelly, Jason. *The Neatest Little Guide to Stock Market Investing, 2010 Edition.* Plume, 2009.

Kristof, Kathy. *Investing 101.* Bloomberg Press, 2008.

Malkiel, Burton G. *A Random Walk Down Wall Street: The Time-Tested Strategy for Successful Investing.* W.W. Norton & Company, 2007.

Maranijan, Selena. *Investment Clubs: How to Start and Run One the Motley Fool Way.* Motley Fool, 1998.

Mizrahi, Charles. *Getting Started in Value Investing.* Wiley Publishing, Inc., 2007.

Mobius, Mark. *Mutual Funds: An Introduction to the Core Concepts.* Wiley Publishing, Inc., 2007.

Northcott, Alan. *The Complete Guide to Investing in Short Term Trading: How to Earn High Rates of Returns Safely.* Atlantic Publishing Company, 2008.

O'Neil, William J. *How to Make Money in Stocks: A Winning System in Good Times and Bad, Fourth Edition.* McGraw-Hill, 2009.

Paulson, Henry M., Jr. *On the Brink: Inside the Race to Stop the Collapse of the Global Financial System.* Grand Central Publishing, 2010.

Peters, Josh. *The Ultimate Dividend Playbook: Income, Insight, and Independence for Today's Investor.* Wiley Publishing, Inc., 2008.

Sander, Peter, and John Slatter, CFA. *The 100 Best Stocks You Can Buy 2010.* Adams Business, 2009.

Siegel, Jeff, Chris Nelder, and Nick Hodge. *Investing in Renewable Energy: Making Money on Green Chip Stocks.* Wiley Publishing, Inc., 2008.

Siegel, Jeremy J. *Stocks for the Long Run: The Definitive Guide to Financial Market Returns & Long-Term Investment Strategy.* McGraw-Hill, 2007.

Sorkin, Andrew Ross. *Too Big to Fail: The Inside Story of How Wall Street and Washington Fought to Save the Financial System—and Themselves.* Penguin Group, 2009.

Statman, Meir. *What Investors Really Want.* McGraw Hill, 2010.

Stein, Ben, and Phil DeMuth. *The Little Book of Bulletproof Investing: Do's and Don'ts to Protect Your Financial Life.* Wiley Publishing, Inc., 2010.

Swedroe, Larry. *Wise Investing Made Simpler.* Charter Financial Publishing Network, 2010.

Swedroe, Larry E., Kevin Grogan, and Tiva Lim. *The Only Guide You'll Ever Need for the Right Financial Plan: Managing Your Wealth, Risk, and Investments.* Wiley Publishing, Inc., 2010.

Van Knapp, David. *Sensible Stock Investing: How to Pick, Value, and Manage Stocks.* iUniverse Star, 2008.

Wright, Kelley. *Dividends Still Don't Lie: The Truth About Investing in Blue Chip Stocks and Winning in the Stock Market.* Wiley Publishing, Inc., 2010.

Websites

Listed here are some reputable Internet sites providing investing and financial news, stock quotes, analysis, and other features to help you learn more about investing in the stock market.

Bloomberg (www.bloomberg.com). Includes updated business news and financial information; reports on the stock market, futures, commodities, and currencies; political news; stock market data; financial TV and radio; and more.

BrokerWatch (www.finra.org/Investors/ToolsCalculators/BrokerCheck/index. htm). A listing by the Financial Industry Regulatory Authority, Inc. of firms and brokers that have been the subject of regulatory complaints or action.

CNNMoney.com (http://money.cnn.com/). A comprehensive site, featuring a stock tracker, business news, personal finance resources, real estate news, lists of best jobs and places to live, and other finance-related materials.

Forbes (www.forbes.com). An online source for the latest business and financial news and analysis. Covers the stock market and a wide range of financial topics, and contains lists of the world's richest people and other topics of interest.

Kiplinger (www.kiplinger.com). Provides information on a wide range of financial topics, including personal finance and investing advice, business forecasting, and free tools. Includes lots of investing information on stocks, mutual funds, and exchange traded funds.

MarketWatch (www.marketwatch.com). A subsidiary of Dow Jones & Company, Inc., MarketWatch provides a comprehensive market overview, including stock market quotes and business and financial news.

Morningstar (www.morningstar.com). Packed full of commentary and statistics on stocks, mutual funds, and exchange traded funds, Morningstar is held in high regard by financial professionals. A lot available for free, although some parts of the site are only available for a fee.

The Motley Fool (www.fool.com). A down-to-earth, informative, and educational site with stock news updated hourly. Includes lots of tutorials and articles on a variety of financial topics.

MSN Money (www.moneycentral.com). Contains business news, stock quotes, investment information, news about companies and industries, historical price charts, and a portfolio management tool.

Schwab Equity Ratings (www.schwab.com/public/schwab/research_strategies/ stocks/equity_ratings). Evaluates about 3,000 of the largest U.S. stocks, based on fundamentals, valuation, momentum, and risk, and ranks them from A to F.

TheStreet.com (www.thestreet.com). A good all-around site that includes articles about companies, markets, sectors, and asset allocation. Covers both fundamental analysis and technical analysis. Good for both novice investors and investors of intermediate investing skill levels.

***USA Today* Money (www.usatoday.com/money).** Provides news about financial markets, the U.S. economy, business, and corporations. Its personal finance section covers mortgages, budgeting, savings, loans, stocks, taxes, interest rates, and so forth.

Value Line (www.valueline.com). Provides useful investment news and information. It's best known for publishing "The Value Line Investment Survey," a stock analysis newsletter that's updated weekly in both print and online versions.

Yahoo! Finance (http://finance.yahoo.com). Offers business news, stock quotes, and general financial news, including the amount of dividends being offered by specific companies.

Notable Financial Blogs

As you know, blogs are opinion based, but they can be valuable when from a trusted source. These blogs were ranked among the best 25 in 2009 by *Time* magazine business writers.

Angry Bear (http://angrybear.blogspot.com). This blog is written by six Ph.D. economists, an historian, and financial professionals who, writing from the viewpoints of their individual training, provide perspectives on broad sectors of the economy. Writers look at topics as varied as worldwide trade and industrial production and U.S. government programs and regulations such as Social Security.

The Big Picture by Barry Ritholtz (www.ritholtz.com). A money manager, Barry Ritholtz is a respected economic observer. He provides multiple posts a day on diverse subjects such as criticisms of the business press, digital media, and key economic indicators. The blog incorporates relevant and interesting charts, tables, and graphs.

Bill Cara's Cara Community (http://caracommunity.com). Bill Cara, a widely recognized authority on the markets, analyzes the capital markets, stock movements, and the economy with an eye to technical guides including volatility, cash flows, trading volume, and price performance.

Footnoted (www.footnoted.org). Author Michelle Leder digs through SEC filings to reveal insights about government filings that usually are overlooked. Started in 2003, this is one of the oldest financial blogs.

Infectious Greed (http://paulkedrosky.com). Author Paul Kedrosky is considered one of the best financial market pundits, according to *Time* magazine business writers. This site reflects the perspective of a former technology analyst, institutional money manager, and venture capitalist, and includes commentary on global markets, economic trends, and emerging business trends.

Jim Cramer's Mad Money (www.cramers-mad-money.com). This site provides updates throughout the day of Jim Cramer's stock picks. Cramer, a former hedge fund manager who hosts the CNBC show also called *Mad Money*, provides commentary on the site.

Mish's Global Economic Trend Analysis (http://globaleconomicanalysis. blogspot.com). Author Mike Shedlock shares observations made by those in major media, so-called experts, and government officials and serves up analysis based on his impression of their relevance and validity.

S&P 500 Companies

We've often referred to the Standard & Poor's (S&P) 500, an index of 500 large cap companies that represent a wide range of industries. The stocks of the 500 companies are the most widely held U.S.-based common stocks. The S&P 500 was first listed in 1957.

Companies included on the S&P 500 are listed in alphabetical order here.

3M Company

Abbott Labs

Abercrombie and Fitch

Adobe Systems

Advanced Micro Devices

AES Corp.

Aetna, Inc.

Affiliated Computer

AFLAC, Inc.

Agilent Technologies

Air Products & Chemicals

AK Steel Holding

Akamai

Alcoa, Inc.

Allegheny Energy

Allegheny Technologies, Inc.

Allergan, Inc.

Allstate Corp.

Altera Corp.

Altria Group, Inc.

Amazon.com

Amerada Hess

Ameren Corporation

American Capital

American Electric Power

American Express

American Int'l. Group

American Power Conversion

American Standard

American Tower

Ameriprise Financial

AmerisourceBergen Corp.

Amgen

Amphenol

Anadarko Petroleum

Analog Devices

Anheuser-Busch

Aon Corp.

Apache Corp.

Apartment Investment & Mgmt.

Apollo Group

Apple Computer

Applera Corp.

Applied Materials

Archer-Daniels-Midland

Archstone-Smith Trust

Ashland Inc.

Assurant

AT&T Corp.

Autodesk, Inc.

Automatic Data Processing Inc.

AutoNation, Inc.

AutoZone Inc.

Avalon Bay Communities

Avery Dennison Corp.

Avon Products

Baker Hughes

Ball Corp.

Bank of America Corp.

Bank of New York Mellon

Bard (C.R.) Inc.

Barr Pharmaceuticals

Baxter International, Inc.

BB&T Corporation

Becton, Dickinson

Bed, Bath & Beyond

Bemis Company

Best Buy

Big Lots, Inc.

BIOGEN IDEC, Inc.

BJ Services

Black & Decker Corp.

BMC Software

Boeing Company

Boston Properties

Boston Scientific

Bristol-Myers Squibb

Broadcom Corporation

Brown-Forman Corp.

Burlington Northern Santa Fe

Cabot Oil and Gas

Cameron International

Campbell Soup

Capital One Financial

Cardinal Health, Inc.

Carnival Corp.

Caterpillar Inc.

CBS

CenterPoint Energy

Centex Corp.

Century Telephone

Cephalon

CF Industries

Charles Schwab

Chevron Corp.

Chubb Corp.

Ciena Corp.

CIGNA Corp.

Cincinnati Financial

Cintas Corporation

Cisco Systems

CIT Group

Citigroup Inc.

Citizens Communications

Citrix Systems

Clorox Co.

CMS Energy

Coach, Inc.

Coca-Cola Co.

Coca-Cola Enterprises

Colgate-Palmolive

Comcast Corp.

Comerica Inc.

Compass Bancshares

Computer Associates Intl.

Computer Sciences Corp.

Compuware Corp.

Comverse Technology

ConAgra Foods

ConocoPhillips

CONSOL Energy

Consolidated Edison

Constellation Brands

Constellation Energy Group

Convergys Corp.

Cooper Industries, Ltd.

Corning

Costco

Coventry Healthcare

Covidien

CSX Corp.

Cummins Inc.

CVS Caremark

D.R. Horton

Dana Corp.

Danaher Corp.

Darden Restaurants

Davita

Dean Foods

Deere & Co.

Dell Inc.

DENTSPLY International

Devon Energy Corp.

Discover Financial

Dollar General

Dominion Resources

Donnelley (R.R.) & Sons

Dover Corp.

Dow Chemical

Dr. Pepper Snapple Group

DTE Energy Co.

Du Pont (E.I.)

Duke Energy

Dun and Bradstreet

Dynegy

E*Trade Financial Corp.

Eastman Chemical

Eastman Kodak

Eaton Corp.

eBay Inc.

Ecolab, Inc.

Edison Int'l.

El Paso Corp.

Electronic Arts

Electronic Data Systems

Embarq

EMC Corp.

Emerson Electric

Entergy Corp.

EOG Resources

Estee Lauder

Equifax, Inc.

Equity Office Properties

Equity Residential

Exelon Corp.

Express Scripts

Exxon Mobil Corp.

Family Dollar Stores

Fannie Mae

Federal Home Loan Mtg.

Federated Dept. Stores

Federated Investors, Inc.

FedEx Corporation

Fifth Third Bancorp

First Data

First Horizon National

FirstEnergy Corp.

Fiserv, Inc.

Fisher Scientific

Fluor Corp. (New)

Ford Motor

Forest Laboratories

Fortune Brands, Inc.

FPL Group

Franklin Resources

Freeport-McMoran Cp & Gld

Freescale Semiconductor Inc.

Gannett Co.

Gap

General Dynamics

General Electric

General Mills

General Motors

Genuine Parts

Genworth Financial

Genzyme Corp.

Gilead Sciences

Golden West Financial

Goldman Sachs Group

Goodrich Corporation

Goodyear Tire & Rubber

Google

Grainger (W.W.), Inc.

Great Lakes Chemical

H&R Block

Halliburton Co.

Harley-Davidson

Harman International

Harrah's Entertainment

Hartford Financial Svc. Gp.

Hasbro Inc.

HCA, Inc.

Health Management Assoc.

Heinz (H.J.)

Hercules, Inc.

Hewlett-Packard

Hilton Hotels

Home Depot

Honeywell Int'l. Inc.

Hospira, Inc.

Humana, Inc.

Huntington Bancshares

Illinois Tool Works

IMS Health, Inc.

Ingersoll-Rand Co. Ltd.

Intel Corp.

International Bus. Machines

International Flav/Frag

International Game Technology

International Paper

Interpublic Group

Intuit, Inc.

ITT Industries, Inc.

J.C. Penney

Jabil Circuit

Janus Capital Group

JDS Uniphase Corp.

Johnson & Johnson

Johnson Controls

Jones Apparel Group

JPMorgan Chase & Co.

Juniper Networks

KB Home

Kellogg Co.

Kerr-McGee

KeyCorp

Keyspan Energy

Kimberly-Clark

Kimco Realty

Kinder Morgan

King Pharmaceuticals

KLA-Tencor Corp.

Kohl's Corp.

Kroger Co.

L-3 Communications Holdings

Laboratory Corp. of America Holding

Legg Mason

Leggett & Platt

Lehman Bros.

Lennar

Lexmark Int'l.

Lilly (Eli) & Co.

Limited Brands, Inc.

Lincoln National

Linear Technology Corp.

Liz Claiborne, Inc.

Lockheed Martin Corp.

Loews Corp.

Louisiana Pacific

Lowe's Cos.

LSI Logic

Lucent Technologies

M&T Bank Corp.

Manor Care, Inc.

Marathon Oil Corp.

Marriott Int'l.

Marsh & McLennan

Marshall & Ilsley Corp.

Masco Corp.

Mattel, Inc.

Maxim Integrated Prod.

Maytag Corp.

MBIA Inc.

McCormick & Co.

McDonald's Corp.

McGraw-Hill

McKesson Corp. (New)

MeadWestvaco Corporation

Medco Health Solutions, Inc.

MedImmune, Inc.

Medtronic, Inc.

Mellon Bank Corp.

Merck & Co.

Meredith Corp.

Merrill Lynch

MetLife, Inc.

MGIC Investment

Micron Technology

Microsoft Corp.

Millipore Corp.

Molex, Inc.

Molson Coors Brewing Company

Monsanto Co.

Monster Worldwide

Moody's Corp.

Morgan Stanley

Motorola, Inc.

Murphy Oil

Mylan Laboratories

Nabors Industries Ltd.

National City Corp.

National Oilwell Varco, Inc.

National Semiconductor

Navistar International Corp.

NCR Corp.

Network Appliance

New York Times Cl. A

Newell Rubbermaid Co.

Newmont Mining Corp. (Hldg. Co.)

News Corporation

NICOR, Inc.

NIKE, Inc.

NiSource, Inc.

Noble Corporation

Nordstrom

Norfolk Southern Corp.

North Fork Bancorporation

Northern Trust Corp.

Northrop Grumman Corp.

Novell, Inc.

Novellus Systems

Nucor Corp.

NVIDIA Corp.

Occidental Petroleum

Office Depot

OfficeMax, Inc.

Omnicom Group

Oracle Corp.

PACCAR, Inc.

Pactiv Corp.

Pall Corp.

Parametric Technology

Parker-Hannifin

Patterson Cos.

Paychex, Inc.

Peoples Energy

Pepsi Bottling Group

PepsiCo, Inc.

PerkinElmer

Pfizer, Inc.

PG&E Corp.

Phelps Dodge

Pinnacle West Capital

Pitney-Bowes

Plum Creek Timber Co.

PMC-Sierra, Inc.

PNC Bank Corp.

PPG Industries

PPL Corp.

Praxair, Inc.

Principal Financial Group

Procter & Gamble

Progress Energy, Inc.

Progressive Corp.

ProLogis

Prudential Financial

Public Serv. Enterprise, Inc.

Public Storage

Pulte Homes, Inc.

QLogic Corp.

QUALCOMM, Inc.

Quest Diagnostics

Qwest Communications Int'l.

RadioShack Corp.

Raytheon Co.

Realogy

Reebok International

Regions Financial Corp. (New)

Reynolds American, Inc.

Robert Half International

Rockwell Automation, Inc.

Rockwell Collins

Rohm & Haas

Rowan Cos.

Ryder System

Sabre Holding Corp.

SAFECO Corp.

Safeway, Inc.

Sandisk

Sanmina-SCI Corp.

Sara Lee Corp.

Schering-Plough

Schlumberger Ltd.

Scripps (E.W.)

Sealed Air Corp.

Sears Holdings Corp.

Sempra Energy

Sherwin-Williams

Sigma-Aldrich

Simon Property Group, Inc.

SLM Corporation

Snap-On, Inc.

Solectron

Southern Co.

Southwest Airlines

Sovereign Bancorp

Sprint Corp. FON

St. Jude Medical

St. Paul Travelers Cos.

Stanley Works

Staples, Inc.

Starbucks Corp.

Starwood Hotels & Resorts

State Street Corp.

Stryker Corp.

Sun Microsystems

Sunoco, Inc.

SunTrust Banks

Supervalu, Inc.

Symantec Corp.

Symbol Technologies

Synovus Financial

Sysco Corp.

T. Rowe Price Group

Target Corp.

TECO Energy

Tektronix, Inc.

Tellabs, Inc.

Temple-Inland

Tenet Healthcare Corp.

Teradyne, Inc.

Texas Instruments

Textron, Inc.

The Hershey Company

Thermo Electron

Tiffany & Co.

Time Warner, Inc.

TJX Companies, Inc.

Torchmark Corp.

Toys R Us, Inc.

Transocean, Inc.

Tribune Co.

TXU Corp.

Tyco International

Tyson Foods

U.S. Bancorp

Union Pacific

Unisys Corp.

United Health Group, Inc.

United Parcel Service

United States Steel Corp.

United Technologies

Univision Communications

UnumProvident Corp.

UST, Inc.

V.F. Corp.

Valero Energy

Verizon Communications

Viacom, Inc.

Vornado Realty Trust

Vulcan Materials

Wachovia Corp.

Wal-Mart Stores

Walgreen Co.

Walt Disney Co.

Washington Mutual

Waste Management Inc.

Waters Corporation

Watson Pharmaceuticals

Weatherford International

WellPoint Inc.

Wells Fargo

Wendy's International

Weyerhaeuser Corp.

Whirlpool Corp.

Whole Foods Market

Williams Cos.

Windstream

Wrigley (Wm) Jr.

Wyeth

Wyndham Worldwide

Xcel Energy, Inc.

Xerox Corp.

Xilinx, Inc.

XL Capital

XTO Energy, Inc.

Yahoo Inc.

Yum! Brands, Inc.

Zimmer Holdings

Zions Bancorp

Brokerage Firms

Chapter 15 provides information about what brokers do, and explains the differences between full-service, discount, and online brokers. The information in this appendix is intended to help you choose a broker when you're first getting started in the stock market. Of course, only you can decide what level of help you need and what type of broker works for you financially.

Consider the information provided here when you're making a decision about what type of broker—and what particular brokerage firm—you wish to use. Your broker can't guarantee that your investments will make you rich, or that the market won't continue to be volatile, but should be able to offer you the services you need for a fair price, and features that suit your investing needs.

The brokers mentioned in this appendix have received consistently good ratings in brokerage firm rankings, although some rank higher in certain areas (such as fees or customer service) than others. You can get more detailed information about various brokers, along with rankings, at www.brokerage-review.com. The website rates 27 different brokers based on a variety of criteria, and makes recommendations for which brokers are most appropriate for investors of different needs and levels of investment experience.

Charles Schwab

Website: www.schwab.com

Cost per trade: $8.95 for stocks and ETFs, with options at the same price, plus 75¢ per contract.

Minimum starting balance requirement: $1,000

This brokerage firm is noted for excellent customer service, a great selection of investment products, and a low minimum balance requirement, but not for low brokerage fees. Technology aficionados claim that the firm's website is outdated and cumbersome, and doesn't include the investor community, which allows clients to interact with and learn from one another.

ChoiceTrade

Website: www.choicetrade.com

Cost per trade: $5 per trade for stocks and ETFs, or a $1 minimum per trade for direct access stocks and ETFs. Options are $5 per trade, plus 55¢ per contract.

Minimum starting balance requirement: no minimum for a cash account; $2,000 for a margin account

Recommended for new investors, ChoiceTrade offers a streamlined procedure to set up an account, and its website includes an investor community for clients to interact and exchange information.

E*Trade

Website: www.etrade.com

Cost per trade: $9.99 per trade for between 0 and 149 trades per quarter, or $7.99 per trade for more than 150 trades per quarter. Options trade at the same rate and conditions, plus 74¢ per contract.

Minimum starting balance requirement: $1,000 for a cash account; $2,000 for a margin account

Known for good trading tools and a registration system that allows you to set up an account quickly and easily, E*Trade is noted for powerful trading tools. Some investors are levied a $40 per quarter service fee. If you're considering E*Trade, be sure to check whether that fee would apply to your account. And consider the number of trades you're likely to make per quarter, as there are less expensive brokers for small investors who don't trade frequently.

Firstrade

Website: www.firstrade.com

Cost per trade: $6.95 per trade for stocks and ETFs, and the same price for options, plus 75¢ per contract.

Minimum starting balance requirement: none

Firstrade requires no minimum to open an account, and no annual, inactivity, or account maintenance fees. It has been noted, however, that trading tools are minimal, and customer service can be less than satisfactory.

Just2Trade

Website: www.just2trade.com

Cost per trade: $2.50 for trading stocks and ETFs. Options fees are $2.50, plus 50¢ per contract.

Minimum starting balance requirement: $2,500

Founded in 2007, Just2Trade recommends that only investors with two or more years of experience seek its services. The firm is known for high-tech trading tools, such as stock alerts, notice of daily technical events, and a stock screener.

MB Trading

Website: www.mbtrading.com

Cost per trade: Flat rate of $4.95 for stocks and ETFs, but the cost increases for after-hours trading and trade orders for more than 10,000 shares. Options are traded at 95¢ per contract.

Minimum starting balance requirement: $1,000 for a cash account; $2,000 for a margin account

The brokerage offers social networking for investors, no activity fees, and noted trading tools. Its trading software, although sophisticated and powerful, is noted as being difficult to master, meaning that this brokerage may not be ideal for a beginning investor.

Merrill Lynch

Website: www.ml.com

Cost per trade: $14 for stocks and ETFs and $29.95 for limit orders.

Minimum starting balance requirement: $2,000

One of the most well-known brokerages, Merrill Lynch tends to attract high income investors, and charges a variety of fees not encountered with some other brokerages. Investors whose account balances are $100,000 or more may be invited to participate in IPOs, and Merrill Lynch offers more than 600 offices nationwide; a plus for investors who want face-to-face contact with a broker. However, its fees, both trading and others, are among the highest of all brokerages.

Noble Trading

Website: www.nobletrading.com

Cost per trade: $7.95 for stocks and ETFs. The same price for options, plus $1 per contract for market and limit orders.

Minimum starting balance requirement: $500 for a cash account; $2,000 for a margin account

Noble Trading offers four trading platforms for various levels of investors. It is regarded as having good customer service, but its trading platform fees are considered high. There also is a $25 account inactivity fee for investors who trade less than 10 times a year.

Optionshouse

Website: www.optionshouse.com

Cost per trade: $3.95 for stocks and ETFs and two different prices for options, depending on the number of contracts.

Minimum starting balance requirement: $1,000 for a cash account; $2,000 for a margin account

Although the name may imply this brokerage caters to options traders (and it does), it does not limit its services to those clients. Optionshouse is highly regarded for its customer service and ease of registering an account. Optionshouse has received high reviews during the past several years, and is recognized for the quality of its trading tools.

optionsXpress

Website: www.optionsxpress.com

Cost per trade: $9.95 for stocks and ETFs and varying prices for options, depending on the number of trades per quarter.

Minimum starting balance requirement: none

Noted for exceptional customer service that includes broker-assisted trades at no additional cost for beginning investors, optionsXpress gets high reviews from financial magazines and other sources. Although its trading fees are not among the lowest, investors benefit from the lack of a variety of other fees, such as account inactivity or maintenance. optionsXpress offers free, instructor-led online classes for beginning investors; a definite advantage for those just getting started in the stock market. It also is noted for its fast account registration process, many types of available accounts, and its nearly worldwide availability of access.

Scottrade

Website: www.scottrade.com

Cost per trade: $7 for stocks and ETFs; the same for options, with an additional $1.25 per contract.

Minimum starting balance requirement: $500

With a 30-year-plus history, Scottrade is a highly regarded and trusted business. In addition to a low minimum starting balance requirement, there is a feature that allows you to transfer money directly from your checking account. With a multitude of educational resources and excellent support for beginning investors, Scottrade ranks among the highest for customer satisfaction. The brokerage does not charge inactivity or account maintenance fees, and offers an online, interactive community. This established, trusted firm is highly recommended by financial magazines and other sources.

ShareBuilder

Website: www.sharebuilder.com

Cost per trade: $9.99 for stocks and ETFs.

Minimum starting balance requirement: none for a cash account; $2,000 for a margin account

ShareBuilder is set apart from other brokerages in that it offers automatic investment plans. A basic plan enables automatic investments for $4 per investment, and other plans vary from $12 to $20 per month, depending on the number of investments. ShareBuilder is not known for exceptional trading tools, and complaints about customer service have been noted. It is not particularly recommended for beginning investors, as it lacks the capacity to offer advice from experienced traders or ideas for investing.

SogoTrade

Website: www.sogotrade.com

Cost per trade: $3 per trade for stocks and ETFs; the same for options, plus 70¢ per contract.

Minimum starting balance requirement: $500

SogoTrade offers one of the lowest commissions of all brokerages. Some reviews note that it takes longer than average to open a SogoTrade account, due to additional steps and verifications required. The brokerage's trading platforms are said to be slow, meaning that it can take minutes instead of seconds to complete a trade. Also, frequent technical problems have been encountered. There are no inactivity fees, and SogoTrade allows investors to trade fractional shares for no additional fee.

TD Ameritrade

Website: www.tdameritrade.com

Cost per trade: $9.99 for stock and ETFs; $9.99 plus 75¢ per contract for options.

Minimum starting balance requirement: $2,000

A highly regarded firm, although not among the least expensive, TD Ameritrade is known for its efficient account registration process, which allows customers to link to their bank accounts in order to fund a brokerage account immediately.

TradeKing

Website: www.tradeking.com

Cost per trade: $4.95 for stocks and ETFs; with the same price, plus 65¢ per contract, applying to options.

Minimum starting balance requirement: none

With low trading fees and no minimum amount required to open an account, TradeKing comes highly recommended by broker surveys. There are no hidden fees, and TradeKing has been awarded for its excellent trading tools. It is also recognized for great customer service, and is regarded as having one of the best online investor communities. The online community, coupled with extensive educational materials, makes it a good choice for beginning investors.

tradeMONSTER

Website: www.trademonster.com

Cost per trade: $7.50 per trade for stocks and ETFs; between $7.50 and $12.50 per trade for options, plus 50¢ per contract.

Minimum starting balance requirement: $2,000

Recommended for beginning investors, tradeMONSTER offers an online feature that allows account holders to practice trading stocks and options with virtual money, using all of its educational and trading features and tools. tradeMONSTER includes an extensive variety of tools for charting and tracking trends, along with a powerful trading platform. There are no inactivity, account, or other hidden fees.

TradeStation

Website: www.tradestation.com

Cost per trade: Between $6.99 and $9.99 for stocks and ETFs, depending on the number of shares traded under the brokerage's flat-rate plan. Options trade at $1 per contract with no ticket charge.

Minimum starting balance requirement: $5,000

This brokerage firm is appealing to day traders, as it offers two commission plans and boasts one of the best trading platforms in the industry. The platform, however, is said to be difficult to master, and not recommended for beginning investors. Also, you may encounter fees for market data and other services.

Vanguard

Website: www.vanguard.com

Cost per trade: Varies depending on the amount of money invested and number of trades transacted.

Minimum starting balance requirement: $3,000

Known as a leader in mutual fund investing, Vanguard also offers brokerage services for those invested in stocks and ETFs. Fees are dependent on account balances and trading activity. If your account balance is less than $50,000, for instance, you'll be charged $7 per trade for the first 25 trades, then $20 per trade for additional trades. Fees decrease for larger accounts. Vanguard charges a $20 annual maintenance fee and a $10 a month "low balance" fee for accounts of less than $2,500.

WellsTrade

Website: www.wellsfargo.com/investing

Cost per trade: $19.95 for stocks and ETFs, unassisted; $45 with agent assistance; $9.95 for options; plus 50¢ per contract.

Minimum starting balance requirement: $1,000

A brokerage division of Wells Fargo Bank, WellsTrade is known for excellent banking services, but its fees and commissions are among the highest in the industry.

Reviewers note that applicants are required to fill in, sign, and mail paper forms in order to establish an account. The brokerage does offer educational materials, ratings, company profiles, and so forth, but is not known for exceptional trading tools.

Zecco

Website: www.zecco.com

Cost per trade: Varies for stocks and ETFs depending on account balance and number of trades transacted. Options trade at $4.50, plus 50¢ per contract.

Minimum starting balance requirement: none

Investors with account balances of $25,000 or more can make 10 free trades per month with Zecco. Ten free trades also are offered to investors who make at least 25 trades a month. After the free trades, there is a charge of $4.50 per trade. Zecco offers a virtual trading feature for clients who want to practice trading to improve skills and gain confidence, making it attractive to beginning investors. Account registration is recognized as being fast, easy, and efficient. Zecco is considered to offer one of the best online communities, allowing traders to interact with one another and exchange ideas and advice. There are no account minimum or inactivity fees.

Index